Palgrave Studies in Accounting and Finance Practice

Series Editors
Vassili Joannidès de Lautour, GDF, Grenoble École de Management,
Le Blanc, France
Danture Wickramasinghe, Adam Smith Business School,
University of Glasgow, Glasgow, UK
Aude Deville, IAE de Nice, Université Côte d'Azur, Antibes, France

More information about this series at
http://www.palgrave.com/gp/series/16220

Paul David Richard Griffiths

Corporate Governance in the Knowledge Economy

Lessons from Case Studies in the Finance Sector

Paul David Richard Griffiths
EM Normandie Business School
Métis Lab, Oxford, UK

ISSN 2524-8251 ISSN 2524-826X (electronic)
Palgrave Studies in Accounting and Finance Practice
ISBN 978-3-030-78872-8 ISBN 978-3-030-78873-5 (eBook)
https://doi.org/10.1007/978-3-030-78873-5

© The Editor(s) (if applicable) and The Author(s), under exclusive license to Springer Nature Switzerland AG 2021
This work is subject to copyright. All rights are solely and exclusively licensed by the Publisher, whether the whole or part of the material is concerned, specifically the rights of translation, reprinting, reuse of illustrations, recitation, broadcasting, reproduction on microfilms or in any other physical way, and transmission or information storage and retrieval, electronic adaptation, computer software, or by similar or dissimilar methodology now known or hereafter developed.
The use of general descriptive names, registered names, trademarks, service marks, etc. in this publication does not imply, even in the absence of a specific statement, that such names are exempt from the relevant protective laws and regulations and therefore free for general use.
The publisher, the authors and the editors are safe to assume that the advice and information in this book are believed to be true and accurate at the date of publication. Neither the publisher nor the authors or the editors give a warranty, expressed or implied, with respect to the material contained herein or for any errors or omissions that may have been made. The publisher remains neutral with regard to jurisdictional claims in published maps and institutional affiliations.

This Palgrave Macmillan imprint is published by the registered company Springer Nature Switzerland AG
The registered company address is: Gewerbestrasse 11, 6330 Cham, Switzerland

To the wonderful women who have contributed to shape who I am

Contents

1	Introduction	1
2	Conceptual Framework: Corporate Responsibility, Governance, Business Ethics, Culture and the Knowledge Economy	7

   2.1   Corporate Responsibility (CR) as a Framework for Corporate Governance   7
        2.1.1   Adopting a Sustainable Business Strategy   7
        2.1.2   Corporate Responsibility: A Framework   8
        2.1.3   Stakeholders and Conflict of Interest   11
        2.1.4   Sustainability Measurement   14
        2.1.5   Making Things Happen: Sustainability Implementation   15
        2.1.6   Focus on Corporate Governance   18
   2.2   Corporate Governance, Business Ethics and Culture   18
        2.2.1   Corporate Governance and Compliance   18
        2.2.2   Business Ethics and Its Relationship to Corporate Governance   21
        2.2.3   Doing Business in an International Context: Culture and Corruption   23
        2.2.4   Creating an Ethical Culture in Banking   29
        2.2.5   The Challenges in a World of Intangibles   31
   2.3   The Knowledge Economy: From Physical Resources to Intangible Assets   31

		2.3.1	Characteristics of the Knowledge Economy	31

	2.3.1	Characteristics of the Knowledge Economy	31

- 2.3.1 Characteristics of the Knowledge Economy — 31
- 2.3.2 Effect of Technology on the Knowledge Economy: Social Networks, Big Data, Artificial Intelligence — 37
- 2.3.3 Cultural Change: Incorporating Generation Υ as Consumers and Workers — 41
- 2.3.4 Transparency and Reporting—Integrated Reporting <IR> — 44
- 2.3.5 Bringing It All Together — 46
- References — 48

3 **First Things First: The Hidden Cost of Poor Governance** — 53
- 3.1 Overview — 53
- 3.2 Agents Putting Their Own Interest Ahead of the Corporation's — 53
  - 3.2.1 Introduction — 53
  - 3.2.2 Factors in Selecting an RHQ — 55
  - 3.2.3 Approach — 57
  - 3.2.4 Data Analysis and Development of Location Comparison Criteria — 58
  - 3.2.5 Results — 61
  - 3.2.6 Discussion and Aftermath — 63
  - 3.2.7 Conclusions — 64
- 3.3 The Devastating Effects That Weak Internal Controls Can Have — 65
  - 3.3.1 Introduction — 65
  - 3.3.2 The Company — 66
  - 3.3.3 Approach and Sources — 69
  - 3.3.4 The Incident — 69
  - 3.3.5 Root Causes of the Unethical Behaviour — 71
  - 3.3.6 Lessons Learnt — 72
  - 3.3.7 Looking Ahead — 74
- 3.4 The Waste of Implementing Corporate Standards That the Staff Work Around — 75
  - 3.4.1 Introduction — 75
  - 3.4.2 Approach — 75
  - 3.4.3 The Role of Technology in Orica's Latin American Business — 77

		3.4.4	The SAP Implementation Project Decision Process	78

      3.4.4 The SAP Implementation Project Decision Process 78
      3.4.5 Risk Management 84
      3.4.6 Outcome of the SAP Implementation Project 85
      3.4.7 Project Management Versus Governance 87
  3.5 Lost Opportunities of Poor Corporate Governance Resulting in a Siloed Organisation 89
      3.5.1 Introduction 89
      3.5.2 The Situation 90
      3.5.3 The Response 91
      3.5.4 Implementation 94
      3.5.5 Discussion 95
  3.6 Cross-Case Analysis 97
  References 101

4 Challenges to Global Governance in MNE: Strategy Adaptation to Local Markets 105
  4.1 Overview 105
  4.2 IBM Argentina: Polycentricity in Practice 106
      4.2.1 Overview of the Company 106
      4.2.2 IBM Argentina in Its Context 110
      4.2.3 The Governance Discussion 113
  4.3 Sensible Governance: Global Standards in a High Context Approach 115
      4.3.1 Overview 115
      4.3.2 History of Nobleza Piccardo and Its Relationship to BAT 117
      4.3.3 The Competitive Landscape 119
      4.3.4 The Business Context 122
      4.3.5 The Governance Discussion 124
  4.4 Local Management Misalignment: A Governance Challenge 126
      4.4.1 Background 126
      4.4.2 Overview of Banco Santander in Chile 127
      4.4.3 Banco Santander Santiago and Its Competitive Context 128
      4.4.4 Value Discipline of the Organisation 130
      4.4.5 The Governance Discussion 133

	4.5 Cross-Case Analysis	134
	References	139
5	**Challenges to Local Governance in International Business: The Risks of Corruption**	**141**
	5.1 Overview	141
	5.2 Extortion: To Bribe, or Not Bribe?	142
	5.2.1 Introduction	142
	5.2.2 Context	145
	5.2.3 Embedding Integrity in the Corporate Culture	146
	5.2.4 Transaction Governance Capacity	148
	5.2.5 Discussion	148
	5.2.6 Conclusion	152
	5.3 Laundering Drug Money: Rot from the Tail	153
	5.3.1 Overview	153
	5.3.2 The Organisation: HSBC	153
	5.3.3 The Incident	154
	5.3.4 The Money-Laundering Technique Applied Through HSBC Mexico	156
	5.3.5 Discussion	157
	5.3.6 Conclusions	159
	5.4 Laundering Easy Money: Rot from the Head	160
	5.4.1 The Bank	161
	5.4.2 The Incident	162
	5.4.3 Form of Money Laundering at Danske Bank	166
	5.4.4 Discussion	167
	5.4.5 Conclusions	170
	5.5 Cross-Case Analysis	171
	References	179
6	**To be or Not to be: Principles for Responsible Banking**	**181**
	6.1 Introduction to the Principles of Responsible Banking	181
	6.1.1 Overview	181
	6.1.2 History of Banks and the Climate Crisis	183
	6.2 Drivers for Adoption	187
	6.2.1 Citibank	188
	6.2.2 Mitsubishi UFJ Financial Group (MUFG)	190
	6.2.3 Industrial and Commercial Bank of China Ltd (ICBC)	191

	6.3 Reasons to Refrain from Adopting	194
	6.3.1 JP Morgan Chase	194
	6.3.2 HSBC	196
	6.3.3 Wells Fargo	198
	6.3.4 Synthesis of Reasons to Refrain from Signing	200
	6.4 Operational Challenges	202
	6.4.1 The Long Tail of Environmental Sustainability	202
	6.4.2 The Way Forward	204
	References	208
7	**The Future of Corporate Governance**	211
	7.1 Overview	211
	7.2 Lessons on the Status of Corporate Governance	211
	7.3 Uncovering the Window: Where Is Corporate Governance Heading?	219
	7.3.1 Introduction to Scenario Planning	219
	7.3.2 Scenario Structure No. 1	222
	7.3.3 Scenario Structure No. 2	227
	7.3.4 Scenario Structure No. 3	233
	Reference	239
8	**Final Reflections and Concluding Remarks**	241
Index		245

LIST OF FIGURES

Fig. 2.1	Elements of a sustainable business model of the transition to the knowledge economy (*Source* Author)	8
Fig. 2.2	CR implementation model (Griffiths, 2008)	17
Fig. 2.3	GLOBE's ten cultural clusters (*Source* House et al., 2004)	24
Fig. 2.4	Rizzuto model: Bringing it all together	26
Fig. 2.5	Protagonist fourth factor of production: Knowledge & Sustainability	32
Fig. 2.6	The increasing weight of intangibles	35
Fig. 3.1	Wells Fargo—product density per client (*Source* Wells Fargo Norwest annual report)	67
Fig. 3.2	Content analysis of annual report for 'cross-selling'. Lafferty Group for RBA workshops in Buenos Aires and Bogota. Based on (*Source* Norwest and Wells Fargo annual report)	68
Fig. 3.3	Orica's operations in Latin America	76
Fig. 3.4	Methodology adopted for the business case	80
Fig. 3.5	IS architecture for MW CPG	92
Fig. 3.6	Top-down transition to final architecture	93
Fig. 3.7	Inputs for arriving at Standard Business Processes	94
Fig. 3.8	Tracking benefits to the BSC	95
Fig. 4.1	IBM Argentina's business units (Rizzuto, 2016)	108
Fig. 4.2	BAT Southern Cone Business Units	116
Fig. 6.1	History of banks' engagement with the environment (Griffiths & Baudier, 2021)	187

Fig. 6.2	Number of companies that engage in climate impact disclosure (*Source* Climate Disclosure Project [CDP] https://www.cdp.net/en/companies/companies-scores)	204
Fig. 7.1	Inter-construct influence and interaction model	220
Fig. 7.2	Economy versus awareness for the environment	221
Fig. 7.3	Changes in approach to corporate reporting and in a Gen-Y society	222
Fig. 7.4	Interaction of the development of AI and the governance of social networks and Big Data	227
Fig. 7.5	Interaction of sensitivity towards the climate crisis and the PRB	233
Fig. 8.1	Corporate governance as the great integrator	244

List of Tables

Table 3.1	Summary of interpreted importance of RHQ location factors in Africa	56
Table 3.2	Classification of factors (identified by number) by their role and degree of importance	56
Table 3.3	Variables of the two-dimensional model	57
Table 3.4	Operations and regional HQ locations	59
Table 3.5	Relative weights of Quality of Service factors	60
Table 3.6	Relative weights of Cost of Delivery factors	61
Table 3.7	City scores on the *Quality of Service* dimension	62
Table 3.8	City scores on the *Cost of Delivery* dimension	62
Table 3.9	Overall score scenarios	62
Table 3.10	Benefits of Regional SAP Implementation	81
Table 3.11	Total cost of ownership	82
Table 3.12	The base case and sensitivity analysis (NPV in US$ thousands)	83
Table 3.13	Analysis of risks and mitigating strategies	84
Table 3.14	Synthesis of cross-case analysis	100
Table 4.1	IBM Argentina's mission, vision and value statements (Rizzuto, 2016, citing IBM Argentina 2012 dossier)	106
Table 4.2	Brands sold by Nobleza Piccardo in Argentina	121
Table 4.3	Summary of cross-case analysis	138
Table 5.1	Synthesis of cross-case analysis	176
Table 6.1	A stakeholder view of the evolution of responsibility in banking	185

Table 6.2	Signatories ranking table of fossil fuel financing since the Paris agreement—in billion US dollars (extracted from Banking on Climate Change, 2020)	189
Table 6.3	Categories in which JP Morgan Chase heads the league table of fossil fuel financiers since the Paris Agreement—in billion US dollars (extracted from Banking on Climate Change, 2020)	196
Table 6.4	Non-signatories ranking table of fossil fuel financing since the Paris Agreement—in billion US dollars (extracted from Banking on Climate Change, 2020)	196
Table 6.5	Fossil fuel financing as a proportion of total assets	201
Table 6.6	Governance factors in relation to the principles of responsible banking	207

CHAPTER 1

Introduction

With the transition from the Industrial Economy into the Knowledge Economy a formidable series of new challenges come to the corporate governance space. Although this transition has been happening gradually for close to five decades, there was an abrupt inflexion point in 2007–2008 that revealed to us how outdated many of our methods in management and governance are. Until then, the old Industrial Economy methods developed over 200 years and fine-tuned as part of the new world order that was established after the Second World War worked reasonably well.

Three key global phenomena happened in the 2007–2008 moment in history, each of which individually would have accelerated the transition but would not have caused a step change—it was that they happened simultaneously that made us change gear from evolution to revolution, particularly so in the financial services sector. The three phenomena are, first, the advent of the Great Recession with the devastating effect it had on the reputation of the financial sector that spilled over to the rest of business. The second is the technological revolution that came with the coming of age of cloud computing and the advent of the first i-phone and the other smartphones that followed. This led to the creation of social networks and their unplanned side-effect of uncontrolled growth in data that we understatedly called *Big Data*. Finally, at approximately the same

© The Author(s), under exclusive license to Springer Nature Switzerland AG 2021
P. D. R. Griffiths, *Corporate Governance in the Knowledge Economy*, Palgrave Studies in Accounting and Finance Practice, https://doi.org/10.1007/978-3-030-78873-5_1

time we had the Millennium generation or Generation Y with the cultural change they bring, having reached adulthood and making their footprint felt in the workplace and consumer markets.

The conjunction of these three phenomena revealed the preeminence of intangible assets over physical ones, for which our accounting and reporting systems are not prepared. As will be seen in Sect. 2.3.1 in 1975, 83 percent of assets in the Standard & Poor 500 companies were tangible, and only 17 percent were intangible. By 2015 the relationship at the S&P 500 flipped to only 13 percent tangible assets and 87 percent intangible ones, the majority of which are in the form of intellectual capital. How can we govern organisations with reporting systems that give us granular visibility of only 13 percent of assets? Even more important than this from a governance perspective is the fact that intangible assets being shareable radically changed the competitive landscape. While in the industrial era success depended to a great extent on taking control of physical raw materials and other resources and thus confrontational competition, in the knowledge economy no organisation creates value on its own but requires collaboration with multiple other organisations. This requires a radical change in the approach to governance and gives way to the following point.

The occurrence of the three phenomena reinforced a trend that was already happening, that is that the financial sector like the rest of the business needs to become sustainable, by which we mean that businesses need to integrate socially in their community and physically in their environment. As a result of this companies, especially in the Anglo-Saxon financial systems, could not focus only on the interests of shareholders but had to prioritise the interests of a multitude of other stakeholder groups many of which have opposing interests. Managing the priorities between stakeholder groups is a whole new challenge for governance.

Some of the regulatory changes that came after the 2007–2008 crisis such as Open Banking made incumbent banks lose power and become vulnerable to Fintech. This was reinforced by regulatory changes demanding banks increase their reserve capital, which derived in banks letting go their riskier young clients (none other than Gen-Y!) who quickly adopted the Fintech alternative. As a result of this the traditional standards for the governance of the financial sector, based on a relatively small number of licenced and highly regulated financial institutions, whose activities were circumscribed to the borders of a nation state, were no longer adapted to the new reality of a sector with a far greater number and diversity of players operating under varying degrees of regulation and many of whom operate cross-borders.

Returning to the happening of the three simultaneous phenomena, through push of the Fintechs and pull of their Gen-Y customers, was triggered the need for financial services to become far more digital in a world of data tsunami where risks in cybersecurity are a reality. Cybersecurity, thus, created a series of new demands on corporate governance.

Although the issue of globalisation has been deeply researched in the strategy and operations domains, its impact on corporate governance is far less so. Organisations involved in the international business face a specific set of challenges arising from the clash between their governance standards and values defined at the corporate centre, and the societal culture of the host countries where they have subsidiaries or do business. This is particularly relevant in countries where formal institutions are weak and the voids they leave are filled by informal institutions. This has many implications and challenges from the corporate governance perspective that have not been tackled in the literature.

Finally, if one takes the generally accepted Governance triangle of shareholders, Board of Directors and CEO/senior management team, there is significant knowledge on the relationship between the shareholders and the Board of Directors, and on the relationship between the Board of Directors and the CEO/management team. However, there is a third critical relationship in corporate governance which is that between the CEO/management team and the rank & file of the organisation. This relationship is extremely important to develop an ethical corporate culture and one that protects and enhances the intellectual capital of the organisation.

So, the objectives of this book are (a) to shed needed light on the new challenges for corporate governance that derive from the transition to the knowledge economy as described above, and (b) to fill the gaps in the literature on corporate governance in an international context and on the 'CEO vs rank & file' governance relationship.

To focus on the issues, this book addresses the following question: *What changes need to be incorporated into corporate governance to cope with the challenges posed by the transition to a knowledge economy?*

To facilitate its response, that question is broken down into the following sub-questions:

- How can corporate governance deal with the advent of the predominance of intangible assets such as intellectual capital?
- How does corporate governance need to be adapted to deal with the reality of multiple stakeholder groups many of which have opposing interests?
- How does corporate governance need to be adapted to cope with the challenges of digitalisation in the era of Big Data and risks of cybersecurity?
- How can multinationals deal with the tension between the headquarters and the subsidiary due to the need to combine the corporation's ethical culture and corporate governance values with the institutional forces of the subsidiaries' host market?
- What is the role of the 'CEO vs rank & file' relationship in achieving effective corporate governance in the knowledge economy?

These questions are tackled in the context of financial services, in the new banking and Fintech landscape that has resulted from the phenomena described above that took place in 2007–2008. The method followed is to develop a series of case studies around four challenges in governance: the hidden cost of poor governance, the adaptation of multinational strategy to local markets, the risks of corruption and the adoption of the Principles of Responsible Banking. The findings of each case study will be mapped onto extant theory in corporate governance and a cross case analysis within each of these themes is performed in search of new insights. Finally, these insights are combined to propose new theoretical conjectures and a series of scenarios of possible developments in corporate governance are produced.

Many of the case studies come from personal experience working as a consultant for blue-chip companies in over 15 countries—such are the cases of Glamorgan FS, Orica, Wells Fargo, MW CPG and the four bribe situations described under corruption. Other cases were developed throughout my academic career either as personal research cases (i.e., Santander Chile, HSBC Mexico, Danske Bank and those on the Principles of Responsible Banking) or by my doctoral research students (i.e., IBM Argentina and BAT Argentina).

The rest of the book is organised as follows. Chapter 2 presents the current status of relevant theory on corporate governance and the knowledge economy. Chapter 3 presents the four case studies and discussion on the hidden costs that result from having poor corporate governance in place. Chapter 4 presents the three cases on strategy adaptation to local markets and contrasts the outcomes of good and not so good governance practises to extract lessons on how to bridge across different societal cultures. Chapter 5 goes deep into the issue of corruption with four real-life situations on bribing and two cases on money laundering, to emphasise the need to build a corporate culture of performance with integrity. Chapter 6 uses the recently adopted Principles of Responsible Banking to present some thirty years of history of banks working for environmental sustainability and some interesting insights are extracted from comparing three large banks that have enrolled on the principles with another three that have not done so. Chapter 7 synthesises the prior chapters into theoretical conjectures on corporate governance in the financial sector, and develops twelve possible scenarios of corporate governance going forward in a horizon of some fifteen or twenty years. Finally, Chapter 8 presents the conclusions.

It is recommended that the reader goes through the book in the order presented, but it is pointed out that after having read Chapter 2 the reader could alter the order in which Chapters 3–6 are read as they are self-contained. However, all chapters need to be read before moving onto Chapter 7 and Chapter 8.

CHAPTER 2

Conceptual Framework: Corporate Responsibility, Governance, Business Ethics, Culture and the Knowledge Economy

2.1 Corporate Responsibility (CR) as a Framework for Corporate Governance

2.1.1 Adopting a Sustainable Business Strategy

Legitimacy is a prerequisite for private sector business if it is to contribute to society and thus maintain a licence to operate. Unfortunately, over the last two or so decades trust in business has seriously deteriorated in even the most pro-market economies. Departing from the negative aura that emanated from what are perceived as failed privatisations of the 1990s in many regions, through the e-bust and accounting scandals such as the Enron incident of the early days of this century; the role of the financial sector in the Great Recession of 2007–2008; the outrageous 'diesel-gate' scam of 2015 at car manufacturer VW; highly visible money laundering cases at HSBC Mexico and Danske Bank; the cross-selling and false customer account openings that emerged at Wells Fargo in 2016, to the still unravelling accounting (again) case of Wirecard. Businesses are now under pressure to gain legitimacy: the main route they are following is the adoption of corporate responsibility (CR) principles and making promises of commitment to sustainability (Kusnetsov et al., 2007).

© The Author(s), under exclusive license to Springer Nature
Switzerland AG 2021
P. D. R. Griffiths, *Corporate Governance in the Knowledge Economy*, Palgrave Studies in Accounting and Finance Practice,
https://doi.org/10.1007/978-3-030-78873-5_2

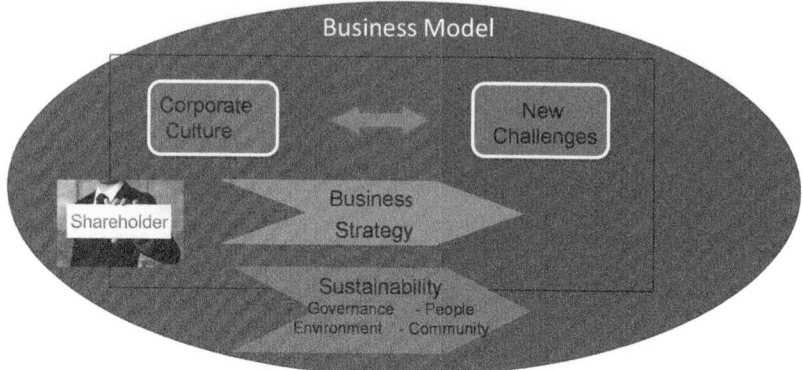

Fig. 2.1 Elements of a sustainable business model of the transition to the knowledge economy (*Source* Author)

In this context, adopting a sustainable business strategy is becoming ever more imperative, and this requires thinking on who are the stakeholders of the organisation, what are their expectations and, above all, recognising that different stakeholder groups often have conflicting interests. Sceptical analysts will be watching out for signs of greenwashing, window-dressing and smoke-screening. Overcoming this requires moving sustainability away from a standalone programme to incorporating the principles of CR into shaping the business model, into building the culture of the organisation, into the setting of new challenges and into the formulation of corporate strategy, as is represented in Fig. 2.1.

The following sections will develop the concepts required to formulate and implement a sustainable business strategy.

2.1.2 Corporate Responsibility: A Framework

Corporate responsibility comprises a series of management principles that enable and facilitate an organisation to fit harmoniously into its social and physical contexts (Capriotti & Garrido, 2006; Griffiths, 2006). Perera's (2003) framework on corporate social responsibility proposes managing and monitoring corporate citizenship behaviour along four dimensions:

a. Corporate governance and ethics;
b. People;
c. Environment; and
d. Contribution to Development.

To take these in turn, Corporate Governance and Ethics in the realm of CR refers to the processes of adopting and maintaining corporate values and objectives, of ensuring transparency, of accepting accountability and of confronting corruption. The need for aligning core business investments with social responsibility requires that the evaluation of fit with corporate values be part of the investment evaluation methodology (Griffiths, 2006, 2007).

Under the dimension of People come issues such as the safety of products and working conditions, labour standards, human rights of its staff and equal opportunities. It has been said (Handy, 2002) that people should be treated as assets (to be nurtured and helped to grow) and not as costs (which are there to be reduced). Key within this dimension of CR is giving staff opportunities for professional development taking into account that the organisation cannot ensure long-term employment, but it should enable the future employability of its staff.

The environmental dimension of social responsibility requires actions and investments in preserving the local and global environment, on cleaner production processes, on eco-efficiency and on environmental technologies. Paramount here is the migration towards non-fossil sources of energy, pursuing a neutral carbon footprint, reducing its water footprint. In other words, the organisation needs to internalise all its environmental costs and not transfer them to society.

Finally, the 'Contribution to Development' dimension of corporate responsibility is about showing contributions to education and healthcare, to the development of local small and medium enterprise (SME) suppliers, to closing the digital gap, to promoting community development and other similar initiatives. Peinado-Vera (2006) cites Prahalad (2005) when he talks of the 'Base of the Pyramid Model' that 'combines profits with improving poor peoples' lives'.

So, what is the relationship between CR and sustainability? Sustainability is the operationalisation of the CR principles into a sustainable business model. As such, it is about actions and behaviours, not principles. A sustainable business model balances financial returns with the principles of CR. This balance is achieved when management performance is measured, monitored and assessed based on indicators that represent at least some of the four dimensions of CR. This leads to the definition of sustainability as:

> Business behaviour that creates the trust and commitment of stakeholders, both now and in the future.[1]

This is a powerful statement with strong words such as 'behaviour', 'trust', 'commitment', 'stakeholders', 'now' and 'future'.

The MacMillan SPIRIT Model (where SPIRIT is an acronym for Stakeholder Performance Indicator and Relationship Improvement Tool) assists in formulating a sustainability model focussed on the stakeholders. The model is applied to define the organisation's sustainability priorities in terms of stakeholder interests, and in designing how to incorporate those priorities into the business strategy.

The application of SPIRIT departs by understanding the external pressures on the organisation and does so by focussing on issues and stakeholders. The external issues vary significantly over time. Over the last forty years there have been tectonic movements that have required organisations to adapt vigorously or succumb. Some of these have been:

- Deregulation and privatisations in the 1980s
- Advent of Total Quality Management at the end of the same decade
- Globalisation and consolidation in the 1990s and onwards
- Industrialisation of emerging economies in the 1990s and 2000s
- Relocation of manufacturing to the newly industrialised world
- Global population growth, with great disparity across regions
- Reduction of extreme poverty but growth of wealth inequality
- Consciousness for the climate crisis as from the 2000s
- Awareness of and unacceptability towards pollution
- Terrorism at an unheard-of scale since 9/11
- Unstoppable migration waves at great volume, especially in the 2010s
- Advent of mobile technologies, social networks and Big Data with its impact on cyber-security
- Threat of Water-wars in several parts of the world

---

[1] This definition was proposed by the late Prof MacMillan at the Institute of Reputation, Henley Business School.

- Pending US—China commercial war
- Pandemics such as the current Covid-19.

These trends did not come alone. They have been accompanied by significant changes in laws and regulations; new demands on companies by investment funds; voluntary but morally obliging codes particularly in the environmental space; the proliferation of increasingly assertive third sector organisations such as NGOs, consumer protection and community groups.

So, these are the external issues that need to be dealt with in applying the SPIRIT model, but these issues must be related to the different stakeholder groups as is developed in the next section.

2.1.3 Stakeholders and Conflict of Interest

As will be seen later in this chapter, in the Knowledge Economy where assets are mainly intangible and no organisation creates value on its own but collaborating with others, companies are expected to integrate into their physical and social context. This is the essence of corporate responsibility: development of relationships with key stakeholders in order to simultaneously create social and financial value (Marquis & Velez Villa, 2012). It follows that stakeholder management cannot be left aside from a key decision as is stated in the SPIRIT model.

Stakeholders are defined as 'any group or individual who can affect or is affected by the achievement of an organizational purpose' (Freeman, 2010) or that contribute, voluntarily or involuntarily, to the value creation process of the company and are either 'beneficiaries or risk bearers' of its activities (Post et al., 2002).

CR in the SPIRIT vision calls for a stakeholder-centred approach to management which does not mean that stakeholders make the decisions. It does not mean, either, that the organisation needs to bend backward to satisfy all stakeholder groups. In fact, it is quite the contrary. It means that the organisation is sensitive to the impact of its activities on the different stakeholder groups and uses that as input for defining its priorities. One of the interesting things about CR, and possibly the reason why the issue does not go away as a resolved problem or as a passing management fad, is that stakeholder groups have opposing interests.

Often there is confusion between CR and philanthropy, but it must be stated clearly that these two concepts are radically different. In fact, philanthropy with corporate funds is corporate irresponsibility. A stakeholder-centred management approach is based on that maintaining appropriate relationships with stakeholders is to the long-term benefit of the organisation; that is why organisations increase social benefits or mitigate social problems to groups external to the company. Companies invest in CR because they expect that will lead to company-favouring responses from their stakeholders (Bhattacharya et al., 2009; Marquis and Velez Villa, 2012). Philanthropy is virtuous but it should be done from the agents own wallet, not that of the shareholders.

Marquis and Velez Villa (2012, p. 20, exhibit 1) classifies stakeholders into employees, customers, governments, investors, community and civil society and suppliers. There is a lot lumped together under some of those categories, but this classification will work for the sake of analysing stakeholders at this stage.

There is evidence to support that CR and involvement of staff on the organisation's CR activities generates organisational identification that in turn is highly correlated with improved job performance. The logic behind this is that organisational identification leads to higher commitment to the company's mission and to higher motivation. It connects the employees' values and identity to the values of the organisation (Ashforth & Mael, 1989; Dutton & Dukerich, 1991; Jones, 2007).

There is overwhelming evidence to support that the adoption of clear CR values operationalized into a sustainable business model will help attract high calibre professionals, from MBAs to Gen Y graduates, and that they will select a CR company over a non-CR one at equal pay, and in fact may even accept a lower pay to become part of a more responsible organisation (Bhattacharya et al., 2008; Greening & Turban, 2000; Sen et al., 2006; Turban & Greening, 1997). It is sometimes lost of sight that by 2025 Gen Y will comprise 75 percent of the workforce, and it is little known that 70 percent of them see themselves working independently at some point, so if firms do not make a significant effort to retain them they will suffer from a lack of staff. This situation is even more alarming in emerging markets where 82 percent see themselves as independents at some stage (Deloitte, 2014; Islam et al., 2011).

The second stakeholder group is that of customers. Customers are increasingly inquisitive into the CR standards of the companies they do business with. It is too early to say what the effect of the current Covid-19 crisis will trigger in terms of customers' buying habits but it may be surprising when data becomes available—in the 2007–2008 financial crisis in the UK the demand for sustainable products actually increased, surprising the analysts who anticipated that in a crisis consumers would be more focussed on price. The importance of customers as a stakeholder group depends to a significant extent on the value discipline of the organisation. When the value proposition to clients is based on customer intimacy and best total solution, the customer will rank very high up on the stakeholder group hierarchy; if the value discipline is of operational excellence and the value proposition of best total cost, maybe customers will rank further down. If, on the other hand, the value discipline is of product leadership and the promise to clients is of the best product, ensuring that the product incorporates sustainability throughout seems a must.

The third stakeholder group mentioned above is that of government. Governments are a particularly sensitive stakeholder group in highly regulated industries such as financial services and robust sustainability standards are essential in maintaining a productive relationship with this stakeholder group, particularly in times when the government is under pressure of scrutiny by a disgruntled population. Under these conditions governments are highly sensitive to flares in sustainability that will contribute further to population unrest, so it is key to keep this front under control for a smooth relationship.

With respect to CR and its connection to investors, there is much literature. The literature is mixed in that there is evidence that CR reduces company risks and increases its reputation, both of which translate into a positive outcome for shareholders; but there are other studies that arrive at that the impact of CR on shareholder value is not so clear; and yet some other studies that have arrived at that in companies with low innovativeness capability CR actually reduces customer satisfaction levels which in turn harms market value. An increasing number of investors are sensitive to social value creation, and many others are positive towards CR as long as it is demonstrated that it does not detract from shareholder value. What everyone agrees with is that investors do value transparency and expect that management in the companies they invest in are vigilant in keeping costs under control (Bhattacharya et al., 2009; Dowell et al., 2000; Luo & Bhattacharya, 2006).

Community and Civil Society engulfs a multitude of organisations such as environmental groups, charities of different natures, local NGOs and international NGOs, consumer defence groups, the traditional media and, highly relevant these days, social media groups. These stakeholder groups have weight, but even more so because they can have an impact on all the other stakeholder groups and their relationship with the organisation.

Finally, suppliers are an important stakeholder group because the host organisation is responsible for sustainability end-to-end, and it therefore needs to be closely integrated to its suppliers to be able to monitor and ensure that it has clear visibility of the standards being supplied. With the past trend of off-shoring production and establishing integrated supply chains across many organisations and countries this issue became even more sensitive.

Once the stakeholder groups have been identified, the SPIRIT model requires each one of them to be assessed in terms of how they influence the organisation by looking at three dimensions of the relationship: Power, Legitimacy and Urgency (P,L&U). This analysis is vital to ensure that the organisation's priorities are not overrun by those stakeholders with most power and urgency, leaving aside those with the most legitimacy.

With the P,L&U analysis in sight, the stakeholder analysis continues with two questions in mind:

- How are the stakeholders being treated?
- How are conflicts of interest between stakeholder groups dealt with?

The main objective of SPIRIT is to clarify the links between value and attitudinal alternatives, and the expected outcomes of an effective sustainability plan that will enable the best future performance. The dimensions of success of the future performance are retention, extension, advocacy, lack of subversion, development of trust and positive emotions with the stakeholder groups.

The next section gives an introduction to the challenges of metrics on sustainability.

2.1.4 Sustainability Measurement

It is undeniable that corporate reporting on sustainability has increased dramatically over the last few years as shown by the Climate Disclosure

Project (CDP).[2] The Economist (20 June 2020, p. 65) reports having analysed emissions disclosures from over 5000 publicly held companies that in total represent approximately 90 percent of the value of the world's stock markets, and found that the number of companies disclosing their emissions has risen steadily. In America, disclosure has risen from 53 percent of the S&P 500 companies five years ago, to 67 percent in 2020; during the same period disclosure of the Euro Stoxx 600 has gone from 40 to 79 percent, and of the Nikkei 225 it has gone from 13 to 46 percent. The study confirmed that the largest emitters are companies that burn fossil fuels in their key processes (i.e., fossil-fuel power generation, airlines running fleets of aircrafts, steelworks that need to burn coal in the production of steel), and specifically singled out Exxon as the largest emitter in America and ArcelorMittal in Europe. However, the study also confirmed that corporate reporting on sustainability is based on highly idiosyncratic Environment, Social and Governance (ESG) indicators calculated by external consultants in a relatively non-standard and often opaque way. This seems to be corroborated by the European Banking Authority (EBA, 16 July 2020)[3], when it calls for 'promoting internationally consistent disclosures of key metrics Green Asset Ratios to support the identification, assessment and measurement of sustainability financial risks'. These measurement difficulties in conjunction with the need to respond to social pressure and marketing incentives could lead to wooliness of arguments and overstating emissions controls.

Notwithstanding the limitations in metrics that need to be addressed, the implementation of sustainable business strategies needs to be pursued with those tools available today. The following subsection will present a model to facilitate this.

2.1.5 Making Things Happen: Sustainability Implementation

Three clear lessons emerge from the research with companies that implemented a sustainable business model. First is the need to focus on 'materiality' in CR programmes: Which are the really important issues the

---

[2] See the Climate Disclosure Project (CDP), https://www.cdp.net/en/companies/companies-scores, Figure 1.

[3] See EBA (16 July 2020) *EBA supports EU Commission's actions towards a more sustainable European economy* (https://eba.europa.eu/eba-supports-eu-commission%E2%80%99s-actions-towards-more-sustainable-european-economy).

company needs to confront? This requires getting to grips with what are the negative impacts of the organisation on society and the environment and defining how the organisation is going to do something about them. For example, a tobacco company should address issues around smoking and health; and financial services organisations should refrain from discussions on animal rights and CO_2 emissions (unless there is evidence to show that they are material). Perera's four dimensions of CR, mentioned above, give a useful framework for underpinning this.

Surviving in today's demanding markets requires that owning up to having a negative impact on some aspect of the business context should be accompanied by credible evidence that something is being done to neutralise these harmful effects. So, the second lesson is the imperative need for implementation. Companies need to move on from CR talk and resolutely tackle the question of its implementation. This will require defining metrics to measure progress—but it must do so with parsimony, avoiding the problem of too many metrics to manage, a trap that many companies in the early days for CR fell into. It must also embed the CR values in its business processes, so that the indicators based on the referred metrics emerge from the processes rather than having to be elaborated as ends in themselves. For implementation to be successful, the organisation must carefully plan a change management programme to tackle stakeholder management, organisational impact, training and communications initiatives. Finally, it needs to put in the information systems that will enable all this to happen.

Prioritising and applying this parsimony is an effective strategy for achieving results, but this gradual approach should not be interpreted as a lack of ambition, nor should it lead to complacency. So, the third lesson is the need for continuous improvement. Continuous improvement takes the form of adding more indicators and metrics to monitor once initial results are achieved. Furthermore, once the essential dimension of CR is well covered, moving on to other new CR dimensions is critically important.

The model in Fig. 2.2 brings together the concepts discussed above and the lessons learned in a way that helps management visualise the issues required to implement CR values in their organisations.

The design of CR implementation starts with the input from the SPIRIT model to prioritise stakeholder groups and initiatives. Departing from these CR opportunities the challenge is to arrive at a Sustainability Model founded on those CR values that are truly material to the

2 CONCEPTUAL FRAMEWORK: CORPORATE RESPONSIBILITY ...

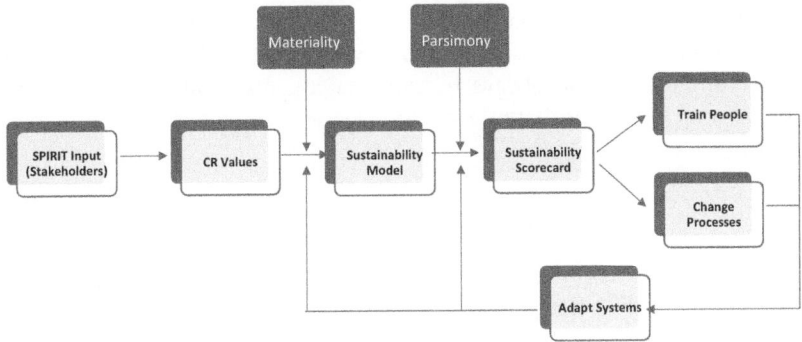

Fig. 2.2 CR implementation model (Griffiths, 2008)

company and the business strategy it is pursuing. The emphasis will be on those CR investments that, in the long run, strengthen the organization's competitiveness.

A common mistake is that organisations become impatient or overambitious at this stage and fall into the temptation of attempting to measure their progress using hundreds of indicators. That is a recipe for failure. Parsimony is required to ensure that at least in the initial stages, the organisation uses only a few indicators to track progress and to measure management performance in the CR space. These indicators then need to be structured and disaggregated in a form that allows the monitoring of all the units in the organisation. Although the dimensions are different to the Balanced Scorecard, the principles are almost exactly the same and therefore Kaplan and Norton's methods can be applied (Kaplan, 2010).

The next step is to allocate resources to the implementation. Two types of resources are required: People and ICT. On the people side it is necessary to identify what type of communication is needed, what training is required and how it is going to be delivered. There are two loops in the model. The first to be activated is the one on Metrics and Sustainability ScoreCard. Once progress has been made it is worth discussing the possibility of reviewing the Scorecard to include more indicators and reviewing the Sustainability Scorecard. The objective here is to achieve more granularity and depth in the information on the current CR initiatives, but not adding new initiatives. This review would typically be done every 6 months to a year.

The other loop is about selecting more processes to include in the Sustainability Model, in other words to achieve more breadth in the CR effort. But this should always be done taking materiality into account. This review would probably activate once a year or certain number of years.

2.1.6 Focus on Corporate Governance

So, this section has introduced the principles of CR and a framework that helps visualise them through four dimensions, namely, Corporate Governance and Ethics, People, Environment and Contribution to Development. It then moved onto presenting the relationship between CR and sustainability, the latter being about actions and behaviours that put CR into practice. Stakeholder analysis and management were presented as critical for any sustainability initiative, and the SPIRIT model was introduced as a means for stakeholder analysis and for formulating corporate strategy that incorporates sustainability at its core. Finally, there was a discussion on reporting and metrics, and a model for the implementation of sustainable business model.

In the next section the Corporate Governance and Ethics dimension of CR and sustainability will be developed.

2.2 CORPORATE GOVERNANCE, BUSINESS ETHICS AND CULTURE

2.2.1 Corporate Governance and Compliance

In Sect. 2.1.2 corporate governance was characterised as the processes of adopting and maintaining corporate values and objectives, of ensuring transparency, of accepting accountability and of confronting corruption. There are many important terms in this characterisation that will be expanded on throughout the following subsections in this chapter. One important one is transparency that refers to the openness of an organisation to sharing information with its inner-circle stakeholders (i.e., shareholders, staff, financiers, tax authorities, the community) and with other actors in its business context (i.e. Clients, consumers, regulators, NGOs, analysts). This does not mean 'carte blanche' disclosure to all, but each of these groups is entitled to the information directly relevant to sustainability compliance in its field (Griffiths, 2008).

In the Anglo-Saxon financial systems, the corporate governance triangle plays a key role: Shareholders, Board of Directors and Management (i.e., CXOs or executive directors) and there is a well developed legal framework defining the roles, rights and responsibilities of these three groups, as well as the relationships between them. Amongst these two relationships are key: Shareholders with the Board, and the Board with the CEO and executive team. These two relationships are intensely studied in the literature and are firmly embedded in the legal and regulatory frameworks. A third governance relationship is that one of the CEO and executive team with the rank and file of the organisation. Indeed, the operational relationship between senior management and the staff in the organisation is amply studied and defined, but not this relationship from a governance perspective. This is an important point to keep in mind as it will emerge in several parts of this book and constitutes a gap in the literature that this book intends to close or at least reduce.

In the Anglo-Saxon financial systems the shareholder has a privileged status amongst stakeholders and hence its pivotal role in this governance triangle. Complementing this, the legal framework goes into great detail in the protection of the minority shareholder. In the Continental financial system (i.e., Franco-German) and the Asian financial systems (i.e., Japan, South Korea) that strong position of the shareholders amongst stakeholders is diluted in different ways, amongst them by having a strong presence of union representatives, bankers and in some cases even government representatives or ex-officials on the Board of Directors. This can partly be explained by the higher relative weight of financial markets with respect to banks in the Anglo-Saxon financial systems.

Many will support that it is this significant role of shareholders amongst stakeholders and the clarity in direction that this gives, that has made the Anglo-Saxon financial systems highly successful—but, is the current trend towards CR and sustainability promoting a dilution of the role of shareholders? Will this have an impact on the future performance of the Anglo-Saxon financial systems?

The International Compliance Association (ICA) defines compliance as 'the ability to act according to an order, set of rules or request'; these orders, sets of rules and requests provide binding constraints under which the employees of a bank must operate with a threat of penalties if they are violated. As opposed to the adoption of an ethical banking culture that, as will be seen later, has a voluntary component, compliance is about abiding by the law. Compliance in finance has two levels:

- Level 1: The bank complies with regulations
- Level 2: The staff of the bank comply with internal systems and controls defined by senior management that are designed to lead to compliance with level 1.

It is the role of the compliance officers in the organisation to interpret national and global regulations and translate them into internal policies. The objective of this exercise is to give clear directives to staff that will lead to honesty and integrity and, ultimately, to an ethical banking culture.

Compliance laws, rules and standards cover matters such as observing proper standards of market conduct; managing conflicts of interest; treating customers fairly; and ensuring the suitability of customer advice, all of which refer to the fiduciary responsibility of a financial institution. Some of the cases to be seen in the following chapters of this book will illustrate the conflicts that emerge and the compliance risks that they pose.

More explicitly, compliance risk (BCBS, 2005) according to the Basel Committee of Banking Supervision (BCBS) refers to the 'risk of legal or regulatory sanctions, material financial loss, or loss to reputation a bank may suffer as a result of its failure to comply with laws, regulations, rules, related self-regulatory organisation standards and codes of conduct applicable to its banking activities'. It is the risk of impairment of the bank's integrity resulting in damage to the bank's brand (i.e., reputation risk) as well as sanctions and financial loss that can affect future business with existing clients and create substantial difficulty in acquiring new customers. It is more than just reputation risk since it can have lasting effects on the bank's integrity and customer trust. Based on this perspective, it is typical for a bank's compliance function to be part of the strategic risk management framework of the organisation and will have Board level involvement in its monitoring.

There are three specific sources of compliance breeches: Client related such as failures in 'Know your customer' (KYC) or transaction monitoring, money laundering and terrorist financing; Business related such as staff behaving in self-interest rather than that of the customer, conflict of interest of Bank Directors, data protection and privacy failures, harassment towards employees or customers; or Bank related, such as flaws in internal controls to meet Level 1 compliance, underfunded and weak compliance units, lack of independence of the compliance units, slow reporting of non-compliance incidents. Several of the cases to be seen in following chapters will address these issues.

Clearly in today's complex organisations senior management and the Board have many blind-spots that are barriers to imposing compliance top down. Furthermore, it is a rule of language that regulations have a degree of ambiguity. Thus, there needs to be a corporate culture of trust that leads to ethical behaviour. The next subsection will delve into some of the decisions that need to be made to make this happen.

2.2.2 Business Ethics and Its Relationship to Corporate Governance

What is business ethics? Clearly it is not about having or not having a set of rules to guide behaviours, as the Enron case demonstrated. Enron had a highly developed code of ethics that every employee and external stakeholder had access to, in which the foreword signed by its chairman, Kenneth Lay, read:

> We want to be proud of Enron and to know that it enjoys a reputation for fairness and honesty and that it is respected.

This did not stop it from grossly misrepresenting its financial situation.

Ethics is about what *should* be done and is defined by a series of values, not by rules. The absence of values will lead to bending the rules and abiding by the rules does not necessarily mean that the person is ethical, but it can be said that an unethical person will be prone to non-compliance of the rules. More specifically, business ethics can be defined as the study of standards of business behaviour that promotes human welfare. It is a systematic study of values.

While morality is a societal issue, ethics refers to a group or the individual, but morality underpins business ethics. An action is said to be ethical 'when it promotes the good of society or more specifically, when the action is intended to produce the greatest net benefit (or lowest net cost) to society when compared to all of the other alternatives' (Schwartz & Carroll, 2003). In other words, moral behaviour is about being unselfish, it is about not putting one's own interest ahead of the interest of others. Moral behaviour is about one's behaviour with respect to others and moral conflicts arise due to self-interest conflicts between individuals. In this context, two schools of moral philosophy need to be highlighted.

The first is Consequentialism. According to this school the ends justifies the means and the morality of an action is judged only by the consequences arising from that action. It requires the individual to analyse a decision in terms of the harms and benefits it causes to multiple stakeholders, and finally incline the decision towards the option that provides the greatest good for the greatest number of people.

The other school is Deontology. As opposed to the prior one, it focuses on the intentions or moral duty of the decision-maker, rather than on outcomes. It is about doing the right thing for its own sake; the individual in this school will not ask how much profit was made, but how was that profit made. The means are far more important than the ends. There is a separation between the consequences of an action and the moral principles guiding that action. The business decision-maker will ask the question: what are my moral obligations?

So, the question that arises here, is whether a bank should go for Consequentialism or for Deontology. Deontology sounds ethically attractive but, almost ironically, what are the consequences? Can doing the right thing have a negative impact on the interest of the customer, and thus breech the bank's fiduciary responsibility? Besides, in an activity that is already so highly regulated, can you add an additional constraint? And, how can an external entity keep check on whether the bank's staff is really being deontological? Like in many ethical situations, maybe there is not a Universal answer to this, and the important thing is that the institution develops an ethical stance, with little regard to which, and thus operates in the best interest of its customers.

There is evidence that stakeholder trust is the key for long-term financial performance and there is research that supports that ethics in banking leads to stakeholder trust (Brickley et al., 2002).

Conversely, research supports that customers are wary of unethical behaviour by bank representatives and that 'while trust and confidence are steadily increasing overall, [there is] lingering discontent toward mortgage lenders' (Khan, 2002). Data shows that even people morally opposed to strategic default said they would be more likely to default on their mortgage loan if they knew their lender or bank had been accused of predatory lending. The 2007–2008 financial crisis revealed numerous instances of overly risky behaviour on the part of bank executives that have had catastrophic consequences for society at large.

It is telling about the limitations of accounting systems that despite trust being so important for bank performance, it does not show up in its financial statements. Like many other intangibles such as reputation and intellectual capital, it is excluded. In the following subsection these business ethics concepts will be applied to doing business internationally. Are there absolute moral standards or do they depend on the frame of reference such as culture or social norms? And if the frame of reference evolves over time, does ethical behaviour change? This is a test of ethical relativism.

2.2.3 Doing Business in an International Context: Culture and Corruption

The radical changes in economic structures over the past two decades that have come as a consequence of globalisation and of the transition from an industrial economy to a knowledge economy have completely changed the landscape for multinational enterprises (MNE) and demand a shift in strategic models and magnify the needs for strategic adaptations. This shift in strategic models requires MNEs to focus their inner view of integrating business strategy with corporate culture in a way that was not imagined a short time ago. It also requires MNEs to take into account the new macroeconomic/political/regulatory frameworks in each country where they decide to operate, in what can be seen as an outer view of the firm. Not only do they need to respond to the formal institutional forces described, but also to informal ones such as societal culture in the host country. In this new economic structure, there is also a need to accommodate for cooperation between organisations to optimise resources, achieve sustainability and share intangible assets. Finally, MNEs need to consider changes in power structures that require them to operate more as polycentric networks of distributed power than the classic hierarchical organisation. All these factors have a significant impact on the governance of the MNE and will be fleshed out in the following paragraphs.

The first large change in approach in MNE has been the shift from a *low context* approach to a *high context* one. While in the past MNE could approach their international development in a one-strategy-fits-all-markets format, where they would not have any considerations for local differences, now they need to be highly sensitive to local differences and thus need to adapt their corporate strategies.

One of those local differences would be, typically, culture. The concept of societal culture was developed strongly by the GLOBE project (House et al., 2004) that used Hofstede's nine dimensions of culture to classify the 62 countries studied into ten cultural clusters as indicated in Fig. 2.3.

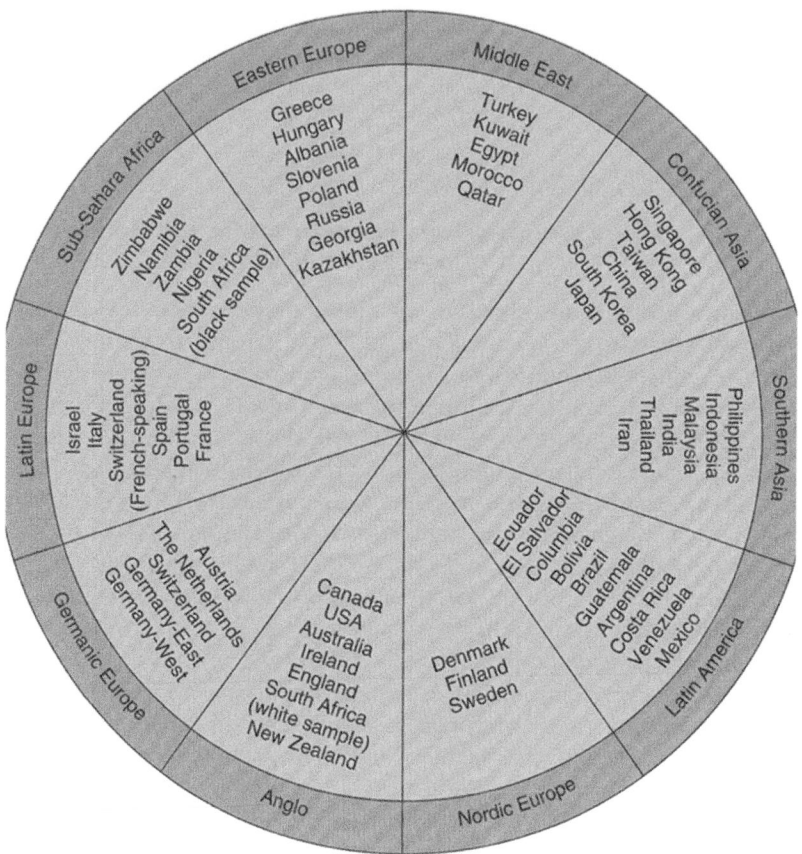

Fig. 2.3 GLOBE's ten cultural clusters (*Source* House et al., 2004)

These clusters are such that cultural similarity is large within a cluster and the cultural differences increase with the distance between clusters on the disc. That is, for example, that the cultural similarities are significant between Eastern Europe and the Middle East, but vastly different between Eastern Europe and Nordic Europe.

Another significant change was the moving away from monocentricity or centralised political system. The concept behind this is what Naim (2013) called the end of power but that can be more adequately described as the democratisation of power or lowering the barriers of power. In governments this movement takes the form of decentralization and devolution; in markets that were once controlled by banks take the form of being controlled by hedge funds and others; in corporations it manifests itself in that old behemoths cannot stand up to agile startups; in religion it is the end of unquestioned authority; another form is the proliferation of NGOs taking up roles previously exercised by governments. And more specifically in the world of MNEs, subsidiaries do not simply accept decisions taken in the centre, and host countries do not simply accept their culture to be overridden by the corporate culture of the MNE. Ostrom (2010) conceptualised this new model of governance as polycentricity, with distributed power and institutional forces leading to diverse strong decision centres that interact with each other in a democratic relationship.

Institutional forces are another significant factor that MNEs need to adapt to in each host country. In many of these host countries the formal institutional forces such as the political institutions, the economic organisation, the financial systems and the regulatory frameworks are deep and well developed and will clearly define the boundaries for the MNE's activities in that market. In other cases, these formal institutional forces are not well developed and informal institutions such as local culture and idiosyncrasy have a significant say upon the MNEs activities.

MNEs also need to deal with the fact that they are foreigners in their host markets. Sometimes being foreign is an advantage and other times it is a significant disadvantage. This does not depend only of specificities of the host market, but of some sort of cultural relationship between the head office country and the host country. For example in Brazil foreignness is often a disadvantage as the Brazilian culture is nationalistic, there are policies to develop local suppliers, and the tax system is incredibly complicated to understand. Chile, on the other hand, values foreign products if they come from the Anglo-Saxon or Germanic worlds, but on the other hand is negative with regards to products/services coming from Spain or other Latin American countries.

Rizzuto (2016) applies Miles & Snow's model to represent the strategy of the MNE. This model consists of three dimensions of adaptation (i.e., Entrepreneurial Problem, Engineering Problem and Administrative Problem) and four types of strategy to adopt (i.e., Prospector, Defender, Analyser and Reactor). Through her research Rizzuto bridges across all these domains and synthesises them in a model of strategy adaptation, as shown in Fig. 2.4.

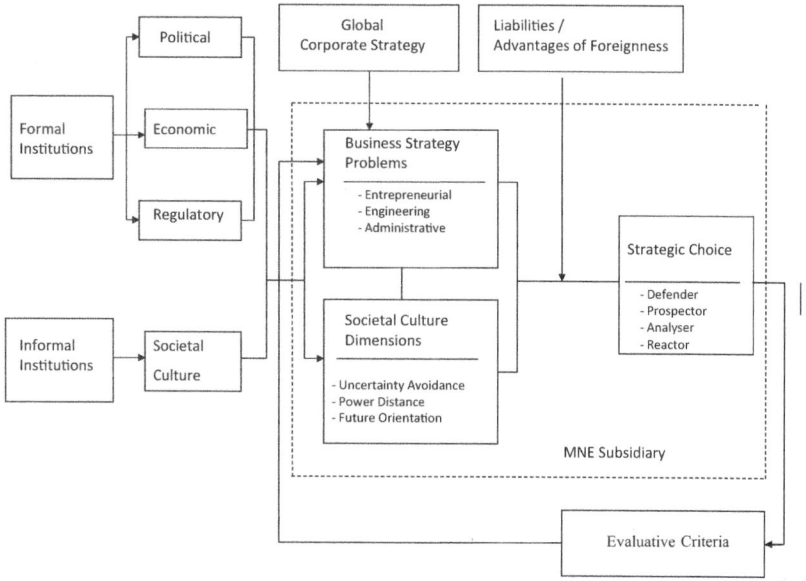

Fig. 2.4 Rizzuto model: Bringing it all together

The dotted line is the boundary of the subsidiary. In the top-centre is the Global Corporate Strategy of the MNE that influences the subsidiary strategy but is competing with other forces such as the Formal and Informal institutions on the left, and the societal culture dimension from underneath (as can be seen the model emphasizes three of Hofstede's dimensions of societal culture, namely *uncertainty avoidance, power distance* and *future orientation*). Liability/advantage of foreignness acts as a mediator between local strategy and strategic choice and there is a loop of evaluative criteria.

Corruption is a strong impediment for democracy and the rule of law. In a democratic system any institution that falls in malpractices loses legitimacy and as a country it leads to depletion of national wealth in the form of allocating resources to suboptimal projects, usually very large ones and obstructs the markets. At an individual level, it undermines people's trust in the political system, in its institutions and its leadership. It often leads also to environmental degradation.

Is there a change in the trade winds of corruption? Many countries have become increasingly concerned with the issue. New laws and international agreements seek to create a worldwide shift towards the reduction of corruption, and this means that business leaders operating internationally must deal with changes in ethical norms and laws and their responsibilities on this front are continually evolving. However, they do have resources to assist them in entering new markets as there are organisations such as Transparency International and the World Bank that provide estimates of the relative pervasiveness of corruption in different countries.

Transparency International conducts annual surveys in countries throughout the world to elicit opinions concerning the extent and nature of corruption in each country. It publishes a Corruption Perception Index (CPI) score for 180 countries that indicates the degree of public sector corruption as perceived by business people and country analysts, which ranges between 10 (highly clean) and 0 (highly corrupt).[4] Transparency International claims to be active on several fronts to curb corruption, especially of the public sector, around the world.

The World Bank says that it leverages its lending activities to empower its role in the investigation of corruption within its bank financed projects and programmes. It has created an Integrity Vice Presidency (INT)[5] that investigates allegations of fraud and corruption in Bank-financed projects. According to the website it claims that since 2001, INT has handled more than 3000 cases of alleged fraud, corruption or other wrongdoing, resulting in the public debarment of 351 companies and individuals whose names have been listed on the Bank's website. It says to provide extensive analytical work and diagnostics on governance and anticorruption and to set up global partnerships to fight corruption and help countries recover stolen assets.

Research by these organisations and others arrive at that corruption is everywhere but it is not the same everywhere which poses the need for firms and their managers to understand how local corruption works and how to adapt to it. Levels of corruption in each country evolve over time and it has been found that corruption tends to reduce in countries that

---

[4] See the 2019 results at https://www.transparency.org/en/cpi/2019/results.

[5] See https://www.worldbank.org/en/about/unit/integrity-vice-presidency#:~:text=The%20Integrity%20Vice%20Presidency%20%28INT%29%20is%20an%20independent,fraud%20and%20corruption%20in%20World%20Bank%20Group-financed%20projects.

have become recipients of higher levels of foreign direct investment (FDI) flows. Conversely, the greater the degree of government regulation, the higher the levels of corruption as public servants hold greater power over corporate success.

Two useful dimensions of corruption are *pervasiveness* and *arbitrariness*. On the one hand, pervasiveness refers to the likelihood that a firm will encounter corruption in its normal interactions with government officials (frequency and degree). On the other, arbitrariness relates to the degree of uncertainty concerning the size, the target and the number of payments necessary in any situation requiring government approval.

Returning to the issue of culture and finding its links to corruption, there are three of Hofstede's cultural dimensions that appear to be predictors of a country's level of corruption. The first point is that in national cultures that are low in *power distance* the people are prone to question the leaders' actions, and so there is less opportunity for corruption; while cultures with high power distance involve a hierarchical system that may encourage corruption. The second is that a culture that is high in *individualism* emphasises performance outcomes and therefore gives less weight to personal connections that could involve corruption. Finally, in countries with a *universalistic culture*, people believe that laws should apply to everyone equally, in contrast to *particularist* societies, where corruption may be commonplace as part of a well established favouritism and special privileges for the elites. Other studies (Conklin, 2011, p. 43) found that there is a clear relationship between disillusionment with democracy and the degree of corruption.

To close this reflection on culture and corruption it is important to mention that a national authority does have tools to counteract the effects of corruption through formal processes independently of the characteristics of its culture. For example, *transaction governance capacity* (TGC) is the capacity of a society to guarantee transparency in the processes of economic transactions and the ability to enforce commercial contracts. A high degree of TGC is achieved by fulfilling three primary criteria:

- giving stakeholders access to information;
- designing and implementing clear processes that eliminate selective interpretations; and
- speedily completing processes.

Complying with these three criteria is a way of building trust in the system.

With all these elements of ethics, culture, compliance and corruption in place, the next section will shed light on what needs to be done to create an ethical banking culture.

2.2.4 Creating an Ethical Culture in Banking

Corporate culture refers to a set of beliefs and behaviours that determine how a company's employees and management interact, handle relationships with stakeholders and perform business transactions. This has a special significance in banks, where an ethical bank culture provides a reference against which individual actions and decisions are evaluated on a continual basis. This means that individuals in a bank look to leadership for guidance on what is acceptable behaviour, and through experiences these patterns of behaviour are internalised by the employees who use them as a guide for future actions.

In line with the latter, research in the area identifies two dimensions to an ethical banking culture (ILM, 2007, p. 58), namely, an ethical stance and a cultural operational model. By an ethical stance is meant that the leadership needs to communicate its ethical position to its staff to give clarity for decision-making. Without this clarity, staff will face ethical dilemmas and be prone to making decisions misaligned with the organization's course. One area of those dilemmas is in the priority that is to be given to different stakeholder groups. As mentioned above on stakeholder management, different stakeholder groups have conflicting interests so if the staff focuses exclusively on optimising shareholder interests (i.e., short-term or long-term) it can lead to excessive risk-taking by managers at the expense of other stakeholder groups. For example, aggressive cost cutting may improve short-term profitability but may place undue stress on employees; or commission-based selling may increase short-term earnings at the expense of customer satisfaction. Another example is that increased risk-taking is likely to be preferred by shareholders who keep realised profits, but debt holders and depositors would be let down as they would rather more cash flow stability. So, bank executives should declare and communicate the bank's ethical stance to all stakeholders in order to ensure that there is clarity at the time of decision-making.

In terms of the other dimension, the bank's cultural operational model, it is about how to steer all these aspects of the bank's operations to meet its stated ethical stance. This is a structural issue and essentially covers four components of the structure. The first is culture, which as was mentioned above, is the collective set of core values, beliefs and norms of the bank. The second is about behaviour, which refers to the individual actions and reactions of employees in their dealings with each other and with customers. The third is knowledge or intellectual capital, which in turn can be subdivided into *human capital* that is what people know; *structural capital*, which refers to a set of systems and processes that enable banking operations; and *relational capital* that can be summarised as the network of contacts that the bank has with external stakeholders. Finally, there is the tangible infrastructure, which refers to the visible aspects (such as branch offices and ATMs) of the bank. So, all these components of the operational model need to be tuned to enable a sustainable strategy and prop up the ethical stance as described in the previous paragraph.

The ethical stance and cultural operation model conform the reference framework of the bank that acts as a moral compass for all its employees. They synthesise the values and behaviours that need to be shared across all units in the institution and will lead to ethical individual behaviours aligned with a strong bank corporate culture—it is this alignment that creates what is called an ethical bank culture. This ethical bank culture means going beyond mere compliance within the bank and its decision-making. It is the leaderships' job to create the culture ensuring employees *do the right thing, because it is the right thing to do* and in the best interest of the prioritised stakeholders. Without this guidance, good people can and do make bad decisions. It requires that senior management sets the example and relentlessly communicates to all employees the values of the bank and the standard of behaviour that is expected from them.

In summary, achieving an ethical bank culture requires a proactive, day-to-day, effort from the bank's leadership team. It needs to implement and monitor training and communications on the bank's values and conscientious moral judgement. It needs to promote diversity within the bank with the intention that this will translate into a balanced relationship with the institution's different stakeholder groups. The leadership team must permanently refer back to the bank's objectives when making decisions on products, interest rates, remuneration schemes and communications with the external world. It must implement training on confronting dilemmas in decision-making, promoting openness and discussion between employees and raising employees' awareness of the effects of their behaviour. The leadership team, must put in place a scheme for giving direct employees feedback on results of their behaviours. Furthermore, it should set up an ethics committee to monitor progress and establish a communications channel to the committee or other body for individuals to refer to *ex-ante* when confronted with ethical dilemmas.

2.2.5 The Challenges in a World of Intangibles

Complementing the view on CR and sustainability seen before, this section focussed on the Corporate Governance dimension of sustainability. It delved deep into the challenges of corporate governance and the issues related to compliance, so critical in an extremely sensitive and regulated industry as financial services. It then did an overview of the principles of ethics and how they apply to banking. That was followed by the challenges of doing business internationally where societal culture plays a significant role and different views on what corruption is come into play. Finally, it was shown that financial services confronts professionals in banks with many dilemmas, and therefore there needs to be in place an ethical banking culture that contains as much as possible making inadequate decisions.

The fact that the world has transitioned, or is transitioning, from an industrial economy to a knowledge economy, with its predominance of intangible assets and the surging of collaboration over competition, poses to the corporate governance of banks a series of new challenges. That is what will be addressed in the next section.

2.3 The Knowledge Economy: From Physical Resources to Intangible Assets

2.3.1 Characteristics of the Knowledge Economy

Up to the 1980s the Economics 101 course at any university would start with the introduction of students to the three factors of production: *Land*, *Capital* and *Labour*. Unknown then, there was something missing that started becoming significant two-hundred or so years earlier: a fourth factor that is now articulated as *Knowledge & Sustainability* (K&S). The incidence of K&S was marginal in the agricultural economy, but with the advent of the Industrial Revolution it rose and manifested itself in what was later called productivity. Together with productivity came massive social changes, prominent amongst them was the possibility to pay people for work and thus the moral demeaning of slavery. It is interesting that for 12,000 years fierce battles were fought for avoiding the wrong end of the relationship, but never was que institution of slavery as such questioned. Not even in the scriptures. Of course, it was only the K of K&S that was acting then; the S kicked in at the very end of the twentieth century—precisely the acceleration of the transition from an industrial economy to the knowledge economy. This can be visualised in Fig. 2.5.

Labour is the great loser in this transition to the knowledge economy, with some astounding contradictions. *Labour* productivity is declining while the contribution of *labour* to gross domestic product (GDP) is also dropping and it is well established that the drop in weight of *labour* with respect to GDP is proportional to the increase in deterioration of wealth distribution. There are no surprises there, but what is surprising is that despite the growth of population and the decrease of incidence of *labour* on GDP, global poverty is decreasing (Rosling, 2018).

In parallel with this change in the relative weights of the factors of production, since the 1990s there has been a new approach to business strategy: a clear trend towards emphasising efficiency in the use of resources as opposed to the traditional industrial economy urge to

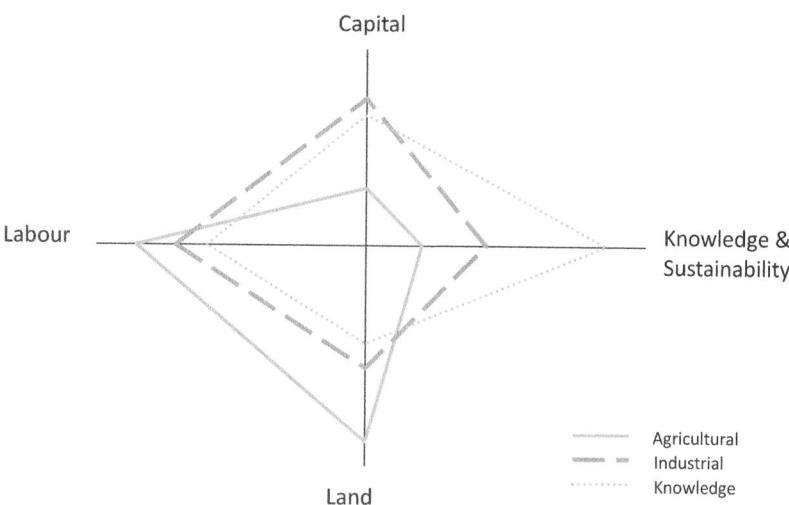

Fig. 2.5 Protagonist fourth factor of production: Knowledge & Sustainability

control raw materials. In other words, leading organisations in all regions of the world are applying knowledge directed towards innovations aimed at increasing efficiency, effectiveness and productivity within a framework of greater sustainability.

The question that springs to mind here is why is labour productivity dropping? This question will be addressed later in this chapter.

So, what is meant by *knowledge economy*? Here are two established definitions[6]:

> ... one in which the generation and exploitation of knowledge has come to play the predominant part in the creation of wealth. It is not simply about pushing back the frontiers of knowledge; it is also about the most effective use and exploitation of all types of knowledge in all manner of economic activity. (DTI Competitiveness White Paper, 1998)

and

> economic success is increasingly based upon the effective utilisation of intangible assets such as knowledge, skills and innovative potential as the key resource for competitive advantage. The term "knowledge economy" is used to describe this emerging economic structure. (Economic and Social Research Council, 2005)

So, from these definitions it can be extracted that success in the knowledge economy is reliant on the effective application of knowledge to solve business problems, to exploit business opportunties, to innovate and thus achieve sustainable competitive advantage. But then, what is knowledge?

The definition of knowledge has entertained philosophers for over two millennia and they still have not come to terms with it. For the purpose of this book the definition of knowledge departs from data. Despite claims that data is the 'black ore' of the twenty-first century and is worth more than oil, data has little intrinsic value. However, data with a structure converts into information, which has not too much intrinsic value either, but when it meets intelligence (i.e., human or digital) that gives an explanation to that information, it turns into knowledge that has, no doubt, intrinsic value. Is this enough? Going back to the DTI definition of

---

[6] http://www.theworkfoundation.com/Assets/Docs/I%20Brinkley%20HE,%20FE%20and%20the%20Knowledge%20Economy.pdf.

knowledge economy given above, it '*is not simply about pushing back the frontiers of knowledge*' but about '*exploitation of all types of knowledge in all manner of economic activity*'. So, it is important to differentiate knowledge per se from knowledge that can be applied to economic activity—this kind of knowledge will be referred to from now on in this book as *intellectual capital* (IC). One day this age will be referred to as the *IC economy* instead of *knowledge economy*!

The next question is who creates knowledge in the knowledge economy? Citing Michael Porter (1998), Sala-i-Martin and Schwab (2004, p. 84) say it is clear that

> *sound fiscal and monetary policies, a trusted and efficient legal system, a stable set of democratic institutions, and progress on social conditions contribute greatly to a healthy economy.*

These border conditions provide the context and opportunity to create wealth but macroeconomic conditions do not themselves create value. Wealth is actually created at the microeconomic level of the economy that is by firms. In excess of 80 percent of the variation of GDP per capita across countries is accounted for by microeconomic fundamentals. Unless microeconomic capabilities flourish, macroeconomic, political, legal and social reforms will not bear fruit (Viedma & Cabrita, 2012).

As a corollary of this, the wealth or poverty of a specific nation is strongly dependant on the number of competitive or excellent companies that the nation hosts, where an excellent or competitive company is the one that achieves long-term extraordinary profits due to the fact that it has a business model with sustainable competitive advantages. Government do not create wealth but they contribute to facilitating or to hindering wealth creation.

A second corollary is that in the knowledge economy sustainable competitive advantages are mainly based on intangibles and because of this strategic management of intangibles or intellectual capital becomes a fundamental task. When asked what his role at Apple was, Steve Jobs responded that it was to manage its IC, by which he meant channelling knowledge assimilated into the organisation towards generating innovative ideas and developing them into final products. He spoke about focussing all his attention on 'invisible opportunity spaces' such as understanding and developing the value of networks. Which was arguably Apple's most successful strategy? Quite possibly the creation of App Store

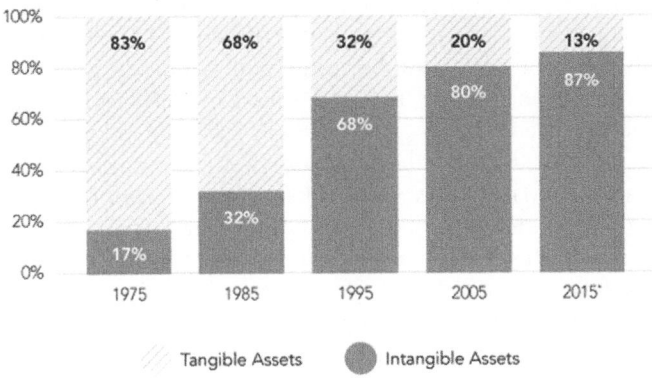

Fig. 2.6 The increasing weight of intangibles

that generates more income than tangible devices and at close to zero marginal cost, that is straight to the bottom line. Ironically, it is said that it took Jobs a long time to accept his Board's idea that Apple's platform should be opened for external developers to provide applications—Jobs the perfectionist believed applications should be developed in-house.[7]

An organisation's value consists of tangible and intangible assets, but intangible assets now constitute by far the majority of assets in most organisations. In the period between 1975 and 2015, the relations between tangible and intangible assets in the Standard & Poor 500 firms, went from 83–17 percent, to 13–87 percent as shown in Fig. 2.6.

Considering that most intangibles are not documented in traditional accounting systems, how can companies in knowledge intensive fields prove their value to investors? Moreover, how can a company's management manage assets that are not accounted for? Clearly accounting and reporting systems need to be reviewed and updated—there will be more on this key governance issue at the end of this chapter.

Having seen that wealth in the knowledge economy is created by companies, the next question that needs to be addressed is how these companies create wealth. The simple answer to this is that they do so

---

[7] See Prasad, Bhaskar (2011) *International Business Times, Octubre*; and Edvinsson, Leif (2012) *Foreword* to Viedma and Cabrita (2012).

through good strategy formulation and superior strategy implementation, which is always a human task and strongly depends on the quality of the top management team and its key professional people. In a continuously changing environment business models quickly get out-of-date and, as a consequence, innovation in business models becomes an urgent and permanent need. This is quite different from the industrial economy where, in its early stages, value creation centred around product innovation; and in its later years the challenge was process innovation and innovation in the service layer (Viedma & Cabrita, 2012).

Amazon is probably the most iconic company in the business model innovation front. It started by creating a revolution in book retailing by taking it from the high street to the cloud; it later introduced the e-book simultaneously disrupting the publishing industry and entering the device business (i.e., Kindle). It then went on to shift part of its workload onto its clients by introducing reader reviews and saving the cost of reviewers; then it applied AI to anticipate the interest of its clients (i.e., 'readers of this book also bought...'). It then exploited a formidable logistics network and supply chain to move into general retail, online. Then came the greatest innovation in business model by exploiting its formidable ICT platform/infrastructure to move into the Cloud computing services business dislodging IBM as the prime corporate computing services provider; then came the handset business, Fire, to get its icon on the mobile screen; and its next step will be to enter the courier business applying drones for the last mile.

Who has made the greatest impact, Apple or Amazon? That question normally triggers a fervent debate. Apple has a stronger reputation for design, but Amazon has had more impact on the operation of the digital world. Both have revolutionised business models, but Amazon seems to have the edge. However, both are examples of companies that have understood the knowledge economy and the importance if innovating business models and are to be kept in mind for benchmarking in financial services.

Another characteristic of the knowledge economy is that companies on their own do not create wealth. They need the collaboration of other companies, of universities and research institutes, of financial institutions, of government and other organisations and institutions and specially the existing ones in the cluster, region or nation where the company is located. In other words, they need to be an active part of a territorial open innovation system and of what some authors call knowledge-based ecologies (Viedma & Cabrita, 2012).

In summary, in the knowledge economy the creation and application of knowledge is key in economic value-building. It is more than merely extending the frontiers of knowledge...economic success depends on the effective use of intangible assets (e.g., knowledge, skills) to obtain a competitive advantage. It is a new economic structure in which all sorts of knowledge is applied in the most effective ways in all kinds of economic activities with a focus on innovating business models. The advent of the smartphone and social networks, through their effect Big Data, have had a significant impact on the structure of the knowledge economy. This will be dealt with in the next section.

2.3.2 Effect of Technology on the Knowledge Economy: Social Networks, Big Data, Artificial Intelligence

Data was described above as not having intrinsic value but being the building blocks of knowledge and IC. The advent of the i-phone and with it the smartphone gave place to social networks and, to all effects, the digitally networked society. The volume of data in the world at the human scale was already on the rise through the proliferation of devices from i-pods, through i-pads and security cameras, to all sorts of devices such as cardiac defibrillators and other remote health monitors, GPS and localization systems, early mobile phones with texting and e-mail capabilities, facial and fingerprint recognition devices, barcode readers,...but the advent of social networks had an explosive effect on the production and capture of volumes of data. Apart from this human-scale data, there were massive advances on sub-human-scale data such as genetic sequencing and supra-human data such as that obtained of the deepest parts of the universe by installations such as the Atacama Large Millimetre/submillimetre Array (ALMA) observatory. To cap it all, there is machine-to-machine or robotic chatter that already 'exceeds that generated by the sum of all human voice conversations taking place on wireless grids' (O'Brien, 2012). All these applications had an unplanned side-effect that is the phenomenon called Big Data. In that sense, Big Data is a self-inflicted phenomenon in the knowledge economy like the *climate crisis* is an unplanned outcome of the industrial economy.

Similarly to how *global warming* or *climate change* are understatements of the climate crisis in the industrial economy, 'Big' data is a colossal understatement—it should be called Data Tsunami. Just to get a feel for its dimension: since the first registration of data, which took the form of writing some 5000 years ago, up to 2003, humans created 5 billion gigabytes of data. In 2011 this same amount of data was created every two days. In 2013 the same amount of data was accumulated every 10 minutes. A recent review of two other sources gave for 2016 similar volumes as those given above for 2011.[8] Does it matter? Not at all—even if these figures have an error of 50 percent, the volumes are staggering.

What is humanity getting out of the Data Tsunami? It is producing knowledge about a Universe covered in metrics and it is learning about itself as could never have been imagined a decade ago. It has metrics for nearly everything—actually for so many things that it appears to be confirming Galileo's famous remark that the language of nature is mathematics; or even Stephen Hawking's more mischievous that mathematics may enable man 'to read the mind of God' (Hannaford, 2006). The volume is so massive that the human mind is not doing this alone—it is relying on artificial intelligence (AI).

As happens with many technologies that have not reached maturity, there is a certain degree of confusion on what is meant by the terms associated with them. This is the case with AI, machine learning, artificial neural networks or cognitive computing. An illustration of this was addressed by Ginni Rometty at her CES 2016 keynote speech when the question '*If Watson is AI?*' was raised. Rometty, CEO at IBM, responded that AI is only one of 27 engines behind Watson, IBM's cognitive computing initiative (Rometty, 2016). In a recent review of the state of AI The Economist (2018) mentioned that deep learning has given 'new life to AI'—if deep learning is linked to cognitive computing, then there is an overlap or even outright confusion in the use of these terms: IBM includes AI under cognitive computing, and The Economist states that cognitive computing is a part of AI. To generate even more distraction, McAffee and Brynjolfsson (2017, pp. 69–70) write about AI being similar to the learning of languages by humans. They state that there are two types of AI; on the one hand there is the rules-based or symbolic like humans learn a second language; and on the other is statistical pattern recognition like a child learns a first language—so for them AI is interchangeable with cognitive computing. This debate on terminology is likely to continue for some time.

---

[8] See http://www.northeastern.edu/levelblog/2016/05/13/how-much-data-produced-every-day/ and http://www.silverpop.com/marketing-resources/white-papers/all/2016/2017-marketing-trends/.

As the roots of AI can be traced back to the 1950s it has been around for many decades before the articulation of terms such as deep learning, machine learning, artificial neural networks or cognitive computing so it makes sense to differentiate the meaning of these terms. Thus, this section will explain what is meant by the terms machine learning, artificial neural networks and cognitive computing, and relate them to the more established concept of AI. To simplify things, in the remainder of this book the terms machine learning, artificial neural networks and cognitive computing will be used interchangeably.

Deep Learning refers to artificial neural networks learning in a fashion that emulates the way it is believed the human brain learns, changing the connections between bits of computer code that are designed to behave like neurons and thus enabling the churning of data to identify and retain patterns. The outcome of this is similar to the human learning cycle: Observe-Interpret-Evaluate-Decide. This can be applied to performing highly complex tasks such as managing a power grid, or a traffic network, or a hospital complex and the equipment within, or even a nuclear arsenal. It is reported that Google reduced energy consumption in its array of servers by 40 percent and it is evident that quantum leaps have been achieved in mundane elements such as bio-recognition, voice-recognition, translation and others (Jarvis, 2012; Kolb & Kolb, 2017; McAffee & Brynjolfsson, 2017, p. 76; Rees, 2018).

Silver et al. (2017) further develop the idea of deep learning by introducing the concepts of supervised learning, unsupervised learning and learning reinforcement. Supervised learning refers to the machine being fed with many examples or cases that it can sieve through when confronted with a new situation, with an objective of finding the one that best adapts to the particular situation. The artificial neural network is improved further by 'playing against itself'[9] and thus registering more use cases in a process they call reinforced learning. In other words, the machine departs from a set of use cases introduced by humans and then plays against itself creating increasing numbers of use cases that 'enrich' its 'experience' on the topic. Finally, in unsupervised learning the machine is given a set of rules of the game and a *tabula rasa* to develop its own 'knowledge' through playing and pattern recognition without any human designed use cases. In a similar vein, Radford et al. (2018)

---

[9] This technique was used in the development of the system which eventually became a world champion at GO.

claim to employ a two-stage training procedure to learn natural language processing (NLP). First, they use a language modelling objective on a set of unlabelled data to learn the initial parameters of a neural network model. In a second stage they adapt these parameters to a target task using the corresponding supervised objective.

As has been seen lately with the Tesla autopilot accidents on March 23, 2018 in Silicon Valley (FORBES, 2018) and on March 18 in Arizona (San Francisco Examiner, 2018) the application of these leading-edge technologies comes with significant risks. They can and do fail. This kind of failure means systemic collapse and potentially tragic accidents.

It has been pointed out that AI-based devices will be able to replace much if not all human professional endeavours. It has already been claimed that AI's performance in some aspects of medical diagnosis is superior to humans. AI's ability in the legal profession will be second to none as the work in this area is largely a matter of being able to rapidly access details of either legislation or case history. AI will certainly be able to produce any mathematical or arithmetical work faster and more error-free than any human. Information and communications technology already play a very significant role in both accounting and finance and this can be expected to grow considerably as more AI is introduced into the systems. The ability of machines to produce graphical representations out-strips that of humans. Medical diagnosis has been substantially improved through the use of AI and this can be expected to increase and produce material productivity gains in the hands of doctors and nurses (Jiang et al., 2017; Kenny et al., 2008). In short, knowledge-based work will be severely impacted. There is likely to be in the medium term a significantly reduced need for knowledge workers in most if not all the professions. This is shocking—a knowledge economy with less need for knowledge workers?

The repercussions of this in society are not at all clear. Historically technology tended to eliminate low skilled work and thus created opportunities for retraining individuals to higher skill levels. There is a real potential that the opposite will happen with the application of AI. It would appear that fewer professionals may be needed and many of those who are already trained may find it increasingly difficult to find work and may have to compromise on lower skilled tasks (Brynjolfsson & McAffee, 2014).

Furthermore, with the development of applications of AI such as driver free vehicles there is a potential to eliminate the necessity for numerous semiskilled jobs. It has been estimated that there are approximately 3.5 million professional lorry drivers in USA alone whose jobs will be threatened by this new approach to transportation (All Trucking, 2018). It is not ridiculous to envisage high levels of structural unemployment for which there may not be any immediate solutions.

It is true that there have been false alarms in the past about how technology will destroy jobs and these predictions have not been realised as suggested. But previous forms of information and communications technology have never been as sophisticated as they are today. They have never been as inexpensive to acquire. They have never been as robust and accessible to large sections of the population. Today the higher probability is that there will be a more profound impact on employment levels of knowledge workers, certainly in the more developed countries. The next section will deal with another dimension of social change.

2.3.3 Cultural Change: Incorporating Generation Y as Consumers and Workers

Several aspects of culture and governance have been discussed in prior sections, but there is one more aspect that needs to be dealt with and that is the effect that incorporating Generation Y is already having on corporate culture and thus governance. This section deals with the impact that Generation Y is introducing by making its footprint in the worlds of work and consumption, giving an additional cultural lever to the Knowledge Economy. Examples of changes in the workplace caused by the incorporation of Gen Y is, on the one hand, the pressure on senior management to use social networks (SN) to communicate with their staff and with the outside world; on the other hand that the growth of Gen Y in the organisation also creates an environment that is far more prone to sharing knowledge and information. With respect to Gen Y as consumers, research has found that in the Fintech space the older generations are followers of their Gen Y peers in the use of mobile financial products and channels, and this can be extrapolated to other industries.

Indeed, lessons for financial services can be drawn from research done in the telecommunications sector (Griffiths & Arenas, 2014). It has found that knowledge networking is being driven by the grass-roots (young people, mostly Generation Y) while the old stock is reluctant to get involved. The young people are pushing the agenda by bringing in their own devices (i.e., being given a device by the company is not considered a perk of the job for Generation Y—they want to use their own device at work) and being permanently connected. This has led to the realisation that the company has minimum control over even the most sensitive information (e.g., commercial proposals) which has triggered great concern particularly for information security officers. This situation is leveraged by the fact that these young people have a far more collaborative mindset which, together with connectedness, strengthens the people-driven knowledge networks within and across organisations. It was also found that there is a need for effective social networking tools that enable people to share their information and knowledge. These tools need to be highly user friendly with the same touch and feel of their personal social networking (SN) platforms. If these are not provided, people will store this information in their own hard discs or in their Drop-box or similar tools.

Senior management's view on SN is paradoxical. On the one hand this group understands the value and benefits of SN and have hard evidence that they are here to stay, as the companies' revenue from SMS traffic has stagnated or dropped due to the widespread adoption of WhatsApp amongst their clients. On the other hand, their adoption rate of SN as a working tool is low and in general senior management does not use SN to mobilise their staff. At the middle management level, particularly amongst the older population, resistance is even higher, which is a significant barrier to implementation of domesticated SN in organisations, particularly if senior management does not support it explicitly. Hurdles to implementation are not only entrenched in the type of people as mentioned above, but also in their incentives that are in most cases not aligned with the need for knowledge sharing.

Prior to the pandemic, high staff turnover and aggressive recruiting rate has caused an increasing number of Generation Ys amongst the workforce. This alone is causing cultural changes with the new generation being far more prone to connectedness and having a more natural tendency to share through SNs. This has helped trigger the ubiquity of connection devises and leverage the network effect. The question that remains to be answered is whether this connectedness and participation in SN has translated into business benefits for the organisation.

On the imprint of Generation Y as consumers, research into the advent of Fintech as a separate industrial sector from banking, found that Generation Y are avid adopters of mobile banking as long as it is easy to use and it poses no excessive risks in terms of data security. Both these conditions were hard to meet for incumbent bankers due to their legacy platforms, but straight forward for the Fintechs. On the other hand, due to the increased capital requirements that fell upon banks after the Great Recession of 2007–2008, banks put great effort into developing CRM processes and solutions that enabled them to strengthen their relationship with their 'valued' (i.e., the older more affluent) customers, and let go their less profitable and higher risk ones, as the Generation Y were seen to be. This opened a segment of great potential to the Fintechs (Boonsiritomachai & Pitchayadejanant, 2017; Lee & Shin, 2018). What banks seem to have overlooked is that Generation Y are not wealthy as individuals (yet) but they are on the way to become the largest demographic group, and as a group they hold $1tn in wealth. So, for example, as investors they are offered by Fintechs passive portfolios managed through robo-advisers at extremely low fees that this generation can monitor fully from remote locations via mobile applications. Worse still than this misjudgement, is that banks did not foresee that Generation Y have great influence over their elder generations' behaviours in terms of adoption of technologies. When the parents and grandparents of the Generation Y saw how effectively their younger were managing their portfolios, they decided to follow the same root—as a result the traditional asset-management/wealth-management sector is under pressure to prove their added value.

In parallel with the above and especially in the Anglo-Saxon world, with Generation Y there emerged a new breed of what were to be called social entrepreneurs whose projects did not pursue a predominantly financial objective and thus were unfit to be assessed in terms of the banks' traditional credit scoring criteria. This new breed of entrepreneurs resort to alternative finance sources such as crowdfunding so became another market opportunity for Fintechs (Kotarba, 2016).

In summary, the incorporation of Generation Y into the workforce is changing the culture and openness to sharing knowledge and accelerating the adoption of SN tools, but the barriers to full deployment are still embodied in the older generation of senior and middle managers. As consumers they are demanding from traditional organisations that they offer mobiletechnology-based services, and as entrepreneurs they are changing the business-to-business landscape. The final section of this chapter will deal with problems of reporting in the knowledge economy and propose integrated reporting as a way forward.

2.3.4 Transparency and Reporting—Integrated Reporting <IR>

As seen in prior sections, the challenge in accountability and reporting is that the traditional accounting systems do not (generally) account for intangibles, thus missing out on the core of an organisation's assets in the knowledge economy. So this needs to be overcome by adopting different approaches to reporting, in particular approaches that will account for intangible assets. One of these approaches is what has been called Integrated Reporting <IR> and an overview of it will be given in the following paragraphs.

What is integrated reporting? Integrated Reporting is a broad-based framework for business and investment decisions that are long term, inclusive and with purpose. It was created by the International Integrated Reporting Council (IIRC), a worldwide coalition with the mission to mainstream integrated thinking and reporting and to change the corporate reporting system so that Integrated Reporting <IR> becomes the global norm. As all reporting it is a communications tool prepared through a process founded on integrated thinking that results in a periodic report issued by the organisation on its value creation over time. More specifically, it is a concise communication about how an organization's strategy, governance, performance and prospects, in the context of its external environment, lead to the creation of value in the short, medium and long term.

The need for <IR> emerged as a response to globalisation and interconnectivity that mean the world's finances, people and knowledge are inextricably linked, as evidenced by the global financial crisis. In the wake of the crisis, the desire to promote financial stability and sustainable development by better linking investment decisions, corporate behaviour and reporting has made evident the need for <IR>. As has already been mentioned above, currently there are significant information gaps in reports, with the organisations such as the World Bank and IMF calling for a greater focus on aspects such as risk, intangible assets and incorporating a future orientation to reporting. The <IR> has emerged as a response to these needs and has been created to enhance accountability, stewardship and trust as well as to harness the information flow and transparency of business that technology has brought to the modern world. It is expected that the <IR> will provide investors with the information they need to make more effective capital allocation decisions and thus promote better long-term investment returns.

In the words of the IIRC Chairperson, Mervyn King, The <IR> Framework.

> ... is a tool for the better articulation of strategy, and to engage investors on a long-term journey to attract investment that will be crucial to achieving sustained, and sustainable, prosperity.

<IR> is, thus, an evolution of corporate reporting, with a focus on conciseness, strategic relevance and future orientation. As well as improving the quality of information contained in the final report, <IR> makes the reporting process itself more productive, resulting in tangible benefits. Because it requires and brings about integrated thinking, the process of its preparation involves many people from across the organisation and enables a better understanding of the factors that materially affect an organization's ability to create value over time. This process itself should lead to behavioural changes and improvement in performance throughout an organisation.

So, the primary purpose of <IR> is to explain to financial capital providers how an organisation creates value over time. The <IR> framework does so by conceptualising the organisation's capital into six categories: *financial, manufactured, intellectual, human, social and relationship* and *natural*. These capitals are stocks of value that are affected or transformed by the activities and outputs of an organisation and the <IR> Framework gives guidelines to express them through a combination of quantitative and qualitative information. Across these six categories, all the forms of capital an organisation uses or affects should be considered.

The six categories of capital are seen as a flow, a flow of capital through the organisation. In other words, an organization's business model draws on various capital inputs and the <IR> shows how its activities transform them into outputs. The structure of the <IR> includes the following eight content elements:

- *Organisational overview and external environment*
- *Governance*
- *Business model*
- *Risks and opportunities*
- *Strategy and resource allocation*
- *Performance*
- *Outlook*

- *Basis of preparation and presentation.*

The General Reporting Guidance for preparation of the <IR> poses a question for each of the content elements that must be addressed by the organisation to prepare its report. It is important to understand that the eight content elements are fundamentally linked to each other and are not mutually exclusive. As such, the order of the content elements can be sequenced in different ways. They are not intended to serve as a standard structure for an integrated report with information about them appearing in a set sequence or as isolated, standalone sections. Rather, information in an <IR> is presented in a way that makes the connections between the content elements apparent.All the information on the <IR> and the guidelines for its preparation are in the public domain.

There is no certainty that the <IR>, an initiative launched in 2013 and thus still in its early years, is the final answer, or if it will achieve what it pursues, or if the international business community will give it the value it deserves. But if it does, it will most probably enable organisations, especially publicly listed ones, to focus on results beyond the quarter. It will also set the focus for companies to make capital-allocations decision based on the value creation capabilities of the organisation. If it is successful at this, it will pave the way to bridging across the different systems.

If <IR> fails the international community will have to search for other reporting systems that build on its philosophy but take it further. Win or lose, <IR> helps to understand that the current reporting systems are far from sufficient for the knowledge economy and a world where intangibles are the bulk of assets.

2.3.5   Bringing It All Together

This chapter has given the reader a solid background on current thinking on CR and its connection to a sustainable business model. It reflects on the need for organisations to connect to their social and physical context and on the role of business in society and *how* successful companies are interpreting this role and adopting it. It also reflects on the challenges that derive from the need to centre their strategy and operations on the needs of different stakeholder groups—but it also makes clear that it is not the stakeholders who decide for the organisation. The organisation needs to define and establish its character but do so in a form that is sensitive to stakeholders. The trouble is that different stakeholder groups have often opposing interests so the corporation must deal with this. Within this context the chapter defined what Corporate Governance is and its relationship to corporate responsibility and a sustainable business model.

It described the components of CG and, what is more important, the relationships between these components. The relationships between the Board and the shareholders; the relationship between the Board and the CEO/Senior Management; and the relationship between the CEO/Senior Management and the rank and file of the organisation. It developed the concepts of Business Ethics and the role that it plays in connection to CG and the demands it puts on senior management and the Board. It then introduced and developed the concept of Institutional Forces, both Formal and Informal. That led on to the issue of Societal Culture and its impact on Corporate Culture and the need for an ethical corporate culture going forward.

The chapter then went on to describe the characteristics of the knowledge economy where innovation is driven more by innovation in business models than in products, services or processes, which puts great demands on corporate governance not to stifle the evolution of the organisation. It is also characterised by the predominance of intangible assets such as knowledge and intellectual capital over the traditional physical resources and raw materials; this changes the business environment from one to compete for resources towards one that promotes collaboration to create value—it shows that this has a significant impact on corporate governance. Another characteristic of the knowledge economy is the advent of social networks and Big Data, which puts security and privacy at the core of corporate governance. Furthermore, the advent of Artificial Intelligence in the form of machine learning and cognitive computing with its potential to polarise the professions and society as a whole puts great demands on governance not only of the corporation, but of the science/technology itself.

Finally the chapter picks up from the argumentative strand of culture to deal with the impact that Generation Y is introducing by making its footprint in the worlds of work and consumption, giving an additional cultural lever to the knowledge economy. Examples of changes in the workplace caused by the incorporation of Generation Y is, on the one hand, the pressure on senior management to use SN to communicate with their staff and with the outside world; and it comments on research that has detected that the growth of Generation Y in the organisation also creates an environment that is far more prone to sharing knowledge and information. With respect to Generation Y as consumers, it has been found that in the Fintech space the older generations are followers of their Generation Y peers in the use of mobile financial products and channels, and this can be extrapolated to other industries.

Most importantly for the issue of governance, it picks up from the transparency and reporting argumentative thread to develop the need for reporting for intangible assets such as Intellectual Capital and Reputation. It describes in some detail the Integrated Reporting (<IR>) initiative that looks far beyond traditional reporting of financial statements and corporate annual reports, as a possible guideline on the future of reporting.

With this theoretical background in place, the next four chapters will present a series of case studies on governance in financial services, and map their findings onto these concepts with the purpose of finding new insights that will advance thinking on corporate governance in the knowledge economy.

References

Ashforth, B. E., & Mael, F. (1989). Social identity theory and the organisation. *Academy of Management Review, 14*, 20–39.

Basel Committee on Banking Supervision (BCBS). (2005, April). *Compliance and the compliance function in banks.* https://www.bis.org/bcbs/index.htm.

Bhattacharya, C. B., Sen, S., & Korschum, D. (2008). Using corporate social responsibility to win the war for talent. *Sloan Management Review, 49*, 37–44.

Bhattacharya, C. B., Korschin, D., & Sen, S. (2009). Strengthening stakeholder-company relationships through mutually beneficial corporate social responsibility initiatives. *Journal of Business Ethics, 85*, 257–272.

Boonsiritomachai, W., & Pitchayadejanant, K. (2017). Determinants affecting mobile banking adoption by generation Y based on the UTAUTM modified by the TAM concept. *Kasetsart Journal of Social Science.* https://doi.org/10.1016/j.kjss.2017.10.005.

Brickley, J. A., Smith, C. W. & Zimmerman, J. L. (2002). Business ethics and organisational architecture. *Journal of Banking & Finance, 26*(9), 1821–1835. https://doi.org/10.1016/S0378-4266(02)00193-0

Brynjolfsson, E., & McAffee, A. (2014). *The second machine age.* Norton.

Capriotti, P., & Garrido, F. C. (2006). Principios de la Responsabilidad Social Empresarial, Fasciculo 1, Editorial, Guia de REsponsabilidad Social Empresarial, Diario Financiero (Chile), p. 3.

Conklin, D. W. (2011). *The global environment of business.* Sage.

Deloitte. (2014). *The Deloitte Millennial survey: Big demands and high expectations*. https://www2.deloitte.com/content/dam/Deloitte/global/Documents/About-Deloitte/gx-dttl-2014-millennial-survey-report.pdf.
Dowell, G., Hart, S., & Yeung, B. (2000, August). Do corporate global environmental standards create or destroy market value? *Management Science, 46*, 1059–1074.
Dutton, J. E., & Dukerich, J. M. (1991). Keeping an eye on the mirror: Image and identity in organisational adaptation. *Academy of Management Journal, 34*, 517–554.
FORBES. (2018, April 16). *Fatal Tesla crash exposes gap in automaker's use of car data*. https://www.forbes.com/sites/alanohnsman/2018/04/16/tesla-autopilot-fatal-crash-waze-hazard-alerts/#60f0606f5572. Downloaded on 17 April 2018.
Freeman, R.E. (2010). *Strategic management: A stakeholder approach* (p. 53). Cambridge University Press.
Greening, D. W., & Turban, D. B. (2000). Corporate social performance as a competitive advantage in attracting a quality workforce. *Business and Society, 39*(September), 254–280.
Griffiths, P. D. R. (2006, September 12–14). The role of information & communications technology as a facilitator for social responsibility implementation. In *Proceedings of the British Academy of Management Conference 2006 (BAM2006)*. Queens University Belfast and the University of Ulster, Paper No. 10457.
Griffiths, P. D. R. (2007). *Why bribe?* TRACE 2007 Essay Contest, Winning Essays. www.TRACEinternational.org.
Griffiths, P. D. R. (2008, September 9–11). Corporate Social Responsibility (CSR): window-dressing, smoke-screening, or the route to legitimacy? In *Proceedings of the British Academy of Management Conference, Harrogate*, Paper BAM-10446.
Griffiths, P. D. R., & Arenas, T. (2014). Entel: A case study on knowledge networks and the impact of web 2.0 technologies. *Electronic Journal on E-Learning (EJEL), 12*(4), 384–394. http://www.ejel.org/main.html.
Handy, C. (2002, December). What's a business for? *Harvard Business Review*.
Hannaford, C. (2006). 473959 (p. 8). Trafford Publishing.
House, R., Hanges, P. J., Javidan, M., Dorman, P. J., & Gupta, V. (2004). *Culture, leadership, and organisations: The GLOBE study of 62 societies*. Sage.
ILM. (2007). *Understanding culture and ethics in organisations* (5th ed.). Oxford.
Islam, A., Cheong, T. W., Yusuf, D. H. M., & Desa, H. (2011). A study on 'Generation Y' behaviours at workplace in Penang. *Australian Journal of Basic and Applied Sciences, 5*(11), 1802–1812. ISSN 1991–8178.

Jarvis, P. (2012). *Towards a comprehensive theory of human learning*. London (eBook version).
Jiang, F., Jiang, Y., Zhi, H., Dong, Y., Li, H., Ma, S., Wang, Y., Dong, Q., Shen, S., Wang, Y. (2017). Artificial intelligence in healthcare: Past, present and future. *Journal of NeuroInterventional Surgery, 2*(4). https://doi.org/10.1136/svn-2017-000101.
Jones, D. A. (2007). *Corporate volunteer programmes and employee responses: How serving the community also serves the company*. In Socially Responsible Values on Organisational Behaviour Interactive paper session, 67th Annual Meeting of the Academy of Management, Philadelphia, PA.
Kaplan, R. S. (2010). *Conceptual foundations of the balanced scorecard* (Harvard Business School Working Paper 10–074).
Kenny, P., Parsons, T., Gratch, J., & Rizzo, A. (2008, July 16–18). Virtual humans for assisted healthcare, PETRA 2008. In *Proceedings of the 1st international conference on Pervasive Technologies Related to Assistive Environments*. Article No. 6, Athens. https://doi.org/10.1145/1389586.1389594.
Kolb, A. Y., & Kolb, D. A. (2017, November 30). Learning styles and learning spaces: Enhancing experiential learning in higher education. *Academy of Management Learning & Education, 4*(2). https://doi.org/10.5465/amle.2005.17268566.
Kotarba, M. (2016). New factors inducing changes in the retail banking customer relationship management (CRM) and their exploration by the Fintech industry. *Foundations of Management, 8*, ISSN 2080-7279. https://doi.org/10.1515/fman-2016-0006.
Kusnetsov, A., Kusnetsova, O., & Warren, R. (2007, September 11–13). CSR, legitimacy and institutions: Some evidence from a transition economy. In *Proceedings of the British Academy of Management Conference 2007 (BAM2007)*. Warwick Business School, Paper No. 10155.
Lee, I., & Shin, Y. J. (2018). Fintech: Models, investment decisions, and challenges. *Business Horizons, 61*, 35–46. https://dx.doi.org/10.1016/j.bushor.2017.09.003.
Luo, X., & Bhattacharya, C. B. (2006). Corporate social responsibility, customer satisfaction, and market value. *Journal of Marketing, 70*(October), 1–18.
Marquis, C., & Velez Villa, L. (2012). *Managing stakeholders with corporate social responsibility*. Harvard Business School, Course Overview Notes, 9-412-121.
McAfee, A., & Brynjolfsson, E. (2017). *Machine platform crowd: Harnessing our digital future*. New York.
O'Brien, K. J. (2012, July). Talk to me, one machine said to the other. *New York Times*.
Naim, M. (2013). *The end of power*. Basic Books.
Ostrom, E. (2010). Beyond markets and states: Polycentric governance of complex economic systems. *American Economic Review, 100*(3), 641–672.

Peinado-Vera, E. (2006). Corporate social responsibility in Latin America. *Journal of Corporate Citizenship (JCC), 21*(Spring), 61–69.
Perera, L. (2003). *Social report: The fourth basic financial statement.* PricewaterhouseCoopers, J.S. Servicios Graficos.
Porter, M. E. (1998). *The competitive advantage of nations.* Free Press.
Post, J. E., Preston, L. E., & Sachs, S. (2002). Managing the extended enterprise: The new stakeholder view. *California Management Review, 45*, 6–28.
Prahalad, C. K. (2005). *The fortune at the bottom of the pyramid: Eradicating poverty through profits.* Wharton School Publishing.
Radford, A., Narasimhan, K., Salimans, T., & Sutskever, I. (2018). Improving language understanding by generative pre-training. *OpenAI.* https://s3-us-west-2.amazonaws.com/openai-assets/research-covers/language-unsupervised/language_understanding_paper.pdf. Downloaded 25 September 2018.
Rees, M. (2018). *On the future: Prospects for humanity.* Princeton University Press.
Rizzuto, D. I. (2016). *The MNE subsidiary challenge: Adapting global strategy to the local cultural context. Two case studies in Argentina.* Thesis submitted for the degree of Doctoral Business Administration, Henley Business School, University of Reading.
Rometty, V. (2016). *CES 2016 keynote speech.* https://www.ustream.tv/recorded/81056340.
Rosling, H. (2018). *Factfulness.* Scepter (Hodder and Stoughton): London.
Sala-i-Martin, X., & Schwab, K. (2004). *The global competitive report 2003–2004.* World Economic Forum.
San Francisco Examiner. (2018, March 22). *Robo-car death a classic example of profit vs. safety.* http://www.sfexaminer.com/robo-car-death-classic-example-profit-vs-safety/.Downloaded on 17 April 2018.
Schwartz, M. S., & Carroll, A. B. (2003). Corporate social responsibility: A three-domain approach. *Business Ethics Quarterly, 13*(4), 503–530.
Sen, S., Bhattacharya, C. B., & Korschum, D. (2006). The role of corporate social responsibility in strengthening multiple stakeholder relationships: A field experiment. *Journal of the Academy of Marketing Science, 34*, 158–166.
Silver, D., Schrittwieser, J., Simonyan, K., Antonoglou, I., Huang, A., Guez, A., Hubert, T., Baker, L., Lai, M., Bolton, A., Chen, Y., Lillicrap, T., Hui, F., Sifre1, L., van den Driessche, G., Graepel, T., & Hassabis, D. (2017, October). Mastering the game of Go without human knowledge. *Nature, 550*, 54–371.
The Economist. (2018, March 31). *GrAIt expectations: AI in business.* Special Report.
The Economist. (2020, June 20). *Briefing: Green investing*, pp. 65–67.

Turban, D. B., & Greening, D. W. (1997). Corporate social performance and organizational attractiveness to prospective employees. *Academy of Management Journal, 40*, 658–672.

Viedma, J. M., & Cabrita, M. R. (2012). *Entrepreneurial excellence in the knowledge economy: Intellectual capital benchmarking systems*. Macmillan-Palgrave (www.palgrave.com).

CHAPTER 3

First Things First: The Hidden Cost of Poor Governance

3.1 Overview

This chapter introduces the issue that when governance has not been properly thought through and implemented, a diverse set of hidden costs emerge that impact different stakeholder groups. The absence of mature governance leads to agents acting in ways that are not aligned with the organisations best interest; or it leads to internal controls being weak and this introducing compliance risks; or it leads to wasted efforts in implementing corporate standards that are then not complied with; or it leads to micro-management and siloed organisations that block a global view of the corporation.

3.2 Agents Putting Their Own Interest Ahead of the Corporation's

3.2.1 Introduction

This narrative started as a case study on the selection of a location for a Regional Headquarters (RHQ) from which to manage the Latin America region of a multinational financial services organisation. This is not a greenfield project as an RHQ in Miami already existed. However, as there was a group of senior managers at the company head office that believed the RHQ should be within the regional territory, and not outside as is the

© The Author(s), under exclusive license to Springer Nature Switzerland AG 2021
P. D. R. Griffiths, *Corporate Governance in the Knowledge Economy*, Palgrave Studies in Accounting and Finance Practice, https://doi.org/10.1007/978-3-030-78873-5_3

case of Miami, the researcher was instructed not to take into account the implications of transferring the actual RHQ from Miami to a new location as it was believed that this would contaminate the study giving Miami an undue advantage. From a governance perspective that is not a minor issue (Uminiski, 2017) as it means ignoring the impact of the project on a significant group of stakeholders as are the company employees in the current RHQ location. However, this was accepted as a premise of the research project.

Due to unplanned events that happened at the end of the research the project turned out to be highly illustrative of the effects of management decisions with disregard for stakeholder groups. In other words, it turns out to be a rare case of non-sustainable behaviour from which rich lessons on sustainability can be extracted.

Glamorgan Financial Services Plc is a leading UK-based multinational in its industry.[1] It is also a significant player in its industry in Latin America where it has a presence in 6 major countries, entering those markets mainly through acquisitions. Although it remains small in Brazil, it is among the top three players in terms of market share in the Latin American markets where it operates, especially Argentina, Mexico and Chile. Notwithstanding, Latin America represents only a small part of Glamorgan's global business (4 per cent by assets).

In its quest for continual improvement in effectiveness, Glamorgan FS Plc found it necessary to review its Regional organisation in Latin America and decide where to best locate its *Regional Headquarters* (RHQ) (Birkinshaw et al., 2006; Hewett et al., 2003). The options were to do nothing and keep its executive team based in Miami or move to one of its major business centres in Latin America. The three shortlisted alternatives were Buenos Aires, Santiago and Sao Paulo.

The executive team at Glamorgan in Latin America engaged a small team of researchers/consultants led by the author to assist it in making the location decision in the most objective and pragmatic way possible. The scope of this study was restricted to corporate services such as strategy articulation, policy implementation and advisory, and it tackled the issue along three streams:

---

[1] This is a real case, but the identity of the company has been disguised by changing the name of the company, the country of its headquarters and its specific sectors in financial services.

(a) Financial services industry hubs and their relevance in defining a preferred location.
(b) Ease and cost of doing business at each of the shortlisted alternatives.
(c) Assessing the impact of withholding tax on inter-company billing.

3.2.2 Factors in Selecting an RHQ

Although there are studies on location criteria for an RHQ in other regions of the world (Chen, 2008; Holt et al., 2000; Laamanen et al., 2012; Luiz & Radebe, 2016) there seems to be a void in the literature on Latin America. Luiz and Radebe (2016) through a literature review arrive at 18 location factors for regional headquarters, and through doing a survey of senior executives of multinationals in Africa and applying Stacey (2005) distribution fitting analysis, rank them arriving at three levels of importance (i.e. Very Important, Important, Less Important) as indicated in Table 3.1.

From the analysis of the eighteen factors of Table 3.1, a great majority of them represent the business context, while four can be associated to cost of service and only three to quality of service. From Table 3.2 it can be seen that four of the six 'very important' factors refer to business context, and business context factors are also highly represented among the 'important' factors. 'Economic IT Infrastructure' is the only cost of service considered a 'very important' factor, and Availability of skilled labour is the only 'very important' quality of service factor. Notwithstanding their low representation, quality of service factors seems to be seen to have more importance than the cost of service ones.

It is surprising that none of these 18 factors seems to address the issues of corporate responsibility (CR) and stakeholder management, a key aspect of corporate governance (Griffiths, 2007a).

Luiz and Radebe's (2016) 18 factors were taken as a point of departure and by comparing with PricewaterhouseCooper's methodology for locating shared service centres in Latin America (reviewed cases for a Latin American finance/accounting/reporting shared service centre for Unilever; for a Finance and IT Latin American shared service centre for Zurich Financial Services; for an HR Latin America shared service centre for P&G; for a Latin America SAP shared service for Orica) and considering the need to comply with CR values, it was decided to re-phrase the factor descriptions and select the top twelve in terms of weighted significance for the success of the business in Latin America. This enabled the

Table 3.1 Summary of interpreted importance of RHQ location factors in Africa

Factor No.	Factor description	Interpreted importance	Ranking
14	Availability of skilled labour	Very important	1
8	Economic IT infrastructure	Very important	2
7	Supportive business environment	Very important	3
15	Size of local market	Very important	4
4	Favourable financial environment	Very important	5
17	Government cleanliness	Very important	6
12	Rule of law	Important	7
11	Government attitude towards business	Important	8
9	Favourable employment relations	Important	9
13	Favourable political climate	Important	10
2	Low operating costs	Important	11
16	Access to regional markets	Important	12
5	Effective regional links	Important	13
1	Favourable Government incentives	Less important	14
10	Political relations between home and host country	Less important	15
6	Compatibility with multinational's home country	Less important	16
18	Geographic position	Less important	17
3	Low living costs	Less important	18

Source Luiz and Radebe (2016, Table 4, p. 85)

Table 3.2 Classification of factors (identified by number) by their role and degree of importance

	Business context	Cost of service	Quality of service
Very important	4, 7, 15, 17	8	14
Important	9, 11, 12, 13	2	5, 16
Less important	6, 10, 18	1, 3	

design of a two-dimensional model for comparing the alternative locations. The two dimensions are *Quality of Service* and *Cost of Delivery*. Each of these dimensions encompasses six factors as depicted in Table 3.3. The precise definition of each of these factors is not included but is available from the author on request.

Table 3.3 Variables of the two-dimensional model

Quality of services	Cost of delivery
Economic freedom	Cost of living
Quality of life	Office space
Education	Salaries
English language	Cost of travel
Quality of telecommunications	Cost of telecomunications
Connectivity	Withholding tax

This two-dimensional framework is useful to conceptualise factors on the basis of which to compare alternative locations, but it is insufficient to carry out the comparison as weightings are necessary to convert this into an applicable model.

3.2.3 Approach

This research draws on published sources to map the FS Industry in Latin America. Thirty-nine multinational competitors, suppliers and closely complementary service companies are reviewed as to how they organise their regional presence and where they set up their RHQ with the intention to identify *Financial Services (FS)* industry hubs in the Region. Further insight is obtained by interviewing the Regional CEO of five of these 39 MNEs.

The philosophy behind this is that location, together with all other organisational decisions, must be subject to, and aligned with, the business objectives and strategy of the organisation. Consistent with this, the methodology applied focuses on envisioning the RHQ as a service organisation that must justify its existence by creating value to its internal customers, namely the Corporate Centre (to which the RHQ reports) and the *Market Business Units* (MBUs, that report to the RHQ). To define this, Treacy and Wiersema's (1995) 'Value Discipline of Market Leaders' is applied to define the RHQ's value proposition.

So, the unit of analysis of this case study is the RHQ as a service unit, and another key premise of the research is that 'customers' have a decisive role in defining the value expected from their RHQ. In accordance with this, three Glamorgan MBU CEOs were invited to express their experience in dealing with a Regional Headquarters—the executive team went beyond the anecdotal experiences to draw lessons shared by the team that gave concrete input to the definition of a location.

The next challenge is to define the relative weights of these factors, for which different approaches are adopted for *Quality of Service* and for *Cost of Delivery* variables. In the case of the former, deep reflection and structured discussions (applying 'knowledge café' and 'Socratic dialogue' techniques) to arrive at a consensual weighting among the members of the executive team was carried out.

With respect to the *Cost of Delivery* dimension factors, the relative weights are defined on an estimate of the incidence that each one of them has on the total operating budget of an RHQ. The specific data is obtained from Glamorgan's accounting books. Of course, these historic costs to be used for the weighting are based on the RHQ being located in Miami. This approach has the advantage of being relatively objective and it is assumed that relative weights would not vary very much across centres.

3.2.4 *Data Analysis and Development of Location Comparison Criteria*

3.2.4.1 *Identification of Regional Hubs*

The review of the FS landscape in Latin America highlights the dominance of the Brazilian market in terms of industry sales in Latin American, accounting for well over 40 per cent. However, even though 33 of the 39 companies had operations in Brazil, only two (one of which is a direct competitor) had its RHQ located there. Then again when assessing not only Glamorgan FS's direct competitors, but also the suppliers and closely complementary service companies, the cluster of players in the Miami area was evident as was the designation of their RHQ there—as seen in Table 3.4. That said, a sizeable number of players (21) opt to manage the Region directly from an EU or other US location, leaving Miami as the #1 RHQ location.

Finally, five companies are selected for in-depth interviews with their Latin American Regional Managers to understand the rationale they applied to setting up their RHQ. In one case the decision is seen to shift with the maturity of the Regional organisation. Whereas originally the US company had sought the 'security' of a Miami base given its depth of skilled resources and communications, over time this approach has given way to a more 'virtual' RHQ concept, where the leading managers were allowed to remain in their chosen 'home' location (so almost eradicating the concept of expatriate manager) and would travel out to the other markets from that home base. In two other companies it was found that the core regional staff would be located wherever the Regional CEO of the moment decided to be based, so leading to changes in the RHQ location every time there was a change of Regional CEO.

Moreover, when the RHQ was in the largest market, it tended towards a concentration of resources to 'subsidize' that same large market, to the detriment of the smaller country offices. It also affected communications across the regional team, reducing the cross-fertilisation of ideas and relationships among the management team. Furthermore, the presence of an RHQ in the country serves to erode the country manager's authority and autonomy, as intermediaries and complementary service providers by-pass local management, going directly over their head to secure a deal or even reverse a local manager's decision.

3.2.4.2 Value Discipline of the RHQ

The application of the methodology led the Glamorgan executive team to converge on that the *value discipline* of the RHQ is one of *customer intimacy*, where the key dimensions of value for its internal customers are *expert advice* and *service reliability*. Without ignoring that in these times of uncertainty keeping costs under control is a virtue to be pursued, what

Table 3.4 Operations and regional HQ locations[2]

All service providers	Country operations			Miami offices	Regional HQs
HQ location	Argentina	Brazil	Chile		
Miami, Florida	7	9	10	11	11
Buenos Aires, Argentina	3	3	2	3	3
Santiago, Chile	1	2	2		2
Sao Paulo, Brazil	2	2	1	1	2
Other locations	11	17	8	7	21
Grand total	24	33	23	22	39

[2] Table 3.4 should be read as follows, taking the first row as an example: Eleven companies have their RHQ in Miami, of which seven have operations in Argentina, nine in Brazil, ten in Chile and 11 have an office in Miami.

will 'make it or break it' for the RHQ is *quality* and not *cost containment* (Ambos & Birkinshaw, 2010; Ambos & Mahnke, 2010; Griffiths, 2007b, 2011; Treacy & Wiersema, 1995).

3.2.4.3 Definition of Relative Weights of Factors
Through applying knowledge management techniques *Socratic dialogue* and *knowledge café* (Griffiths & Remenyi, 2008; Remenyi & Griffiths, 2009) to the executive team of the RHQ plus three MBU Managing Directors, three relevant insights emerged:

(a) *It is detrimental for the region and for the host MBU to have the RHQ sitting side-by-side with an MBU;*
(b) *Moving to a new location has a cost that goes far beyond the 'out-of-pocket' expenditure of finding and refurbishing new premises, in the form of potentially losing talent and disrupting a good executive team and*
(c) *Surprisingly, there is no real benefit in placing the RHQ in a regional FS industry hub.*

The next challenge is to define the relative weights of these factors for which, as mentioned, different approaches are adopted for *Quality of Service* and for *Cost of Delivery* factors. In the case of the former, structured discussions among the members of the executive team on the predictors of performance in terms of *Quality of corporate services* led to the weighting shown in Table 3.5.

Economic freedom of the business environment and *education standard* of the population (representing competences of the support staff pool) comes out top, followed by *connectivity* and *English language* skills of

Table 3.5 Relative weights of Quality of Service factors

Quality of services	Weighting (%)
Economic freedom	25
Quality of life	10
Education	25
English language	15
Quality of telecommunications	10
Connectivity	15
	100

Table 3.6 Relative weights of Cost of Delivery factors

Cost of delivery	Weighting (%)
Cost of living	20
Office space	5
Salaries	48
Cost of travel	4
Cost of telecommunications	0
Withholding tax	22
Score	100

the population. *Quality of life* for expatriate professionals and *Quality of telecommunications* came out as being the factors of lesser significance.

With respect to the *Cost of Delivery* dimension, the relative weights are defined on an estimate of the incidence that each factor has on the total operating budget of an RHQ. The specific data was obtained from Glamorgan's accounting books and the calculations that arrived at these weights can, again, be obtained from the authors. The resulting relative weights can be seen in Table 3.6. Cost of staff (*Salaries*) outweighs all the rest followed by the incidence of *withholding tax* and *cost of living*. *Office space* rental and *cost of travel* have low incidence and, surprisingly, *cost of telecommunications* is immaterial.

3.2.5 Results

Because Miami was the current location of RHQ it was decided to take Miami's value at 100 for all indices. Any value in excess of 100 means that the relevant city scores higher than Miami; and anything below 100 means that the given city is worse off than Miami on that factor. Applying these criteria all cities were scored on the 'Quality of Services' dimension and their scores are included in Table 3.7.

Turning to the 'Cost of Delivery' dimension, the scores obtained by each potential location are given in Table 3.8.

So, from applying the model to the four alternative locations, it emerged that Miami clearly outscored the other three cities on all aspects of the *quality of service* dimension, while Santiago takes the lead on *cost of delivery* scores. Through the testing of several scenarios on weighting the *quality* vs. *cost* dimensions it is concluded that Miami is the location better aligned with the RHQs' value discipline and thus recommended

Table 3.7 City scores on the *Quality of Service* dimension

Quality of services	Weighting (%)	Miami	Buenos Aires	Sao Pablo	Santiago
Economic freedom	25	100	66	72	99
Quality of life	10	100	92	77	88
Education	25	100	36	24	39
English language	15	100	53	47	45
Quality of telecomunications	10	100	64	54	62
Connectivity	15	100	65	64	69
Score	100	100	63	52	72

Table 3.8 City scores on the *Cost of Delivery* dimension

Cost of delivery	Weighting (%)	Miami	Buenos Aires	Sao Pablo	Santiago
Cost of living	20	100	130	90	119
Office space	5	100	133	53	142
Salaries	48	100	109	52	99
Cost of travel	5	100	104	106	99
Cost of telecomunications	0	100	11	5	9
Withholding tax	22	100	144	290	260
Score	100	100	115	112	133

Table 3.9 Overall score scenarios

Overall score	Quality (%)	Cost (%)	Miami	Buenos Aires	Sao Pablo	Santiago
Weights/Scores	75	25	100	76	67	87
	60	40	100	84	76	97
	55	45	100	86	79	100
	50	50	100	89	82	103

that the executive RHQ team should remain there. This analysis is summarised in Table 3.9, where four alternative dimension-weighting scenarios are given.

As can be seen in Table 3.9, if Quality is given 75% weight vs. 25% for Cost, Miami is a clear leader followed by Santiago. If the weight of Quality is dropped to 55% (vs. 45% for Cost) Miami and Santiago lead the pack with an equal score. Anything below Quality weight 55% will position Santiago as the top-ranking city but this would breach the design premise that Quality is a priority over Cost.

So, the primary recommendation is that Glamorgan FS stays put and keeps its RHQ in Miami. Notwithstanding, it should be made clear that the application of the model pinpoints *withholding tax* as a very significant cost element in having the RHQ in Miami (see Table 3.8). Just to clarify, withholding tax has incidence because the RHQ is taken as a service organisation that needs to fund itself by invoicing its services to the MBUs in proportion to the amount of service they give each one. Although the project has a tax consultant on the team, it is believed this issue needs a specialist's treatment and therefore it is recommended that Glamorgan FS brings in their tax advisors to look into this in more detail.

Finally, the *Quality of Service* factor does not vary significantly over time, but in a region where governments frequently use devaluation of their currency as a tool for improving competitiveness, the *Cost of Delivery* variables can be volatile. The results shown in this paper represent the situation at the cost levels of the time when the project was performed.[3] As part of the delivery, the model was handed over to Glamorgan FS so that it can continue monitoring changes over time after the project was concluded.

3.2.6 Discussion and Aftermath

The final outcome of the research was presented to the Host organisation, whom expressed a high degree of satisfaction with the quality of analysis and recommendation that were delivered on time and on budget. However, a few weeks after the study was concluded there were significant changes at Glamorgan FS in Latin America: The Regional CEO who had commissioned the work was replaced by a new CEO hired from outside the company. The new Regional CEO, a Brazilian based in Sao Paulo, immediately moved the RHQ away from Miami. Not to Santiago, nor to Buenos Aires, but to his home city, the lowest scoring location in all scenarios. Did the management team who participated in the study not inform their new boss about the study? Or did the new Regional CEO

---

[3] Date not disclosed for confidentiality.

simply ignore its findings? It is not known for certain, but it is understood that the move was justified on 'strategic' grounds as Brazil is the 'make-it-or-break-it' market for the Region.

The move was so abrupt and obviously decided upon before the new Regional CEO had taken office that it leads to suspect that it was part of the agreed hiring terms for the new Regional CEO. This motivated the author to go back to the field notes to see if any patterns of a more general phenomenon would emerge.

As the notes were revisited it was realised that at one point it had filtered through to the author that the outgoing CEO was under great pressure from his Head Office in the UK to move away from Miami 'into' the Region, and that he had commissioned the study in hope of obtaining objective evidence to support resisting such a move. The notes also revealed that Miami had been picked as RHQ some five years earlier, when the outgoing CEO had taken that posting. Prior to that, the RHQ had been in Santiago where the prior Regional CEO was resident at the time of a restructuring that had led to the creation of the RHQ.

When revisiting the transcripts of the in-depth interviews with senior managers at five of Glamorgan's competitors in the region, three of them point clearly to the fact that their RHQs were set up, respectively in Buenos Aires, Santiago and Mexico City—again, the city of residence of the Regional CEO. The remaining two did not touch on this issue so are neutral in this respect. However, in one transcript was a story of one of the interviewees that, many years earlier when he was a middle manager in a large corporation in the United States, he was in a meeting where a newly appointed CIO had decided to move a 250-strong IT shared service centre from Boca Raton to Houston where she was based, justified merely on personal convenience.

3.2.7 Conclusions

There appears to be hard evidence that the location of an RHQ is used as a management perk. On first thought, some may say there probably is nothing wrong with that—after all, what difference is there between locating one's office close to home and using a company jet? However, the differences are significant. Changing location of an RHQ has implications for at least two groups of stakeholders. On the one hand, the staff. The more senior and specialist staff will have to opt between relocating or losing their job; and the less skilled will not even have that choice—they will be let go. On the other hand, the shareholders. In times of corporate responsibility, need for legitimacy, sensitivity towards stakeholders and enhanced governance it is believed that companies should evaluate the cost and operational impact of this, and not leave it merely as a hidden inefficiency. They need to do this for the sake of transparency.

This study has weaknesses in its design as is the premise that the cost of moving from Miami to another location is not considered. It also has strengths as is the collection of primary qualitative data through structured workshops instead of relying purely on interviews. From this research emerges the issue of RHQ location as a management perk and thus opens a new area of investigation to determine how widespread this phenomenon is.

3.3 The Devastating Effects That Weak Internal Controls Can Have

3.3.1 Introduction

This case study analyses the scandal caused by the excessively aggressive sales culture at Wells Fargo's Community Bank. Many lessons on governance can be extracted from observing the failures that happened at Wells Fargo.

As always in these cases, the causes of disasters such as this are an intertwined series of factors that present themselves more-or-less simultaneously and trigger a series of chain reactions that get out of control with the passage of time. This narrative will combine issues of a flawed corporate culture, of excessively aggressive sales targets set from the centre to be achieved by a vast number of client-facing staff, of inappropriate compensation and incentive plans at all levels of the organisation, of a highly decentralised and fragmented risk and control units, of unethical behaviours towards the customers of the organisation, of misinformation to the Board and the complicity of Board members who do not apply sufficient scepticisms, and of other factors. As will be seen these activities developed over a period that exceeds ten years and came to light as a result of a journalistic investigation by a local newspaper on the activities of the Community Bank in the city of Los Angeles, which was published in February 2014. The outcome of the scandal is severe damage to Wells Fargo's brand and a strong drop in market valuation of the company.

The case will address the following questions.

1. What were the root causes of the improper sales practices at Wells Fargo's Community Bank?
2. What remedial actions were or can be carried out, so these issues are not repeated?
3. What actions can be taken to rebuild the trust customers place in the bank?

3.3.2 The Company

Wells Fargo is one of the top three banks in the USA and possibly the one that had the strongest brand, historically connected to the expansion to the West of the early days of the country. The current Wells Fargo is the outcome of the acquisition of a multitude of community banks, a characteristically American financial institution of limited size, activity and geographic scope in retail banking that emerged as a result of the Banking Act of 1933 (Glass-Steagall) that determined the structure of the industry until its repeal in the 1980s and 1990s; and of its merger with Norwest Bank in 1998. Although it was called a merger, the management team of Norwest headed by its Chairman of the Board and CEO John Stumpf took control of the new Wells Fargo.

Wells Fargo had a policy of conservative lending and aggressive selling. In 2015, that is at the time that the sales malpractice emerged, the bank had a solid position with significant funding through deposits. Its loan-to-deposit ratio at the time was 0.7 comparing favourably with the US high-street banks that averaged a ratio of 0.9, and its tangible-equity-to-assets ratio was high by international standards, at 7.8 per cent. In its financial fundamentals it was a solid and profitable bank.

The bank's problems were on the sales side in its retail Community Bank. The bank was admired at Wall Street for its high tempo sales-driven culture that dominated the bank since its 1998 merger with Norwest. This culture developed over time as a result of its cross-selling strategy that was the foundation stone on which its culture was built. While banks in America had a product (e.g. current account, savings account, credit card, mortgage, vehicle loan, …) density per client of approximately three, Wells Fargo's was double that by the time the crisis flared up. Figure 3.1 shows the progression of its product density since the early 1990s up to 2015. Not even the financial crisis of 2007–2008 made a dent in its progress.

3 FIRST THINGS FIRST: THE HIDDEN COST OF POOR GOVERNANCE

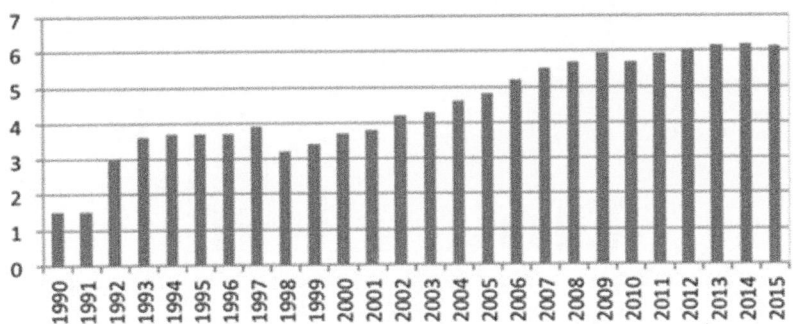

Fig. 3.1 Wells Fargo—product density per client (*Source* Wells Fargo Norwest annual report)

Not satisfied with that, Wells Fargo adopted a central sales target that the CEO summarised in three words: 'eight is great'. The objective for all client-facing staff was to reach eight products per client. This hard sales culture becomes evident in every annual report since the late 1980s as can be seen by the number of times the term 'cross-selling' is used in the annual report—this is particularly aggressive since 2004 as can be seen in Fig. 3.2.

The individuals and entities that played key roles in this incident were:

a. Senior management team: within senior management the key people were John Stumpf who was since the merger with Norwest Chair of the Board and CEO at the new Wells Fargo; Carrie Tolstedt, head of the Community Bank and long time associate with and highly trusted by John Stumpf, who was at the helm of the unit where the cross-selling took place, during the whole period of the scam and Tim Sloan, who served as Chief Financial Officer from 2011 to 2014 and then head of Wholesale Bank until promoted to President and Chief Operating Officer in November 2015. Once promoted to this last position Carrie Tolstedt reported directly to Tim Sloan who until then had no direct contact with the Community Bank activities.

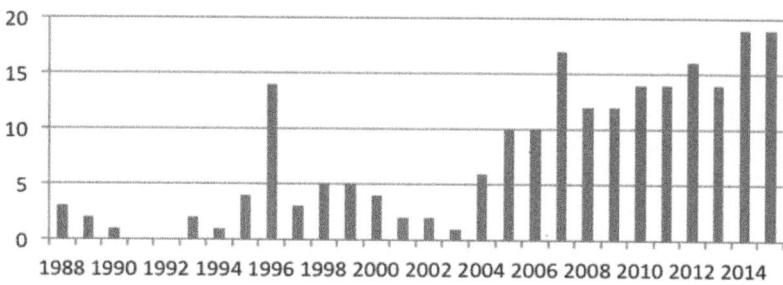

Fig. 3.2 Content analysis of annual report for 'cross-selling'. Lafferty Group for RBA workshops in Buenos Aires and Bogota. Based on (*Source* Norwest and Wells Fargo annual report)

b. Corporate Control Organisations: The control units that had a protagonist role in the cross-selling incident are Corporate Risk, the Law Department, Human Resources and Internal Investigations & Audit. A characteristic of Wells Fargo that would at the end of the day facilitate the loss of control over the Community Bank's cross-selling processes, is that it had a highly decentralised organisation where each of the divisions had their own unit for each of these functions, that reported to the head of their division instead of to the respective corporate function.

c. Board of Directors: The Board and the Risk Committee did not become aware of the sales malpractices until it was in the press in February 2014. As a result of that the Board did receive reports from the Community Bank, Corporate Risk and Corporate Human Resources and they did get involved, especially after May 2015 when the Los Angeles City Attorney filed a lawsuit against Wells Fargo for improper sales practices at the banks branches in Los Angeles and regulatory scrutiny intensified. As from then and until settlements were announced in September 2016 the Board and Risk Committee meetings addressed sales practice issues, resolved the Los Angeles City litigation, responded to regulatory concerns and discussed actions for remediating customer harm. On September 25, 2016, the Independent Directors of the Board of Wells Fargo created an Oversight Committee to conduct a comprehensive investigation of sales practice issues. The Independent Directors on this Committee were Stephen W. Sanger, Elizabeth A. Duke (Vice-Chair of the Board), Donald M. James and Enrique Hernandez, Jr. The Oversight Board retained law firm Shearman & Sterling to investigate and write up the report; Shearman & Sterling, in turn, engaged FTI Consulting to do the forensic and data analytics work. The output is a 110-page report issued on April 10, 2017, titled 'Sales Practice Investigation Report'.

3.3.3 Approach and Sources

This case was developed from secondary sources in two stages. The first stage was done by scanning the press and the web in 2016, for the Retail Banking Academy to be used in two governance workshops for bankers convened by the Argentine Banking Association and by PwC Colombia and the Colombian Banking Association; it was also used for an executive course at Universidad F Santa Maria in Santiago de Chile. The second stage took place in 2017 once the Oversight Committee concluded its report and placed it in the public domain. So, the source for this is the 'Sales Practice Investigation Report' issued on April 10, 2017. Some of the insights included in the case study came out of the discussions held with experienced bankers at the two mentioned workshops and the executive development course.

3.3.4 The Incident

On 8 September 2016 Wells Fargo is fined $185 million to settle a long-running investigation that charged the bank with falsifying millions of customer accounts to boost sales. This was the culmination of a process that started in 2005 and peaked in 2013 when press article in Los Angeles surfaced integrity-related allegations specifically in relation to selling practices to clients.

The aggressive sales targets translated into pressure on frontline staff to sell unwanted or unneeded products to their clients, which proved to be lethal in combination with a compensation and bonus scheme based on cross-selling targets, all along the hierarchical line. Internally, the bank was aware that the high-pressure sales culture was leading to serious wrongdoing as since 2011, by its own admission, the Community Bank had been dismissing employees who sought to boost their sales targets by secretly opening customer accounts unknown to these customers. Despite that, the bank continued to promote these cross-selling metrics to investors without informing them of the false account generation.

It emerges that 5300 staff were ousted due to sales malpractices such as opening unneeded, unwanted and in many cases unknown products to the tune of, in the first instance, 2.5 million accounts that later investigations pushed to over 4 million accounts. Despite these staggering figures, the Community Bank leadership refused to see the problem as a systemic one and blamed junior staff for breaking bank rules. In the Oversight Committee's post-mortem report it is documented that some regional managers and branch managers voiced their concern to Ms. Tolstedt that the targets set at the centre were simply not attainable, but they were not heard. As the years progressed the targets were harder to achieve and thus the quality of accounts opened, measured in terms of the funds deposited in them, deteriorated. The funding rates of these accounts dropped from 90 per cent in 2005 to a low of 80 per cent in 2012; as the situation started to become known and Wells Fargo monitored more closely the sales processes, the funding rate started climbing to exceed 95 per cent by 2016. Low funding rates of new accounts is a clear indicator of unwanted accounts—it would appear that many blind eyes were turned to this indicator at both the senior management and Board level.

It also emerges from the Oversight Committee report that the Board and Risk Committee were not properly informed about the number of people being terminated for improper sales practices. In May 2015 there was a presentation to the Risk Committee that disclosed that 230 employees had been terminated in the Community Bank, and in October 2015 Ms. Tolstedt made a presentation to the full Board in which it is widely viewed by the Directors as having minimised the seriousness of the issues. It was only in September 2016, when the lawsuit was settled, that the Board became aware that it had been approximately 5300 people ousted.

To cap it all, CEO John Stumpf sells $61 million worth of Wells Fargo shares in the month prior to the fraud revelations. As the story unravels Mr. Stumpf is called to testify before the Banking Committee in the US Congress where, in a memorable session, the Chair of the Committee, Senator Elizabeth Warren, questions him mercilessly, ridicules the 'eight is great' mantra and reveals the leadership and governance flaws at this once proud institution. It caused a unanimous chorus of outrage in a Committee that is most often discordant.

The effect of this incident on the market valuation and the reputation of Wells Fargo is revealed by the fact that its share price collapsed, losing $25 billion in value within the week after the September 2016 breaking news of the settlement. On top of that, Wells Fargo is now associated in the minds of consumers with appalling customer mistreatment, and public trust in this once revered bank has been shattered.

As a final comment, it is worth revisiting Stumpf's vision of culture and where it stops and starts, in his own words:

> *If there is one job I must do for our team members, customers, communities and shareholders, it is to be the keeper of our company's culture. It is the role of all team members to understand our culture, internalise it, live it, teach it and reinforce it.*

3.3.5 Root Causes of the Unethical Behaviour

The excessively decentralised structure combined with too much autonomy given to the Community Bank's senior management seems to be a significant part of the root causes of the flawed sales scam. An organisation that relied on mantras such as 'run it like you own it' and developed a culture of strong deference to the management of the lines of business was exposing itself to trouble.

As a result of that, the Community Bank leadership resisted outside oversight and when forced to report minimised the scale and nature of the problems that were brewing; they were also overconfident and unwilling to change its sales model despite having early warnings that it was flawed.

The situation was aggravated by a *laisser faire* style of leadership on the part of the CEO, who did not question the head of the Community Bank and make her accountable. The CEO was the promoter of the 'eight is great' sales-driven model that in his view and the view he could report to the markets, was working. He did not want to risk fiddling with what was, from his point of view, a successful model that implemented effective cross-selling in an environment of, generally speaking, positive customer and staff surveys. The head of the Community Bank did not reveal, and the CEO did not appreciate the seriousness of, the problem and the magnitude of the reputational risk they were exposing Wells Fargo to.

That is not all. On top of that fragile situation, the corporate control functions were dangerously constrained. On the one hand the corporate control units were small, under-resourced and only play some sort of co-ordination role as all the corporate control functions are decentralised to the business divisions with the parallel control units reporting to the head of division rather than their respective corporate control unit. This impeded corporate-level insight and influence over the Community Bank. Another factor related to this, that could be depicted as disparity of power, is the already mentioned culture of substantial deference to the business divisions, augmented by the fact that Ms. Tolstedt was perceived to have strong support from the CEO. A third factor, possibly deriving from the two prior ones, is that the control functions were generally exercised in a transactional approach to problem-solving and thus losing sight of the broader context and systemic issues. As a result, they failed to analyse, size and escalate the sales practice issues.

Finally, another root cause is the weakness of the Board. Indeed, the flawed sales practices were not identified to the Board as a noteworthy risk until 2014; it is also undeniable that the importance of the problem was minimised to the Board; and it is also true that by early 2015 the senior management of Wells Fargo reported to the Board that corrective action taken was working. But the Board revealed minimum or no sense of scepticism and of curiosity. There were glaring signals, such as a high and growing proportion of unfunded new accounts, telling that those accounts did not appear to be wanted. Reading through the sources it is clearly seen that the relationship between the Board and management is too cosy, reinforced by the fact that the positions of Chair of the Board and CEO are unified in a single person.

3.3.6   *Lessons Learnt*

A sales-driven strategy has defined a very particular corporate culture—from this case it appears that strategy and culture are closely linked. This should not be surprising—it is aligned with the concept introduced in Sect. 2.1, that Governance, culture, strategy and a sustainable business model need to be integrated to be successful.

Something that stands out in the case study, applying stakeholder analysis, is that the organisation culture drove one stakeholder group, the employees, to work against another key stakeholder group, the customers.

The effect of working against customers is that it leads to serious reputational damage that in turn leads to loss of market value and thus a severe impact on another stakeholder group, the shareholders. It is rare that an organisation works against its customers, but it does happen. One recent case was that of VW and its emissions scandal, that also ended in great reputational destruction and severe impact on shareholders.

The combination of a hard sales-driven strategy with a highly decentralised organisation can have lethal effects if it is not accompanied by a rigorous, centralised, control function reporting straight to the CEO. In other words, tougher internal controls and possibly a re-thinking of external audit services to ensure they review processes and corporate culture.

Another lesson from this case is that senior management needs to involve the different departments in planning by prompting them to propose objectives, so as to make them realistic and to get their buy-in. Related to this, the outcome of the strategic planning process should be in-sync with the recent trajectory of the organisation—quantum leaps may result in unrealistic objectives. As a general rule, particularly in financial services where it is very simple to grow—simply drop risk management standards—growth objectives should not be a priority to the point of putting at risk service quality to clients.

Senior management needs to ensure there are staff training programmes, joint reflection meetings, that there is staff immersion, by business unit, in the values, mission, vision and long-term objectives of the organisation, with a view at developing an ethical culture centred on the values of the organisation.

Finally, the Board has a key role to play in pulling everyone together, but it can only play that role if its members are critical thinkers with curiosity and scepticism to see straight through management reports to form their own opinions on the issues at stake. One key point is to keep an integral and critical view of the organisation's governance, strategy, culture and sustainable business model. They need to keep permanently in mind the priorities between stakeholder groups and the need to monitor and control the agency problem (Freeman, 2010; Marquis & Velez-Villa, 2012; Sen et al., 2006).

If these guidelines are adhered to, Wells Fargo should be setting the foundations to avoid this kind of event to happen again. With respect to the third question on how can Wells Fargo rebuild its reputation, a few reflections follow.

3.3.7 Looking Ahead

The question that remains to be addressed is *What actions can be taken to rebuild the trust customers place in the bank?* As mentioned in Chapter 2, there are no quick fixes for this. It will require an integrated approach to governance, strategy, culture and a sustainable business model. On the governance side Wells Fargo took a positive step towards transparency by immediately putting the Oversight Committee of independent directors report in the public domain, but it took a long time to reveal all the derivations of the hard sales strategy and sales-oriented culture—information kept dripping out for many months. For example, a year later in September 2017 it was revealed that it had massively sold unwanted insurance to customers that took vehicle loans (*The Economist*, 2017).

On the strategy side Wells Fargo was quick to react. Once the September 2016 settlement was made public, the Community Bank immediately announced it was replacing the broken sales model and eliminating the product sales goals. As culture needs to be aligned with strategy (or vice-versa?) to start working on culture in January 2017 Wells Fargo put in a new incentive programme that focused on customer service rather than selling products.

A radical change in culture requires changing senior management. Over the six months that followed the September 2016 revelations many senior managers were phased out. The first was Ms. Tolstedt and John Stumpf followed shortly afterwards. In February 2017 the Board announced that it was letting go four senior managers deeply involved in the activities that led to the scandal and to keeping the Board misinformed on what was happening: the Group Risk Officer, the Head of Strategic Planning and Finance, who was 'primarily responsible for overseeing the sales goals and incentive plans', and the regional heads of Los Angeles and Arizona 'who had encouraged and deployed especially improper and excessive sales practices'. The Board also engaged on an intense effort to claw-back bonuses already paid or share options not yet vested from the senior managers responsible for the flawed sales and incentive model—according to a source, 40 per cent of the total cost of this event to Wells Fargo was covered by this claw-back exercise (*The Economist*, 2017).

When John Stumpf resigned the Board replaced him by Tim Sloan but his tenure was short-lived: an outsider is required to make the change towards an ethical corporate culture. At the end of the day, trust of customers will be rebuilt only when they perceive that the bankers they are dealing have a professional status—that is that they are highly competent in their knowledge domain and that every piece of advice they give is centred on the client's best interest.

3.4 THE WASTE OF IMPLEMENTING CORPORATE STANDARDS THAT THE STAFF WORK AROUND

3.4.1 Introduction

This case study does an in-depth analysis of the SAP implementation at a multinational industrial and service company. Its aim is to understand the decision process for the investment, the implementation and analyse if it met its long-term objectives. It will interpret the findings from the point of view of corporate governance.

Orica, the mining services business, was segregated from ICI (Imperial Chemical Industries) in 1996 and incorporated as a separate Australian public company. At the time of this intervention, that is the implementation of SAP in the period 2000–2002, Orica operated globally and was the world's leading supplier of commercial explosives, holding close to 25 per cent market share of a USD 6.5 billion market (2002 dollars). Its main rival was a company called Dyno. Committed to innovation, Orica was continuously working with customers to deliver value beyond mere rock blasting.

Mining expertise has been a part of the Orica culture since the company's inception. For over a century, Orica has pioneered the development and implementation of new technology to deliver sustained improvements in mining costs.

Orica has built a platform for continuous development in Latin America. With offices located in Mexico, Venezuela, Brazil, Argentina and Chile (Fig. 3.3), Orica Latin America had become the biggest global solutions provider, in its speciality, for the whole Region.

3.4.2 Approach

This section builds upon a descriptive case study co-written by the author in 2004 which analysed the SAP Latin America project, developed during 2000 and 2001, ex-post its completion (Griffiths & Stern, 2004). Departing from the business case developed in early 2000 to support the decision of whether to carry out the project or not, that paper addressed

Fig. 3.3 Orica's operations in Latin America

the question: 'What lessons can be learned from Orica Latin America's implementation of SAP?' It analysed ORICA Latin America's strategic positioning and the role of technology in delivering its value proposition to Clients and, within that framework, the benefit realisation of the SAP project.

In 2012 the author was engaged by Orica's management in Latin America to review the status of the Standard Operating Model and the degree of adoption of SAP by the users. This case study is developed on the basis of the project notes, internal strategic planning and budget documents, project plans, minutes of the steering committee meetings and others, and maps them onto the case study written on 2004 that was a balance of the short term outcome of the implementation. The focus of this section is to analyse the outcome of these projects from a corporate governance perspective.

3.4.3 The Role of Technology in Orica's Latin American Business

Up until the late nineties, information and communications technology (ICT) development in Latin America had been managed at a local (country) level. This resulted in there being a different business system in each country with no connectivity between them. There was also no consistency of business processes or of data standards across country operations.

A study of the Latin American business units conducted by external consultants identified a range of opportunities for strategic benefit through collaborating across the region:

- Greater integration of key business processes;
- Identification and adoption of best practices;
- Reduction of redundant tasks and information across the region;
- Simplification of processes involved in accounting and general administration functions;
- Achieving a better balance between decentralisation and control so as to avoid duplication and facilitate better performance measurement;
- Implementing shared services for back-office functions;
- Development of areas such as Production Control and Logistics, Customer and Product Group Profitability, Forecasting and planning.

However, the consultant's report stated that the diverse systems infrastructure was a barrier to implementing these innovations in the region. Synergies such as those listed above, would only be achieved if the Latin American businesses were on a common systems platform with consistent and reliable regional processing and reporting.

Orica's, until then, localised approach to ICT was consistent with its business strategy of tailoring services to the requirements of key customers at each market. By the late nineties this was changing rapidly as, on the one hand, globalisation resulted in large, international customers who no longer acted locally without abiding to corporate standards; and on the other new alliances, with the specific intent of exploiting the e-economy, were entered into.

It became clear[4] that consistent information and processes across the business would be essential to meeting the challenges of this new environment, that required timely responses to customers' global requirements, leveraging of Orica's own buying power (either individually or as part of an alliance), and the implementation of extended business processes. It also became clear that this could only be achieved in Latin America by moving to a common business systems platform across the Region.[5]

Due to its ambitious objectives this project had, indeed, significant technical complexities, but far more challenging were the business implications such as moving all business units to a common chart of accounts; agreeing upon and adopting co-ordinated cost-centre and profit-centre structures; uniformly defined dimensions for profitability analysis and a common materials coding standard. Achieving this within the project, and then maintaining it over time in the normal operation, would require a region-wide change management effort.

3.4.4 The SAP Implementation Project Decision Process

Orica's approach to the business case was that it had to meet two objectives. The first was that it should produce the input for making a decision on the SAP investment, which should be based on quantitative data in accordance with corporate requirements. The second objective was to obtain buy-in from senior management in the region which, it was assumed, would facilitate the significant change management process that was to come with the SAP implementation project.

It was key to get the strategic context of the business case right. It was built around the premise that the SAP investment should enable Orica Latin America to align with Orica's corporate strategy, which can be summarised in the following points:

- Latin America must become an integral part of business globalisation.
- It must achieve low cost, operational excellence.

---

[4] Extracted from One SAP Global Instance (Internal document).
[5] Extracted from One SAP Global Instance (Internal document).

- It must pursue growth through acquisitions, joint ventures and exports.
- Technological innovations are to be used to manage products and services.
- It must improve its customer service.
- It must complement its current commodities business with value added services.
- It must pursue knowledge-based business development.

From a functional perspective, the scope of the project SAP modules FI-CO (Finance & Controlling), MM (material Management), PP (production planning), SD (Sales & Distribution) and PA (Profitability Analysis). From a geographic perspective, the analysis should consider all sites of what were defined as the core country operations (i.e. the Brazilian, Chilean and Mexican operations), which should be visited by the business case project team. It should also include a definition of an ICT integration strategy for Orica Export and Orica Argentina.

The fact that the three core country operations were at different departure situations in terms of business and technological development, put significant demands on the business case. For example, the Chilean operation was a remarkably stable business. Its leadership recognised the need to upgrade its information systems and quickly identified a number of benefits in doing so, but prior success led people in the organisation to believe that their extant processes worked. On the other hand, Mexico's management understood the strategic need of a project like SAP to standardise processes across the Region, but it had recently gone through a very tough experience implementing Solomon (another ERP system) and found few benefits to its own operation of adopting SAP. Finally, Brazil recognised the potential of an SAP project and identified certain benefits to come from it, but it had a 'can do' attitude coupled with a low level of exploitation of its legacy systems.

In order to fulfil the objective of attaining senior management endorsement of the SAP initiative, part of the scope of the project was to interview the regional management team and obtain a 'sign off' from the General Managers at each country operation.

An SAP implementation is far from being simply an ICT project—it was then, and still is now, a business transformation project enabled by technology. For this reason, process improvement is at the core of the project, which means adopting leading practices for each business process of the organisation. The methodology followed for developing the business case enacts this, as is described graphically in Fig. 3.4. It departs from defining the business drivers and scope of the project and concludes with target metrics and the expected return on investment (ROI).

The outcome of distilling all the benefits and costs down to dollar amounts is done for both Capex for project implementation, and Opex to arrive at the total cost of ownership.

(a) Tangible Benefits.

Table 3.10 quantifies and summarises the tangible benefits, year on year, for the first five years after launching the project. As can be seen in the table, benefits derive from increased sales (US$ 430 thousand over the five years), reduced cost of sales, (US$ 3.0 million over five years), reduced overhead cost (US$ 1.34 million + US$ 630 thousand = US$ 1.97 million) and financial savings from reduced working capital (US$ 360 thousand). In addition to this, savings deriving from better materials and stock management add up to US$ 1.99 million in the five years. Altogether, these savings add up to US$ 7.76 million over the first five years.

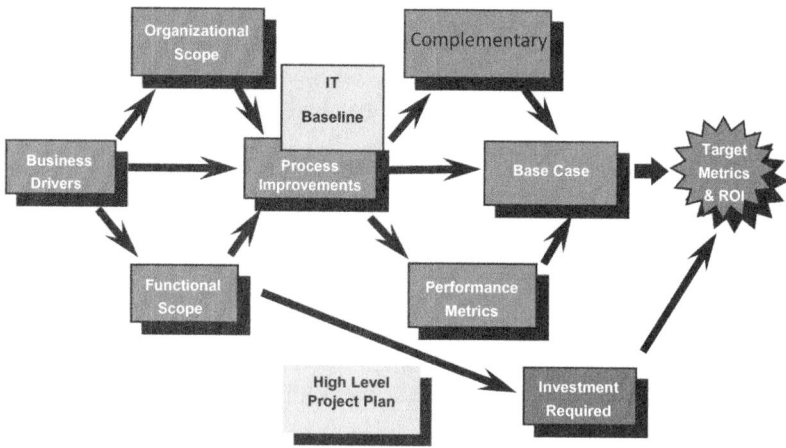

Fig. 3.4 Methodology adopted for the business case

Table 3.10 Benefits of Regional SAP Implementation

Benefit description	Period/Concept					P & L		B/S
	2001	2002	2003	2004	2005	5 Year Acc	Avg. TTB in months	5 Year Acc
Working capital reduction								
Inventories								1.85
Cash flow								0.14
Sales	0.09	0.09	0.09	0.09	0.09	0.43	8	
Costs	0.51	0.51	0.63	0.63	0.75	3.02	9	
Overhead	0.16	0.31	0.49	0.51	0.51			
Agreed personnel reduction	0.03	0.19	0.36	0.38	0.38	1.34	12	
Others	0.13	0.13	0.13	0.13	0.13	0.63	7	
Financial results	0.07	0.07	0.07	0.07	0.07	0.36	12	
Totals	0.82	0.98	1.27	1.29	1.41	5.77		1.99

Base Case (figures in million US Dollars)
TTB = Time To Benefit

(b) Total Cost of Ownership

The costs of acquiring SAP are divided into two types: implementation costs (Capex) and recurring costs (Opex). Implementation costs are the total costs of the project itself. These can be disaggregated in the following categories:

- Internal Team: the cost of all Orica professionals assigned to the project.
- External Consultants: all external consultants' fees. It includes fees for the Business Case, the Business Process Redesign and Change Management initiatives.
- Training: covers all key user training
- SAP & Related Software: regards the cost of the software considering 190 named users. The Export module was left out of the scope.

- Development Costs: represents all implementation costs, including software developments, interface building, customisation, tests, etc.
- Hardware and Peripherals: minimum hardware requirements recommended.
- Expenses & Others.

The cost structure for the SAP implementation is given in Table 3.11.

(c) Cost–Benefit and Sensitivity Analyses

Bringing together the benefits and costs entailed in acquiring a regional SAP implementation, the next step is to apply discounted cash flow analysis to these components. It also analyses the sensitivity of the return of the project to variations in benefit realisation and in cost incurrence. These analyses are summarised in Table 3.12 where it can be seen that the base case has a net present value of US$ 57 thousand, and internal rate of return of 18.4 per cent (which is moderately over the hurdle rate

Table 3.11 Total cost of ownership

		US$
SAP/SOE implementation costs		
Year 1	SAP consultants (PwC)	1,668,000
	SAP licenses and training	221,315
	Hardware	445,169
	Orica Latin America costs	388,700
	Nth America costs: development support	485,580
	Other	148,000
Year 2–5	Exploitaion (e-commerce, B2B, etc.)	400,000
	Reports customization	200,000
	Other	100,000
	Total fixed capital	4,056,764
SAP/SOE yearly recurring costs		
	SOE	341,460
	Nth America costs: server operation and leasing	396,360
	WAN	191,922
	SAP maintenance and 1st line support	119,886
	Other	160,280
	Total recurring costs	1,209,909

Table 3.12 The base case and sensitivity analysis (NPV in US$ thousands)

	NPV	IRR %	Payback years
Base case	57	18.4	3.0
10% Increase in fixed capital expenditure	(202)	8.7	4.0
Country 1 deliver same level of benefits as country 2 and 3	1374	86.0	1.7
50% reduction in infrastructure costs	375	31.0	2.6
50% reduction in working capital benefits	(741)	(7)	6.0

imposed by Head Office of 18 per cent) and a payback period of three years. What stands out of the sensitivity analysis is that improving the benefits in country 1 to the level anticipated in countries 2 and 3 has a significant impact on the returns of the project.

(d) Intangible benefits and some other opportunities

Despite the fact that Orica has decided that its investment decisions on projects like SAP will be based on quantitative, tangible benefits, the analysis of intangible benefits should not be left unattended. Some of the qualitative benefits of the SAP project identified by Orica are the following:

- It would enable *Business Strategy* through more integrated order fulfillment, supply chain and business management processes
- It would provide Orica with an opportunity to create a temporary competitive advantage by enabling it to pioneer new mining technologies before its competitors.
- The global business processes, best practices and agile organisation that would come with the SAP project, would enable developing synergies and facilitate acquisitions and mergers.
- SAP would empower users by making information accessible to them without depending on requests to the IT department.
- It would provide a more flexible technology infrastructure to respond to business changes, and it would help leverage throughout the organisation developments in areas such as Production Control and Logistics, Standardised Product Costing and Coding, Customer and Product Group profitability, Forecasting and Planning.

- It would help meet the demands of major clients to decrease product and service costs and become electronically linked with them in order to exchange information and streamline orders.

3.4.5 Risk Management

Considering the size of the project, the amount of resources involved and the differing perceptions on the initiative held by the country operations, a risk assessment was performed and a change management process was implemented in order to mitigate those risks.

More explicitly, one country operation perceived the project as an essentially information system initiative; another one saw it as a business project and an enabler for growth; and the third country operation understood it as strategic initiative for the Latin American region. These three different views required to be aligned; expectations needed to be managed; and it was necessary for all to understand the risks involved and be prepared to take mitigating actions.

Table 3.13 describes some of the risks identified, the strategies designed for mitigating them, and the actions taken to make these

Table 3.13 Analysis of risks and mitigating strategies

Area	Risk	Strategy	Actions	
People	Top Management must protect and be committed to the project.	Communicate the Business Case results	8/5/2000 General Managers Meeting Publish BC results	
Project	Stakeholder management: What happens if a strategically important project takes priority or competes for the same resources?	Complete the project phase. Orica to put project on a stand by. "Escape clause" in contract with PWC.	Agreement with PWC	Change Management
People	Reward policy. Keep people motivated during the project, and then re-energize them for the exploitation phase.	Define creative solutions in motivating people	Seek external advice	
People	Is the business/site ready? Readiness Assessment for the roll out.	Communicate the Business Case results. General Management agree timing for start to project	8/5 General Managers Meeting Publish Business Case results	
Process	Restrict the temptation for changing the processes during roll out.	Envolvement of Functional Managers and General Managers during Development Phase	Workshops Templates approval and commitment Quality Assurance and Best Practices	
Project & Technical	Australian level of flexibility	Service Level Agreement (negociate a contract with Australia)	Expenditure Proposal to be signed by Australia	

strategies operational and committing the management team with their success.

As an important component of risk management, a communications plan was designed for the project, conveying to senior management that it would require much effort but that the project leadership team knew what it was doing. As another critical component of risk management, the project team defined a set of guidelines aimed at keeping the project simple, minimising complexity and avoiding ever-lasting discussions on the achievement of goals.

Finally, another key factor for the success of the project and risk minimisation, would be people management. A detailed plan was developed with HR that covered everything from communications, through incentives and tying the bonuses of the country managers to the outcome of the project.

3.4.6 Outcome of the SAP Implementation Project

The benefits of a project such as the SAP implementation at Orica Latin America manifest themselves over time (Brynjolfsson, 1993), therefore the success of the implementation should also be measured and evaluated over time. However, it can be said that the project met two objective short-term success metrics: It ended on time and on budget.

The question is whether the project accomplished the financial objectives as they were set forth in the business case. Furthermore, does it enable the strategic imperatives defined, such as facilitating innovation and implementing the global model? As in many projects, some goals were attained, others were not, and still others are in a grey area where it is difficult to determine the causal link between the project and real company improvements.

An area where significant success was achieved is that of overhead cost containment. More explicitly, headcount reductions were executed, without a negative impact on operations, three months after the 'go live' in each country. Other reductions had to be postponed due to technological limitations in some remote locations where the system was deployed. As technologies became cheaper and available (e.g. satellite data links) they were implemented and so were the organisational changes. There are also indications of increased efficiency (both in operations and administrative work), allowing throughput improvement (i.e. manage a bigger business without having to hire new staff). There were cost reductions in audit fees due to standardisation of procedures, and other overheads such as over-time pay at monthly book-closing periods were eliminated.

One area where benefit realisation did not materialise, or at least was not evident in the first two or three years after going live, is that of increasing sales through better information on costs. Related to this, it is not clear that better costing procedures has removed uncertainty with regards to costing of products. In addition to that, two years after the implementation, procurement cost reduction was still slow in showing benefits.

Finally, there are those areas where the project triggered secondary actions or produced intangible benefits. For example, the SAP implementation permitted a better management of inventories, mainly finished products and better production plans, which has helped reduce its trade working capital over sales over the first three years after going live.

Looking beyond hard numbers, there is a general opinion within Orica Latin America that the overall outcome of the project was positive. There are a series of intangible benefits which have not been measured, but probably should have been. An example of this is the convergence of the chart of accounts in Latam with that of Australia/Asia as is as well the standardisation of product costing and of cost centre structures. There are examples of organisational learning that emerged from the project such as the development of a model and methodology for fast SAP implementation in small markets, like Orica Argentina and Orica Venezuela, where it was achieved in some three months; and the company learned how to provide support to regions in different time zones; and to deal with localisation issues, not only in terms financials and taxes, but also with respect to cultural issues.

Likewise, there is little doubt that prior intangible benefits triggered current projects, such as the implementation of one single global SAP instance, and other global initiatives beyond the ICT area (e.g. the implementation of Global Product Managers, which can only exist in a highly integrated global environment).

In summary (a) Orica did not achieve, in the short to midterm, an impact on competitiveness; however, Orica progressed in efficiency, effectiveness and operational performance, leveraging a number of projects that should improve Orica's competitiveness, facilitate acquisitions and create a solid foundation for growth; and (b) Orica did not do a systematic tracking of benefit realisation, particularly of intangible benefits.

3.4.7 Project Management Versus Governance

Shortly after the last country implementation went live the project team was, as expected, disbanded and most staff went back to their old units or were appointed to new positions. The above description reveals an almost "by the book" decision process on the acquisition and implementation of SAP at Orica Latin America, considering its situation prior to its embarking on this project. On the one hand, it also reveals that the short-term objectives had an uncommonly high degree of attainment, and on the other that the short-term objectives not achieved such as increased sales and procurement cost reduction are really beyond the responsibility of the project—those benefits need to be achieved by the respective business units using the new processes and systems, rather than the project itself. So, it is fair to say that the project management had an extraordinary performance. But where does governance come in?

One of the drivers of the project was that Orica's business had changed radically at the turn of the century. While originally it was a product (i.e. explosives and detonators) based business, the market forced it to become a full-service provider to the mining industry. In this new phase, its clients expected Orica to perform rock blasting, and charge per cubic metre of blasted rock produced. So, in a short time it had to incorporate a massive amount of technical/engineering/geological knowledge and invest in equipment to carry out that service. This is a radical innovation in business model. Welcome to the knowledge economy!

To deliver its new service, there had to be major organisational changes that were part of the SAP project. One key component of this is the organisation of a triangular cell distributed throughout the territories where the mines operate. Orica had to set up regional operations offices close to the mines and had to have permanent staff at the mines. The key operational cell was composed of an operations group at the mine site; a materials management group (i.e., procurement, warehouse management, logistics) in the regional office and a sales representative based at the regional office but permanently commuting to the mining sites in its territory.

In the analysis of the organisation performed in 2012 it emerged that, although these triangular cells were operating and delivering their service to clients, a majority of them were doing so in a highly casuistic way. There was no uniformity of processes across cells. SAP was not being used as a process enabler, but actually as a data registration tool, that is the data was input into SAP but not as an integral part of the business processes. Processes were done manually supported by paper and working around the system, and the data was uploaded to SAP at the end of each shift, day, week, month or whatever period was demanded for each category of data. Of course, this defeats the whole point of automating processes and possibly explains why some of the planned benefits indicated above were not achieved.

The driver for the 2012 review was that Orica had defined setting up a global shared service centre in the Far East to perform logistics operations for its subsidiaries all over the world. This was a massive innovation and operational excellence initiative that required all subsidiaries to be delivering on the Standard Operating Model with all their information online real time.

Is that an operational or a governance problem? Operationally the Latam companies were delivering, but they were not abiding by the company standards. So, this is a governance problem. Specifically, it refers to that corporate governance relationship mentioned in Chapter 2 between the CEO or senior management of the Latam operation and its staff. It has a cultural component. The company did not develop a corporate culture that motivated staff to adhere to the corporate standards. Indeed, as proposed by the Rizzuto model in Sect. 2.2.3 and Fig. 2.4 in a high context approach corporate strategy needs to be adapted to societal culture, but that is no excuse for not abiding with corporate standards at an operational processes level.

Going back to the business case described in substantial detail above, it applied a rigorous methodology. However, the methodology applied is an industrial economy approach with emphasis on tangible benefits. It sufficed in that case because Orica was pursuing cost containment, where the benefits of the new processes and systems could be estimated with traditional accounting and cost–benefit analyses. However, in the knowledge economy many of the objectives pursued in business transformation initiatives like the one described, aim at enhancing performance without necessarily reducing tangible costs—initiatives to improve decision-making, improve communications, track greenhouse gas emissions, reduce process and product risks to staff, strengthen cyber-security and other semi-tangible or intangible benefits.

The conclusion of the analysis of this case study is that the absence of governance to ensure the organisation developed a corporate culture that enticed its staff to comply with the corporate standards led to inefficiencies and, thus, loss of profits that were not perceived at the time, but that erected serious hurdles at the time of implementing a corporation-wide innovation as was the global logistics shared services. This caused a direct cost for streamlining the processes in the Latam operations according to the corporate standards, and a delay in the global project. This will have had an impact on several stakeholder groups, but especially to shareholders and possibly to customers.

3.5 Lost Opportunities of Poor Corporate Governance Resulting in a Siloed Organisation

3.5.1 Introduction

This mini-case study describes a situation in a global company where the lack of corporate governance in the ICT function derives in a siloed organisation that becomes a nearly unsurmountable hurdle for exploiting the organisation's international footprint in an agile manner.

The organisation is a leading dairy products company that will be called Milky Way (MW)[6] headquartered in an Anglo-Saxon economy—it is a case where the author was involved as a management consultant to design a global ICT architecture, to select an ERP system to implement in all MW's operations, and to set up an ICT governance scheme.

This project took place in 2006. At that time, MW was organised in two divisions, the traditional Industrial Products and the less established Consumer Packaged Goods (MW CPG) where the company had some strong brands in the country where it is headquartered, and had grown through acquisition so owned in other markets local brands of high visibility. In all, MW reached some 140 countries with its products, but to many of these markets it reached with unbranded industrial products produced in its headquarters. In the case of MW CPG, some international markets were fulfilled from its headquarters, while others were served through local production. In all, MW CPG owned and managed some 100 brands across the world.

---

[6] The real name is disguised as the case is produced from project data. The project was carried out in 2005 so the data herein should not be strategically sensitive, however this is done as a precaution.

The mentioned project, and this case study, focuses only on the MW CPG side of the business. Although there was a CIO who oversaw ICT at both divisions, reality was that the two businesses had very different information requirements so each division had its own IS organisation. Just to give a sense of dimension, in the case of MW CPG its IS organisation (CPG IS) served 3600 users worldwide, it had a headcount of 75, its operational budget for FY06 was US$ 28 million, a capital expenditure for FY06 of US$ 7 million, and was managing at the time a portfolio of 111 projects that had a total budget of US$ 42 million[7] In terms of enterprise resource planning (ERP) systems it had an array of different systems running in multiple instances across the globe: JDEdwards, BPICS, SAP, ACCPAC and MFGPro. They were running on 96 different application servers. This complicated ERP landscape was a reflection of MW CPG having grown by acquisition and not having a corporate standard.

3.5.2 The Situation

MW had many decades of history but had originated as a cooperative owned by the dairy farmers and so its main objective had been to serve its members by collecting and processing their milk. A few years before this project commenced MW had been converted into a corporation and over the years had been changing its corporate culture and becoming more client centric, understanding as such industrial clients and consumers of their products.

In 2005 MW's Board decided that the company should take a decisive step forward in this transformation process and hired an outside CEO for MW CPG. It brought on board a young but highly experienced, fast-paced, marketing and brand manager from one of the leading consumer packaged goods companies in the world to become its CEO. As the CEO was meeting his team to get an understanding of his new company, one of his first questions was 'Who is the largest client?' He got a not very sharp response that it was McDonalds for its cheeseburgers and other dairy ingredients. His next question 'How much does McDonalds buy from us?' received a confusing cacophony of contradictory responses, followed by utter silence when he asked for sales to McDonalds disaggregated by market.

---

[7] All the mentioned figures are in 2005 US dollars.

At the end of the meeting the new CEO asked the CPG IS manager to produce those figures for McDonalds and a few other international clients. Producing them took several days and multiple phone calls to the different MW CPG companies in the world, and the answers obtained were unreliable.

The prior story gives an idea of the status of information at MW CPG. Access to information was slow and management reports required intense Excel-based labour to produce. There were high IS costs due to duplication of functions, multiple handling of data to produce balanced scorecard KPIs and very dispersed and uncoordinated activities that led to a high total cost of ownership of MW CPG's information systems. The data was unreliable leading to outright wrong information and multiple contradicting information (i.e. this was made far more complex due to the number of different brands for each product). It was hard to get a visibility of global CPG IS expenses and CPG IS people as each company used different accounting criteria. There were no standard processes across subsidiaries so it was almost impossible to understand basic information such as global advertising cost for specific brands, or to interpret product pricing in each market.

Clearly, the new MW CPG CEO found this situation unsustainable if he was going to meet his growth and brand development objectives. He instructed his CPG IS manager to come up with a plan to sort this out. The CPG IS manager engaged the author to help him design this grand plan.

3.5.3 The Response

By the mid-2000s there was much experience to build on. In the 1990s and early 2000s the IS world was still haunted by what the economics Nobel laureate Robert Solow called the productivity paradox: IT was being seen everywhere except in the productivity metrics. In retrospect this was due to a series of reasons such as organisational learning on how to use technology, the re-thinking of business in this new digital environment, measurement limitations deriving from accounting systems thought-out for the industrial economy, the advent of intangible assets such as intellectual capital and others. Above all, it was the transition into the knowledge economy as described in Chapter 2.

The solution to MW CPG's problems were relatively simple on paper. It was about materialising standard business processes to be rolled out with minimum adaptations to all MW CPGs operated companies (OpCos) around the world, supported on a global IS architecture. The processes would be automated by transactional systems that would operate on a single instance of one ERP system. These transactional systems would all feed into a data repository from which the CEO and his corporate team could obtain consolidated reports. The architecture can be represented diagrammatically as in Fig. 3.5.

Arriving at an architecture like that from where MW CPG was in 2006 would require a massive amount of work in standardising data (e.g. products' and materials' coding, cost-centre structures, co-ordinated accounts in general ledger, dimensions for profitability analysis, …), in defining common processes from sales-order-to-cash, from purchase-order-to-payment, productions planning, plant maintenance management,…At the time MW CPG was already under severe logistics pressure from retailers in some markets, as supermarkets would give half-hour slots for delivery.

In the normal bottom-up approach, a single ERP would have to be selected and a process module template would have to be developed

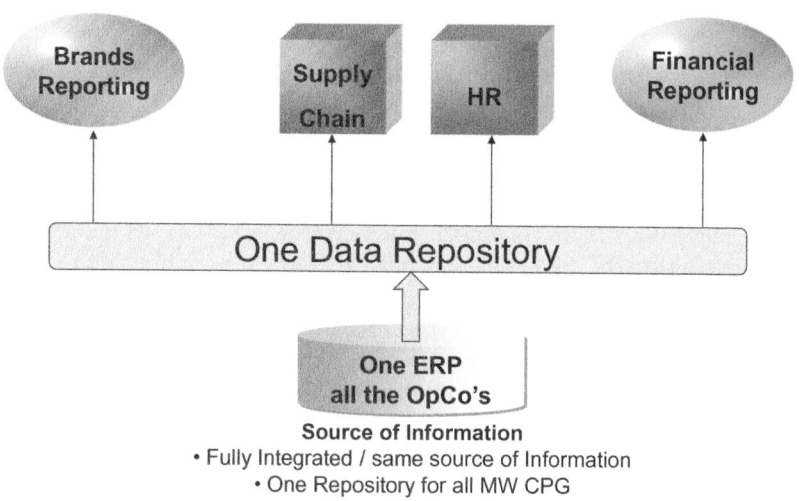

Fig. 3.5 IS architecture for MW CPG

centrally, and then rolled out to all the OpCos. Once that were in place, it would be simple to collect all the transactional data in a single data repository ready to be sliced and diced as senior management wanted to see it. That process would take three to five years! Would the new CEO be prepared to wait all that time to get his first reliable reports? Of course not. His patience span could be measured in weeks or maybe months, not years. So, a different approach had to be proposed.

Keeping the architecture of Fig. 3.5 as the end destination, the only way of arriving at realistic results was to go top-down. That is, start by fitting in the single global repository, and define some rules for all the OpCos, with their current legacy systems, to feed data into the repository. MW CPG management at the centre could then start exploiting information, while the OpCos implemented their new corporate processes, phase out their legacy systems in an orderly manner and start feeding data in with their new ERP as they came live. This is represented schematically in Fig. 3.6.

The reports for senior management that would be obtained during the transition would not be optimal, so an ambitious goal of concluding the whole process within the time frame of three years was agreed, and this should be done while keeping business risks strictly under control. There were to be no, or minimal, order fulfilment disruptions due to the CPG IS plan implementation, for which several measures would have to be put in place. The implementation plan would have to be led by businesspeople at the OpCos, not the CPG IS people. The role of CPG IS was to co-ordinate the definition of standards and then ensure that those standards were enforced. It was the business people at the OpCos that would call the shots on go-live dates in their locations, and it was a joint effort between the business and CPG IS to cleanse the data going into

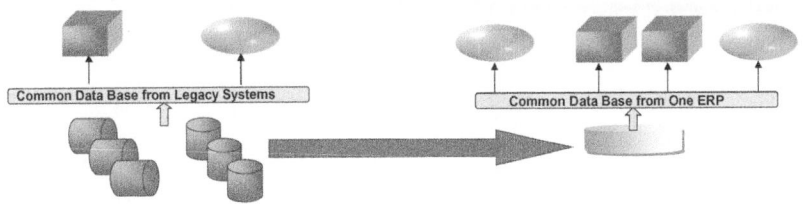

Fig. 3.6 Top-down transition to final architecture

the new ERP system. Finally, it was CPG IS' responsibility to implement testing procedures of the new system before they went live.

3.5.4 Implementation

Once it was agreed what was to be done, the question now was 'How?' The project would be given a name, *Magna*, and it was divided into five key success streams: CPG Business Intelligence (BI), CPG Core Processes, CPG Supply Chain Management (SCM), CPG Innovation and CPG Customer Relationship Management (CRM). To be able to design the business processes that underly each of these streams, the ERP solution had to be selected as the leading practices incorporated in the ERP would be an input to the design. A rigorous selection process was followed, with a quick arrival to a shortlist of two, SAP and JDEdwards, and then comparing the proposals of these two solution providers. The final selection was SAP, and an implementation partner consulting firm was selected as well.

Once the solution was selected, the MW CPG Standard Business Processes were defined with three main inputs: The most effective OpCo's processes were taken as a starting template, to which then were added the best practices in SAP's consumer packaged goods solution, and the input of representatives of the different OpCos. This is represented in Fig. 3.7.

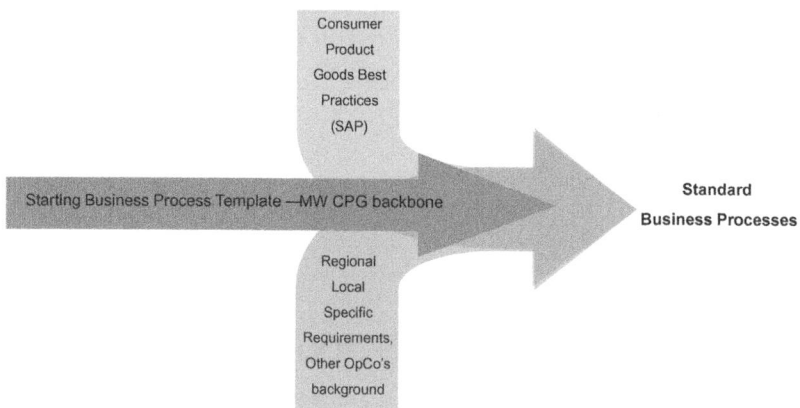

Fig. 3.7 Inputs for arriving at Standard Business Processes

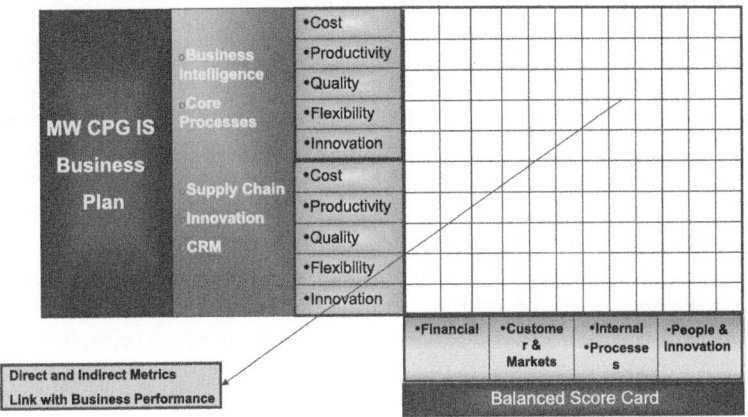

Fig. 3.8 Tracking benefits to the BSC

Finally, the CPG IS governance was designed to ensure that there would be full visibility of all ICT investments and expenses across the OpCos, especially those non-*Magna* initiatives. The policies here were to design an IS portfolio strategy for MW CPG, where all non-*Magna* initiatives would be categorised along the four portfolio components: Infrastructure, Transactional Systems, Informational Systems and Innovation Systems. Policies were designed to distribute Opex according to each IS component's position in the portfolio. Policies were also defined for non-*Magna* IS investment decisions and source of funding for Capex. And, to finish, all the prior policies were rolled up into a methodology to link each project/initiative to MW CPG balanced scorecard, as described in Fig. 3.8.

3.5.5 Discussion

There is a lot to learn from a governance perspective from this case. There was no corporate systems architecture, let alone policies; nor were there corporate standards in terms of data and processes. The old cooperative culture where the priority was to serve the co-op members by collecting their milk production had never changed despite the organisation having adopted a corporate structure and a commitment to be customer (i.e. consumer and industrial) centric. This confirms an old adage that an insider cannot change an organisational culture—the change needs to be led by an outsider. It was the Board's move to appoint an outsider that catapulted the change.

In its intent to create a customer centred culture, the Board appropriately selected a marketing and brand expert. This was an expensive hire for the organisation, however his effectiveness was constrained by the lack of information that derived from the absence of ICT governance and process governance, together with a culture that each subsidiary had total autonomy. It is understandable that an organisation in such an idiosyncratic business as the dairy one, adopt a high context approach, but as the Rizzuto model shows, that does not mean forfeiting corporate strategy and a distinct corporate culture, let alone giving the subsidiaries total autonomy.

Which stakeholder groups were affected? Clearly the shareholders—the company invested in an expensive, world class CEO, and could not reap the benefits in a fast turnaround. And in retrospect, timing was of the essence in this case. If the new CEO had been able to operate with agility, he might have achieved some significant changes before the effects of the Great Recession were felt in 2008—as it happened, the company was caught flat-footed by the crisis. By the time of the crisis the business context was one of full-knowledge economy, but the company had not had time to develop its intangible assets. There had not been time to build intellectual capital in the form of corporate streamlined processes (i.e. structural capital) and a culture that embraced a data-driven management style.

One last view to take on this case is from the lens of the corporate governance triangle and key governance relationships mentioned in Sect. 2.2.1. The 'third relationship', that between the CEO and the rank and file of the organisation failed. It failed to create the corporate culture required for operating in the knowledge economy and becoming customer centric. The failure of this relationship led to the activation of the 'second relationship', that one between the Board and the CEO, which took the form of replacing the CEO by an outsider.

With this in mind, the next section does a cross-case analysis of this and the prior three cases, to attempt to arrive at a degree of abstraction and fresh insight.

3.6 Cross-Case Analysis

The four cases analysed bring to light, in different ways, the hidden cost of poor governance. Interestingly, stakeholder analysis (as seen in Sect. 2.1) applied to the four cases results in one theme in common: Poor governance always seems to negatively affect one stakeholder group, the shareholders, and often times also negatively impacts another one, the client (i.e. Wells Fargo). In the Glamorgan case, shareholders were affected through the agency problem—the lack of governance standards manifested in the form of asymmetry of information between shareholders and managers, led to a transfer of resources from the former towards the latter. In the other three cases the impact on shareholders derived from governance flaw resulting in failed corporate culture. In the case of Wells Fargo it was the failure to build an ethical culture that finally caused massive reputation damage and loss in market value; in the cases of Orica and MW CPG it was the failure to create a culture of adherence to corporate standards that became a barrier to implementing innovation in detriment of shareholder value.

Although damage to shareholders is the constant across all cases, it is not the only stakeholder group affected. In the Glamorgan FS case the employee stakeholder group was also deeply affected, while at Wells Fargo it was the customers who took a strong direct hit, and the severity of both impacts was serious.

Observing the cases from the perspective of the governance triad (i.e. Shareholders, Board of Directors, CEO/Senior Management) and the three key governance relationships (Shareholders vs Board, Board vs CEO, CEO vs Rank & File) seen in Sect. 2.2 it is in the CEO vs Rank & File relationship that issues of poor governance seem to manifest themselves most vividly. It is when this relationship fails that an organisation fails to develop an ethical culture and a culture that entices people to adhere to corporate standards. In the case of Wells Fargo, it was the ethical side that failed because the CEO prioritised sales outcomes over doing the right thing; in the case of Orica it was the CEO that did not communicate with his staff the need for adhering to defined corporate processes that impeded innovation; and in MW CPG it was the CEO that did not demand the definition of information standards and that allowed excessive autonomy, that crippled the organisation when it attempted to become customer centric in a global way.

In the case of Glamorgan FS the situation is more complex. It appears that the Board was not informed of the implications of relocating the RHQ which is a failure in the Board vs CEO relation, and this set a bad example within the organisation that would affect the future effectiveness of the CEO vs Rank & file relation in creating an ethical culture that would abide by corporate standards.

Culture comes up systematically as a factor in all the cases. As anticipated in Sect. 2.2 building an ethical culture is a consequence of effective governance and of the utmost importance in financial services. As the Wells Fargo case shows, its absence opens the organisation to serious wrongdoing when combined with a management style that emphasises performance and subjects staff to highly demanding performance goals. This was made even worse by a culture where business managers had a strong prominence over the controllers, which no doubt led to the disaster at Wells Fargo. If there is not an ethical culture in place, staff will fall into the temptation of cutting corners and accepting that the ends justify the means, even when these are unethical. But the cases show that is not the only aspect of culture in a context of poor governance that becomes significant. There is also the issue of a culture that does not entice staff to abide by the organisations process and information standards. In the Orica and MW CPG cases this has consequences for the shareholders. Linking culture to the governance relationships mentioned in the previous points, a culture that fails on the ethical or organisational fronts results from a deficient CEO vs Rank & File governance relationship. Interestingly, the Wells Fargo and MW CPG cases show that a corporate culture that needs a shift, needs an outsider to come and steer that shift. So, if the CEO vs Rank & File governance relationship fails, the Board vs CEO governance relationship needs to be activated and normally results in replacement of the CEO by an outsider.

Transparency and reporting are at the essence of corporate governance, as seen in Sects. 2.1 and 2.3, and that comes straight through from the Glamorgan FS case. The selection of the new regional headquarter location in complete disregard of the research, locating it in the least convenient location as a perk for the new regional CEO, without specific communication to the Board and other stakeholders, is a breech in transparency. At Wells Fargo, the information on staff being terminated for opening unwanted client bank accounts was held away from the Board and other stakeholders—even after the information on unlawful sale practice emerged through the press, the Board was misguided on its seriousness and led to believe that the measures taken had the problem under control. The Board is not free from responsibility on this case—its members should have been a lot more inquisitive. Notwithstanding, they did correct their course when the Board commissioned and published the independent report on the incident produced by the Oversight Committee. At Orica there was a lack of transparency on the degree of implementation of the Standard Operating Model even at the senior management level. Finally, at MW CPG there was no explicit status comments on the ICT strategy and governance in the Annual Reports. This is not exclusive to this company as that was common practice at the time of the research, but with the importance that digital is taking in business today, it should be standard practice to include in Annual Reports the status of the ICT plan and its implementation.

Multinational Glamorgan FS demonstrated a proactive strategy adaptation stance at the time of creating a regional headquarters, precisely to be closer to the markets—however it failed in execution in the way it defined its locations. The Wells Fargo case shows that a market-driven strategy needs to be complemented by strong internal controls and central oversight. Excessive autonomy of the Community Bank and as seen above, the prominence of the business managers over the controllers, contributed to the disaster at Wells Fargo. Orica has a well thought out strategy adaptation for its operations in Latam, but its governance failed it through not creating a culture of abiding by corporate processes and standards. At MW CPG the strategy for international growth was by acquisition but without thorough plans to integrate new acquisitions into its corporate fabric—this derived in excessive autonomy of the new subsidiaries with very weak controls imposing corporate values that eventually became a hurdle to innovation in marketing and brand building.

Complementing prior points, as seen in Sect. 2.3, in the knowledge economy success requires companies to manage their intellectual capital and innovate deeply in their business model. By despising the effect that the move of the RHQ would have on its employees, Glamorgan FS risked losing the sophisticated human capital that it had built in the Miami RHQ—building a new knowledgeable team in Sao Paulo would take time, effort and resources—in the meantime that could have negatively impacted regional performance. At Orica and MW CPG the failure to implement corporate processes and information standards (i.e. structural intellectual capital) led to barriers to implement new business models. This is summarised in Table 3.14.

Table 3.14 Synthesis of cross-case analysis

Factor/Case	Glamorgan FS	Wells Fargo	Orica	MW CPG
Stakeholders affected	Shareholders and employees	Shareholders and customers	Shareholders	Shareholders
Governance triad + 1, and governance relationship failure	Board vs CEO and bad precedent for CEO vs Rank & File	CEO vs Rank & File	CEO vs Rank & File	CEO vs Rank & File
Culture failures		In creating an ethical culture	In creating a culture of adherence to corporate processes	In creating a corporate identity and adherence to corporate information standards
Transparency breaches	Informing the Board and other stakeholders on the implications of relocating RHQ	Misinforming the Board on seriousness of implications of sales malpractice	On the degree of implementation of the Standard Operating Model	No explicit comments on the status of ICT strategy and governance
MNE Strategy adaptation	Creating an RHQ is positive, but its relocation is questionable	Aggressive sales strategy not accompanied of appropriate controls	Good strategy adaptation formulation, but poor implementation	Through acquisition but without plans to integrate new subsidiaries in corporate fabric
KE—Business model innovation & intangible assets	Risk of losing sophisticated human capital		Failed to materialise structural capital; unprepared for business model innovation	Failed to materialise structural capital; unprepared for business model innovation

A reflection that is triggered by the analysis of these four case studies refers to the role of the Board in its service to the shareholders. When thinking about this it is mostly connected to protecting the shareholders from the agency issue, that is from the transfer of wealth from the shareholders to the management team enabled by the asymmetry of information, between these two groups, on the workings of the organisation. However, this analysis leads to believe that even more important than that is for the Board to watch closely how the CEO vs Rank & file relation is functioning to create an ethical culture and one that entices the members of the organisation to abide by corporate standards. In close connection to this, the cases confirm that if a corporate culture needs to change at a fast pace, the process of change must be led by an outsider to the organisation. Finally, the analysis of the cases confirms how closely integrated Governance, Culture, Strategy and Sustainable Business Model, as shown in Fig. 2.1, need to be.

The next chapter will analyse another three cases to advance understanding on the challenges to global governance in MNEs.

References

Ambos, T. C., & Birkinshaw, J. (2010). Headquarters' attention and its effects on subsidiary performance. *Management International Review, 50*(4), 449–469.

Ambos, B., & Mahnke, V. (2010). How do MNC headquarters add value? *Management International Review, 50*(4), 403–412.

Bhattacharya, C. B., Korschin, D., & Sen, S. (2009). Strengthening stakeholder-company relationships through mutually beneficial corporate social responsibility initiatives. *Journal of Business Ethics, 85*, 257–272.

Birkinshaw, J., Braunerhjelm, P., Holm, U., & Terjesen, S. (2006). Why do some multinational corporations relocate their headquarters overseas. *Strategic Management Journal, 27*(7), 681–700.

Brynjolfsson, E. (1993). The productivity paradox of information technology. *Communications of the ACM, 36*(12), 66–67.

Chen, Y. C. (2008). Why do multinational corporations locate their advanced R&D centres in Beijing? *The Journal of Development Studies, 44*(5), 622–644. https://doi.org/10.1080/00220380802009092.

Freeman, R. E. (2010). *Strategic management: A stakeholder approach* (p. 53). Cambridge University Press.

Griffiths, P. D. R. (2007a). *Corporate social responsibility (CSR): Window-dressing, smoke-screening, or the route to legitimacy?* A critical analysis of how companies approach CSR. Finalist in the Second Annual IFC/FT Essay Competition.

Griffiths, P. D. R. (2007b). The application of market power theory as a value driver for information technology investment decisions: A Study of Six Chilean Banks. In *Proceedings of the Conference on Strategic Management in Latin America*, Santiago, 4–5 January 2006, co-Organised by the Pontifica Universidad Catolica de Chile and The Journal of Business Research.

Griffiths, P. D. R. (2011). *Strategy-technology alignment: Deriving business value from ICT projects*. Academic Publishing International (API). http://www.acade mic-bookshop.com/ourshop/prod_1511198-lt100gtStrategyTechnology-Alignment-Deriving-Business-Value-from-ICT-Projects.html.

Griffiths, P. D. R., & Remenyi, D. (2008). Aligning knowledge management with competitive strategy: A framework. *Electronic Journal of Knowledge Management*, Special Edition, Edited by Prof Rembrandt Klopper, 6(2), 125–134. http://www.ejkm.com/volume-6/v6-2/v6-i2-art5.htm.

Griffiths, P. D. R., & Stern, B. (2004, November 11–12). Orica Latin America—Converting a major IT-based transformation into shareholder value. In D. Remenyi (Ed.), *Proceedings of the 11th European Conference on Information Technology Evaluation* (pp. 155–168). Royal Netherlands Academy of Arts and Sciences, Amsterdam.

Hewett, K., Roth, M. S., & Roth, K. (2003). Conditions influencing headquarters and foreign subsidiary roles in marketing activities and their effects on performance. *Journal of International Business Studies, 34*(6), 567–585.

Holt, J., Gray, S. J., Purcell, W., & Pedersen, T. (2000). *Decision factors influencing the regional headquarters location of multinationals in the Asia Pacific*. Australian Centre for International Business.

Laamanen, T., Simula, T., & Torstila, S. (2012). Cross-border relocations of headquarters in Europe. *Journal of International Business Studies, 43*(2), 187–210.

Luiz, J. M., & Radebe, B. (2016). The strategic location of regional headquarters for multinationals in Africa: South Africa as a host country. *Business Administration and Management, 3*(XIX), 75–90.

Marquis, C., & Velez Villa, L. (2012) *Managing stakeholders with corporate social responsibility*. Harvard Business School, Course overview notes, 9-412-121.

Remenyi, D., & Griffiths, P. D. R. (2009). *The socratic dialogue in the work place: Theory and practice. Electronic Journal of Knowledge Management, 7*(1), 155–164. http://www.ejkm.com/volume-7/v7-1/v7-i1-art15.htm.

Sen, S., Bhattacharya, C. B., & Korschum, D. (2006). The role of corporate social responsibility in strengthening multiple stakeholder relationships: A field experiment. *Journal of the Academy of Marketing Science, 34*, 58–166.

Stacey, A. G. (2005). Reliability and validity of the item means and standard deviations of ordinal level response data. *Management Dynamics, 14*(3), 2–25.

The Economist. (2017, April 7). *Stick in the Mud: A year on, Wells Fargo cannot shake off its mis selling scandal.*

Treacy, M., & Wiersema, F. (1995). *The discipline of market leaders.* Addison-Wesley.

Uminiski, D. J. (2017). *It's your move—Critical considerations when relocating corporate headquarters.* Area Development Site and Facility Planning, Eston, Vol. 52, Issue 1, Q1/2017.

CHAPTER 4

Challenges to Global Governance in MNE: Strategy Adaptation to Local Markets

4.1 Overview

This chapter exposes the reader to the challenges that are present in international business from the need to make corporate strategies designed at the Centre of the corporation adapted to the specifics of each host market where the corporation does business. The challenges that are focused on are those that pertain to the Governance of the corporation. In particular, it will highlight that dimension of governance that refers to the relationship between Corporate Management with senior management at the subsidiary and the latter with the operations and client-facing staff at the subsidiary.

The author is extremely grateful to Dr. Rizzuto for the use of the two cases (IBM Argentina and BAT Argentina) that have been edited by the author to highlight the issues in strategy adaptation pertaining to governance. All merits for these cases are credited to Dr. Rizzuto, while the author takes full responsibility for any shortcomings.

© The Author(s), under exclusive license to Springer Nature Switzerland AG 2021
P. D. R. Griffiths, *Corporate Governance in the Knowledge Economy*, Palgrave Studies in Accounting and Finance Practice, https://doi.org/10.1007/978-3-030-78873-5_4

4.2 IBM ARGENTINA: POLYCENTRICITY IN PRACTICE

4.2.1 Overview of the Company

IBM Argentina is a subsidiary of the IBM Corporation and was founded in 1923, so at the time of this research IBM Argentina had been in the country for 90 years and employed approximately 8000 people. Its products and services are related to business transformation enabled by information and communications technology (ICT). In terms of geographic scope, IBM Argentina supplied the domestic market with products and services, and it exported services to more than 180 clients in 20 countries on five continents. It focuses on the business-to-business domain where its clients are typically government agencies, large MNEs and small and medium enterprises (SMEs). Its vision, mission and value statements are depicted in Table 4.1.

Despite some high-profile unethical incidents in Argentina in the past, IBM is considered a model firm in terms of corporate citizenship, a concept that is reflected in the organisation's ethical management and transparency in its dealings with different stakeholders, and which sets corporate goals compatible with sustainable development. From its beginnings, IBM Argentina has shown a strong institutional commitment with the community. This is illustrated by its contribution to areas such as education, integration of disabled people, digital inclusion and promotion of scientific, academic, cultural, economic and environmental activities.

IBM Argentina has a long and successful track record despite the inherently uncertain environment of its local market. The company not only survived but has positively thrived over the decades. One of its strengths

Table 4.1 IBM Argentina's mission, vision and value statements (Rizzuto, 2016, citing IBM Argentina 2012 dossier)

Mission Statement	To help its clients achieve their business objectives, supplying them with innovative services and solutions for companies of all sizes
Vision	To become the IT supplier of choice as an innovative company as a result of its solutions, products and services; and in recognition of the professional and human quality of its people
Values	• dedication to the success of every client • innovation that matters, to our company and the world • trust and responsibility in all relationships

is that it does not only serve the market in Argentina through the sale of hardware, software and services, but had been for many decades an exporter of manufactured products and at the time of the research for this case study was an exporter of services and know-how.

Throughout the twentieth century IBM Argentina prospered. As mentioned, IBM was founded in Argentina in 1923 but its predecessor—The Computing-Tabulating-Recording Company (CTR)—had started to sell its products (such as dial recorders) in that market as early as 1916 through a distributor under the name of International Time Recording Company. A few years later, IBM acquired weight and time measurement equipment agencies and started its operations in Buenos Aires. In 1927 the first punch card plant was established in Buenos Aires while in 1928 IBM opened new large premises in the capital. Later, in 1933, the first IBM Service Office was opened in Buenos Aires and in another major city.

In the 1950s there were remarkable developments at IBM Argentina. In 1950, during a visit to Buenos Aires, IBM President Thomas J. Watson suggested that a manufacturing plant should be built in the county. In 1955 IBM Argentina manufactured its first machines for export: rotating key punches for Norway, Australia, South Africa and various clients elsewhere in South America. In 1956 for the first time IBM Argentina manufactured IBM 8500 Mechanical Time Clocks for local markets and for export. Finally, in 1958 the Buenos Aires plant made its first export shipment of IBM 8600 Mechanical Time Clocks. During the following decades IBM Argentina continued its expansion and international growth. The 1980s was another noteworthy decade for the subsidiary to the point that by 1991 the plant exported 34 percent of its production to Japan and Australia, 17 percent to other countries in the Asia–Pacific region, 23 percent to other Latin American countries, 15 percent to North America and 6 percent to Europe. So, only 5 percent of the plant's production was sold in Argentina.

In 2008 IBM Argentina celebrated 85 years of uninterrupted commitment to the country by announcing three new service export centres. A year later the Service Export Centre in Argentina was awarded the eSCM level 5 certification (Carnegie Mellon University eSourcing Capability Model for Service Providers) which meant that it was the first IBM business unit to achieve this level of excellence. In 2010, the Olivos III plant was created, a new Service Export Centre facility with capacity of 2000 people and that year IBM Argentina was awarded the Ibero-American Quality prize.

As far as export services are concerned, IBM's capabilities together with the talent and quality of the professionals available locally, have enabled it to offer services from Argentina to clients throughout the world. This includes services such as operating systems technical support, operations, maintenance and monitoring; human resources and financial process consultancy; application development and asset management.

At the time of the case study IBM Argentina was organised into four business units, as depicted in Fig. 4.1, which are Global Technology Services (GTS), Global Business Services (GBS), Software Group and Systems Technology Group (STG).

The GTS business unit satisfies the needs of clients with technological operations in six key areas, Technical Support Services, Business Continuity and Recovery, Network and Connectivity Services, System Infrastructure and Management Services, Outsourcing and Integrated Communications.

Global Business Services was created in 2002 when IBM consolidated its leadership in professional services with the acquisition of PricewaterhouseCooper's global consultancy business and technology

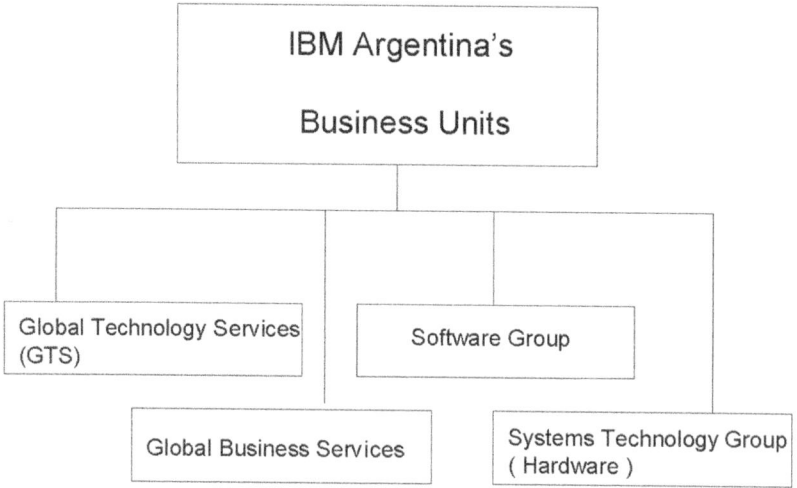

Fig. 4.1 IBM Argentina's business units (Rizzuto, 2016)

services—PwC Management Consulting Services. Within GBS a new global business unit was created, IBM Business Consulting Services, with the incorporation of over 30,000 professionals worldwide who came across from PwC. Through that acquisition IBM positioned itself as one of the main consultancy companies worldwide and Ginni Rometty, the head of GBS at the time, catapulted her career to become the first woman CEO of IBM ten years later.

The strategy of the Software Group business unit was built around alignment of technology to the changing needs of the client's business, supplying middleware products and first-class solutions tailored to the industry. IBM's aim was to build long-lasting relationships with clients, helping them develop more competitive business models capable of being flexible and highly responsive.

Finally, in the Hardware space, the STG offered the most advanced solutions in servers and storage. The IBM products range is characterised by offering flexibility, innovative technology, reliability and the necessary security to boost the transformation of its clients towards a more intelligent world (Rizzuto, 2016).[1]

IBM Argentina appears to follow the *transnational* form under the corporate strategy umbrella. This means that the subsidiary plays an active role in terms of responsiveness to the local context and at the same time participates fully in a highly integrated global corporation (Faulkner, 2003). By highly integrated global corporation is meant that, for instance, the company may close a business deal in Switzerland, or in Israel, or in the United States that requires an array of services and multitude of skills to fulfil. Certain skills and knowledge may be found in IBM Argentina and in that case that part of the project is transferred to Argentina, while another part to Manila in the Philippines, another part to India and so on. Everything flows globally and projects are run from wherever on the planet the corporation has the expertise. Teams are developed at Centres of Excellence at different subsidiaries around the world, giving the corporation a polycentric distribution of knowledge and decision-making. For this to work the company follows standards and IBM in China, in the Philippines, in Spain or Argentina, for example, can work together in project because standards are common. They sell the same products and

---

[1] Citing IBM Argentina dossier, 2012.

solutions in the same way. The parameters of commercial behaviour are the same, as well as ethics, transparency and quality of human resources.

4.2.2 IBM Argentina in Its Context

To say that formal institutions are weak in Argentina is an extreme understatement. Its business environment is characterised by strong political and economic swings, pendular movements that require local leadership teams that read them and adapt their organisations to them. At the time of the development of the original case study in 2013 the country was going through a period of high government intervention in the markets where corporations were required to have a foreign trade surplus in order to be allowed to import products. The power of government was highly centralised with decision-making concentrated in just a few hands and unpredictable criteria. Since then the pendulum swung towards the extreme of openness and promotion of inward investment in one administration, and in 2019 swung back to a highly controlled environment in the current administration.

The cycles are short and the *rules of the game* are not clear. Informality prevails in Argentina's formal institutions, where excessive written regulations and red tape coexist with implicit communications. Moreover, there is a heavy heritage especially in the way rules are written that comes from the Spanish colonial tradition, which is still reflected in Argentina's current bureaucracy. Despite expanding government red-tape IBM Argentina had not suffered a major impact on operations and the company had managed to adapt. In a few years prior to the time of the original case study, market regulation had spawned implicit and explicit rules. A file in government's hands could be dealt with quickly and efficiently, or an official could delay it as long as she wanted. In some areas, the more complex the question involved, the more it was subject to the discretionary decision of a particular official. This turns the process particularistic and far from universalist. Regarding implicit or explicit forms, there is agreement on certain prohibitions, in which civil servants will provide the general framework in writing, followed by specific applications that they communicate verbally and will never put in writing.

IBM has survived and flourished for over 90 years in this environment by exercising a strong embeddedness in the market through a combination of stringent financial management and cementing close relationships with clients, sticking together through flexibility in times of crisis and sharing the benefits in times of growth and positive economic cycle. This market is hard to understand for foreign executives so embeddedness comes in a strong measure through developing local managers to lead the subsidiary.

Understanding between headquarters management and the subsidiary's management team needs to overcome the barriers of distant societal cultures. The *future orientation* dimension of societal culture embodies this as planning in Argentina is sensitive to the short term and in permanent revision, which is hard to follow in the United States. Notwithstanding, from the interviews it emerged that planning is vital within an organisation that shows mostly long-term orientation with a good inclination towards change, while at the same time upholding the status quo. This demonstrates a large degree of adaptation to the local context. Some managers and directors' perspectives reflect their position towards the future, which in turn, results in a mix of corporate guidelines adapted to the pronounced swings of the Argentine business pendulum. In this regard, when asked to discuss the dilemma between planning for the future and accepting the status quo, most of the informants emphasised that planning was vital. In connection to this issue, one of the main values of the company is that it is in a constant state of transformation. The company is large and slow but it manages to stay one step ahead of the market. There may be areas that are not easy to transform, where the status quo is preserved, but the company looks for transformation and does not change its strategy constantly. The managers and directors are obliged to plan, despite day-to-day pressures, which indicate that the organisation is extremely well planned.

Similarly, *uncertainty avoidance* puts great pressure on local management to balance the need for order and coherence with the need for innovation. In a large and complex organisation such as IBM Argentina order and coherence are needed to hold the organisation together, and because it is dealing in advanced technologies, innovation is needed, too. These two apparently contradicting needs are reconciled by areas—for example, on the one hand in service order provision the terms are agreed with the client and there is no room for innovation, but on the other in software development areas creativity and innovation are pursued. In line with the global policies, IBM Argentina is extremely process oriented, with its processes completely compatible with those of the global corporation, which enables order and coherence at the subsidiary. It also offers employees channels for proposing innovations that are analysed and decided upon by local management—of course, being a large organisation, innovation proposals need to go through several approval stages.

In terms of *power distance*, there is good communication between managers and direct reports, especially in the sales culture. IBM Argentina has many subcultures and other areas such as services are more formal. In sales a more informal and communicative culture is found but it is expected that disagreement or criticism must be constructive and in the spirit of finding a solution. People are expected to make a contribution at the strategy articulation phase, but once a strategy is decided upon and moves to implementation everyone is expected to stand behind it, and do not accept that strategies or decisions be open to discussion for ever. Nonetheless, at IBM there is significant room for reports to discuss strategies and work methodologies with their managers.

With respect to the business strategy problems as depicted in the Rizzuto model in Fig. 2.4, the *entrepreneurial problem* in IBM Argentina is centred around growth in the domestic market where it needs to overcome the vicissitudes of the market and changes in the rules of the game, and competitiveness in the international markets where it competes with other IBM subsidiaries. Having an export market has become crucial to the success of IBM in Argentina. Its solution stack from hardware to enterprise systems and process consulting requires importing hardware and software from other IBM operations where they are produced more efficiently. In times where companies could only import if they had a foreign trade surplus, the fact that IBM Argentina exports services has proven to be a key for success in its domestic market. Two stakeholder groups are vital for IBM Argentina to solve its entrepreneurial problem: clients and suppliers. It needs to cement relationships with these two groups to overcome times of crisis through flexibility in its arrangements with them, in a partnership style.

IBM Argentina was dealing with the *engineering problem* by deploying resources across the country, opening commercial offices and service centres, appointing sales and technical people to them and adapting technologies to the needs of the local markets. This leveraged that IBM Argentina had a strong position with regards to product portfolio, well regarded in the market as well as by their competitors. But what executives thought that differentiated them, and was essential, is what they called *product roam up*. This means a continuous upgrading of products, services and overall solutions.

The *administrative problem* was solved by reinforcing its corporate processes and fitting into the global matrix structure and reinforcing the national matrix. The dominant coalition in IBM Argentina was composed of the marketing and engineering functional areas. Planning was being done at the business unit area and objectives were being pursued by putting in place rigorous controls oriented at achieving results.

The IBM brand was seen as incredibly valuable for success in Argentina, together with the access to technological capabilities that came with being part of the multinational. The fact of being an American multinational was a handicap in many circles within Argentina where foreignness is a liability, but the company was astutely overcoming that hurdle by emphasising the 'Argentina' part of the 'IBM Argentina' name, and highlighting its commitment to the country as demonstrated through its long history and its investment in service centres oriented to exports as much as to the local market. Its embeddedness to Argentina was reinforced by employing local people who know the local culture and can read the subtleties in implicit and tacit communications, to lead the operation. A challenge for local management was that IBM Argentina needs to strictly comply with Argentina and US laws and regulations, which of course at times can constrain its activities.

4.2.3 The Governance Discussion

The importance of two local stakeholder groups, clients and suppliers, to smooth out the effects of the pendular economy through flexibility of their contracts in times of crisis has been acknowledged above. Local management needs to invest significant time in cementing these relationships to activate them when the crisis calls—conveying reliability is key for this but that is one of the strengths of IBM Argentina due to its track record. Leveraging the IBM brand is another factor that the subsidiary uses to achieve this goal—IBM has a highly trustworthy brand in the country.

Corporate leadership at headquarters is another key stakeholder group for the subsidiary. This stakeholder demands a great deal of reporting and is essential in communicating well with them in a context where societal culture in Argentina makes many factors hard to understand at headquarters. The headquarters are also important in that the subsidiary needs to comply with US laws and regulations and it needs support from headquarters to understand the nuances of the law. A third factor for which head office is critical is the functioning of the international matrix organisation through which IBM Argentina con reach out to global resources and export its products and services through other subsidiaries. Finally, the corporate headquarters is a key stakeholder in that it orchestrates the functioning of the global polycentric governance system of which IBM Argentina is a component and a beneficiary.

Despite B2B technology being a completely unregulated sector in Argentina, the government is a key stakeholder due to the informal aspects of the formal institutions and its potential to affect aspects of the market to which its operation is overly sensitive. Examples of this are foreign exchange meddling that can instantly make IBM Argentina lose competitiveness in exports or imports; import controls such as demanding that a company has foreign trade surplus to be able to import products; forbid the transfer of royalties to foreign associates; labour regulations, and many others.

Finally, another key stakeholder group is the company's employees who become ever more important to deliver as IBM Argentina becomes more service oriented. The management team at the subsidiary needs them to stay abreast of the latest technologies with which they are working, ensure that the Centres of Excellence they are assigned to perform, that they go the extra mile on the projects where they are involved and above all, to absorb and live the corporate culture that is essential for IBM Argentina to operate on international projects.

With respect to the three governance relationships, the one that is key in this case study is that of the CEO with management at the subsidiary and through them to the rank and file of the organisation. This is key to ensure that the IBM corporate culture works its way down throughout the organisation. At the time of the research it was clear that this was working well as it is quite evident that the IBM corporate culture is palpable in every corner of the IBM Argentina building.[2] This was not

---

[2] IBM Argentina is located in a highly visible tower in an upmarket business sector in the city centre of Buenos Aires, very close to the coast of the River Plate. It is a peculiar building in that it is suspended on a narrow shaft or stem at least three or four stories high, that then opens out to the full-size office floors. On enquiry of why this particular shape had been selected the response was that the President of IBM Argentina at the time had acquired the plot of land that through city planning required buildings to be of a minimum height equivalent to approximately 16 stories. However, when he submitted the building project for approval in head office the response was that he was only aloud to build a 12-story building. Typical Argentine creativity solved the conundrum!

only in the way people behave, but also in the relentless way in which people abide by the corporate business processes for every activity.[3] The corporate culture also reflects the ethical standards of the corporation, which is remarkable for an organisation operating in a societal culture that scores badly in corruption indices.

IBM Argentina has embarked on the knowledge economy full-heartedly. It has migrated from selling boxes to delivering knowledge-based solutions. Despite the fact that factors such as a sound fiscal and monetary policies, a trusted and efficient legal system and progress on social conditions that greatly contribute to a healthy economy and border conditions for companies to create wealth in the knowledge economy are not given, IBM Argentina manages to thrive. One explanation is that they have become effective at managing intangibles such as intellectual capital. The concept of product and solution 'roam up' as a means of balancing the need for order and coherence with a need for innovation. Another complementary explanation would be the polycentric model through which IBM Argentina can access technologies, solutions, skills and resources from other subsidiaries. These are clear signals of effective structural intellectual capital management. On this front there are also some setbacks that were too early to detect in the original case study, as was IBM's late reaction to cloud computing services and thus losing ground to new service providers such as Amazon. There are also other possible positive effects that again were too early to detect in this case study, as IBM's commitment to cognitive computing. Keeping its people abreast with the latest competencies to operate on international projects is a show of good human intellectual capital management, and the mentioned strong relationship to key stakeholders reflects excellent relational intellectual capital management.

4.3 Sensible Governance: Global Standards in a High Context Approach

4.3.1 Overview

Nobleza Piccardo is the Argentine subsidiary of British American Tobacco (BAT). In 2013, Nobleza Piccardo celebrated the 115th anniversary of

---

[3] The author worked for IBM for a period so experimented this first hand, including in Buenos Aires where he travelled to and worked multiple times.

its foundation. The subsidiary employs approximately 1200 people and it belongs to the tobacco industrial sector where its products are cigarettes of various types and flavours. The company basically sells to the local market. There have been changes in the way Nobleza operated until 2009. As from 2010, Nobleza became part of a business unit that brought together the four markets that make up the Southern Cone business unit, that is Argentina, Chile, Peru and Paraguay. Each country keeps its own individuality and keeps its own market objectives but management and some operational synergies are sought across the Southern Cone business unit, which reports consolidated results to the regional and thence at global level. The four markets report to the Southern Cone business unit which is physically located in Santiago, Chile, where management and support teams for the area are based. Southern Cone Business Units are indicated in Fig. 4.2. The staff is composed of nationals of the four countries that are part of the business unit. Remote work was already being implemented at the time of the original case study which means that, for instance, Argentine executives do not necessarily have to live in Chile and are able to perform their jobs from Argentina, flying to Santiago when required.

Nobleza Piccardo's strategy is in line with its parent company, BAT. The strategy is based on growth that seeks to increase market share with

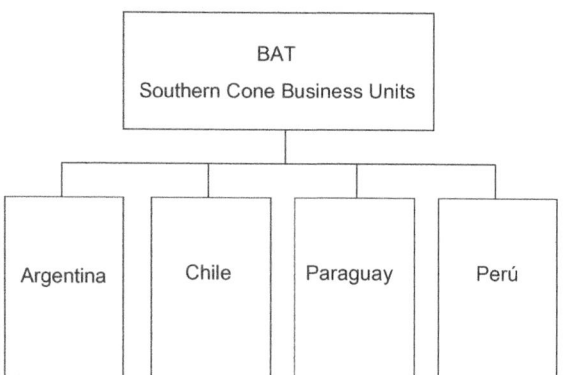

Fig. 4.2 BAT Southern Cone Business Units

a focus on global brands. Their vision states that they wish to achieve leadership in the global industry of snuff.[4]

Nobleza Piccardo's business model is focused on putting together the skills and abilities, experience, drive and passion of its team to meet the goal of transforming the company into the leading tobacco operation in Argentina. Nobleza Piccardo's Key Success Factors are the talent, energy and diversity of the people who are part of its team. This policy is backed by the company's firm belief in the need to recruit the best candidates for diverse positions without considerations for genre, race or religion.

4.3.2 History of Nobleza Piccardo and Its Relationship to BAT

Nobleza Piccardo, BAT's Argentine subsidiary, has its origins in two local companies. Piccardo y Cía. founded in an attic in Buenos Aires in 1898, and Compañía Nacional de Tabacos, which was created in 1913 and was renamed Compañía Nobleza de Tabacos in 1933. As it can be observed, this subsidiary has a long tradition in Argentina. In 1977, these companies merged and gave rise to Nobleza Piccardo, which held a dominant position with a 63 percent market share in Argentina. At the time, Nobleza's principal shareholder was BAT with a 70 percent stake in the merged company, Piccardo held the remaining 30 percent (Nobleza Piccardo website [Online]. Accessed 12 December 2012). BAT currently holds a 98 percent stake in its subsidiary.[5]

BAT is the parent company and defines itself as 'the second largest quoted tobacco group by global market share with brands operating in 180 markets' with a responsible approach to doing business from crop to consumer. In 2011 BAT supplied those markets with 705 billion cigarettes under 200 brands which had been produced at 46 cigarette factories operating in 39 countries (British American Tobacco website [Online]. Accessed 20 January 2013).

The *Born Global* concept is not entirely new as BAT, which started life in 1902, is considered by some authors to have been a company that was born as a global enterprise, as it started life purely as an overseas business operation. At the time, the business was hardly global but, from

---

[4] Rizzuto (2016) citing British American Tobacco 2010 financial statements website. Accessed 22 January 2013.

[5] Rizzuto (2016) citing British American Tobacco 2010 financial statements website. Accessed 22 January 2013.

its beginnings BAT 'was a truly international business' (Wilkins, 2009, p. 19). BAT was founded as a joint venture (JV) between British Imperial Tobacco and the American Tobacco Company whose logic was to end the trademark war between both organisations. This gave rise to a period in which the new company was able to grow exponentially on an international basis. The original purpose was not to compete in their respective home markets, the USA and the UK. Its aim was to develop foreign markets such as Asia, Africa, Latin America and Europe. The strategy along the years and in different territories was based on offering superior quality products and employing quality people to develop them.

In recent years BAT has invested more than 50 million US dollars in Nobleza Piccardo's new plant employing state of the art technology, administrative offices plus a distribution centre that will function separately from the plant. This investment shows a major commitment on the part of the parent company to Argentine operations, especially as the plant is aimed at expanding the company's market share rather than exports. The company has moved from producing locally 85 percent of products sold in Argentina, to producing 99.6 percent locally. This means that the company is focused on the domestic market where it intends to grow its market share and improve its ratios.

At Nobleza Piccardo, those who are committed and are ready to do their job, have equal opportunities for growth. Compensation policies are designed to be competitive and ensure a real differentiation between individual and team performance. Staff earn their salaries on the basis of challenges the business offers, the professional opportunities they experience and the positive team relationships they develop. The company cares about people and their professional development. Nobleza generates training that promotes knowledge and the development of abilities (from Nobleza Piccardo's brochure, Innovation and Commitment chapter). Nobleza Piccardo firmly believes in its right to communicate information about the brands to adults. Conscious of the harm to health, they emphasise the message that 'Smoking causes harm to Health', as they are aware that they are part of a controversial industry. Nobleza Piccardo considers itself a successful organisation, working in a responsible way which in turn, seriously seeks to reduce the risks produced by its products.

After following a multidomestic corporate strategy for decades, in the mid-2000s BAT started a process of globalisation which shows more centralised and global strategies. Local brands have started to decline to give rise to brands with a global footprint. Now the strategy is global while implementation is regional. As mentioned, in 2010 Nobleza Piccardo started a process under which it became part of the Southern Cone business unit, which is now fully integrated and shows a move towards a degree of centralisation within the corporation.

The way they formulated strategies in 2009 displayed a cascade effect with the global strategy, then the regional strategy, where the global strategy is adapted to the characteristics of the region, and finally they have the local market strategy. They align their local strategy with the global and regional strategies. Their local strategy may be somewhat different from the global or regional strategy because they face different circumstances. For example, the regulatory framework in Argentina is different from other countries, so they must act differently under a specific regulatory or financial objective.

4.3.3 The Competitive Landscape

The Corporate Affairs director states that,

> *This is a highly regulated industry worldwide and so it is in Argentina too, where tax pressure is extremely high, for example 70% of the selling price to the consumer represents tax. Some government players, such as the Health Ministry, which is highly influenced by organizations that wish to control tobacco, are under considerable pressure.*

Furthermore, worldwide tobacco regulations are getting notoriously tougher and are being driven by tobacco control groups that influence government health authorities to continuously restrict the activities of tobacco companies. In line with this, Argentina started reviewing its tobacco regulatory framework in 2012.

The market is divided into two major players, Nobleza Piccardo and Philip Morris, with Philip Morris holding 72 percent market share and Nobleza Piccardo 26 percent. In addition, there are small players such as a Jujuy tobacco cooperative that operates regionally in the North West of the country, and another four or five that are based in Greater Buenos Aires, which hold a total of 2–3 percent market share. Apart from that there is a black market that represents 4–5 percent of the market and emerges from a combination of smuggling, counterfeiting and tax evasion.

Phillip Morris' (PM) current market leadership was built on the acquisition in 1965 of a local company that had been founded in 1900. The acquired company was named 'Massalin & Celasco', and PM's leadership was cemented by the acquisition of two further local tobacco companies in 1980.

Interaction takes place through the Tobacco Industry Chamber that brings together both major players to discuss the issues that affect the industry; it is important for them to sit at the same table to discuss regulatory and other industry issues. That is basically what the Chamber is for. Apart from this forum, they monitor the industry, the local market, the Argentine economy and they try to understand how the global and local macroeconomic environment is developing so the company executives can establish to what extent they can achieve the goals that have been set on them.

A total of over 44 million cigarettes per year are sold in Argentina, 42 million of which are done so on a legal basis and approximately 2 million represent the illicit trade. Out of those 42 million, 30 or 31 million are sold by Philip Morris, 10 million by Nobleza Piccardo and the other 2 million by the small players. Illicit trading is a considerable problem which severely affects company profits, as tax evading traders selling smuggled or counterfeit cigarettes can undercut legitimate tax bearing products. This results in a loss of revenue to the company and a loss of tax to the state, but the sale of counterfeit goods additionally damages the company reputation and undermines the credibility of its products. From the evidence collected it appears that prices are increased in unison between both big players in the market. For instance, in mid-January 2013, there was a 4 percent increase in price implemented by both companies of which, as mentioned above, 70 percent goes directly to the state in the form of tax. Is this not a breach in anti-trust legislation?

The World Health Organisation foresees that by 2050 there will be more smokers than today because of a natural growth in the population. Nobleza Piccardo executives assert that demand will not disappear because, despite people being conscious and aware of the damaging effects of their product, 25 or 26 percent of the population in Argentina chooses to smoke. The management team at Nobleza Piccardo does not believe that one brand can be sufficient to satisfy everyone. The portfolio of over 200 brands is aimed at different strategic segments—premium, fresh flavour and adult smokers under 30.

Table 4.2 Brands sold by Nobleza Piccardo in Argentina

Brands	Description
Dunhill	Created in London in 1907. It was introduced in Argentina in 2010 in the super premium segment
Lucky Strike	Launched in 1871, it is one of the oldest international brands in the world. In Argentina it has been competing in the international premium segment since the 1980s
Camel	Camel is an international brand that has been in existence in the world market since 1913 and has been sold in Argentina by Nobleza Piccardo since 1981
Parisiennes	Parisiennes is the leading brand in the dark tobacco segment in Argentina, where it has been established since 1970
Kool	As a leading brand in the segment, Kool uses menthol flavoured tobacco
Viceroy	This is one of the main worldwide brands for British American Tobacco and for Nobleza Piccardo in Argentina. Launched in the United States in 1936 and in Argentina in 2002
Jockey	Jockey is a local brand launched in the 60s which quickly achieved market leadership, becoming number 1 in the 80s and 90s. The Argentine brand with the longest track record in the market
Derby	Since its launch in 1988, Derby has been one of the leading brands on the Argentine market, with the widest reach across the nation
Other brands	Other brands are sold locally such as Gitanes, Gold Leaf, 43/70, Winston and Conway

Source Nobleza Piccardo website. Accessed 14 February 2013

British American Tobacco's four global brands—Dunhill, Kent, Lucky Strike y Pall Mall—cover the premium and low-price segments. While the development of these global brands is fundamental to the corporation's strategy, they have also been raising the profile of Vogue (a brand targeted on women) in the premium segment and Viceroy, one of the main international brands in the low-price segment.[6] Table 4.2 describes the main brands sold by Nobleza Piccardo in Argentina.

[6] British American Tobacco Central America [Online]. Accessed 14 February 2013.

4.3.4 The Business Context

As portrayed in the IBM case, formal institutions in Argentina have a high degree of informality. Over and beyond the mid-term challenges deriving from the pendular behaviour of the political and economic systems, the day-to-day activities are also undermined by uncertainties caused by the governments idiosyncratic form of decision-making on issues that affect business. The excessive concentration of government power in an extremely centralised manner, where no more than four to six individuals call the shots for the whole state, and where government insists on intervening in the microeconomy to cover for the shortcomings in its macroeconomic policies, causes havoc for the management of a multinational subsidiary. The challenges are even greater for BAT than for IBM due to that the tobacco business in Argentina is, like in most countries, highly regulated, exposing the subsidiary to the whims of erratic government regulations. Apart from written regulations being highly detailed and intricate, they are cast over by clouds of unwritten rules.

Under the umbrella of complicated formal institutions described in the prior paragraph, rules of the game are unclear and everchanging. Red tape conditions many aspects of business and only insiders know the rules. Two areas that affect Nobleza Piccardo particularly seriously are that of import controls and outbound international payments, as some critical ingredients are imported; and price controls where implicit and tacit controls overlay explicit ones. Informality prevails, the criteria applied by the authorities are particularistic, and in communications with the authorities the implicit and explicit coexist and are hard to read. It is common for messages from the authorities to be contradictory, with a strong discrepancy between statements and actions. Surviving in this regulatory environment requires employing multiple resources simply to understand reality and Corporate Affairs units need to be highly developed.

In the absence of robust formal institutions, the informal in the form of societal culture take a high-profile role. In terms of *uncertainty avoidance*, Nobleza Piccardo's management team show a great deal of tolerance to uncertainty. Managers are almost permanently in short-run reaction mode solving pressing problems, leading to an uncertainty avoidance company that articulates and develops short-term strategies to cope with its context. It needs to co-ordinate closely with BAT headquarters to thrive in this peculiar environment. In the dilemma between 'orderliness and consistency' versus 'innovation', it generally lies off-centre towards the former. The need for orderliness and for compliance with strict regulations, limits the potential for innovation.

In terms of *power distance* Nobleza Piccardo has open-door policy where it is relatively easy to obtain access to the CEO in Argentina. Communication between management and staff is fluid and it has an egalitarian culture as staff have space to express opinions divergent from those of the manager, and as evidenced by the fact that senior managers and staff all have meals in the same cafeteria where the CEO queues up like everybody else. It is generally accepted that directors are accessible and listen to managers, and managers do the same with their reports. Rather than a work methodology, it is an integral part of Nobleza Piccardo's culture. The subsidiary's CEO discusses complex issues with the management team but in the final instance it is he who makes the decisions.

With respect to *future orientation*, this is a hyperactive planning organisation. Of the twelve managers interviewed, eleven stated that planning is central to the success of Nobleza Piccardo, and only one expressed that there is excessive planning. Their strategic plan is developed for ten years, but with significantly more detail in the first 24 months. The ten-year plan is reviewed annually, but there is also much activity monthly in tracking progress and reviewing forecasts for the first 24 months of the plan.

Continuing with the application of Rizzuto's model, the next factor to analyse is the subsidiary's strategy applying the Miles and Snow model. Observing the three strategic problems of resolution factors, it emerges that with respect to the *entrepreneurial problem* Nobleza Piccardo operates in the mass market B2C for which it produces locally, with increasing proportion of national ingredients to avoid import restrictions. It is focused on the local market where it needs to ramp up market share to be carved out of its main competitor and market leader, Philip Morris. Its response to the challenge of domestic market growth is through understanding the needs of the consumer and improving the image of the firm and its products, applying a methodology they called *Dialogue*. Another aspect of its effort to increase market share is to build on its product excellence and international brands, and leveraging innovations developed abroad by BAT corporation. One of the issues it needs to deal with is the illicit cigarette market that erodes sales and can compromise the brands through forged cigarettes. Relationship with stakeholders such as distributors, retailers and suppliers is another important component of the growth campaign.

Solutions to the *engineering problem* are based on a permanent effort for improving efficiency through streamlined and automated processes applying technological tools such as SAP. BAT has made heavy investments in its production plant in Argentina, distribution centres, commercial centres and in its distribution fleet, all of which show commitment to the market.

Nobleza Piccardo tackles the *administrative problem* through inserting its largely functional organisation in Argentina into the matrix organisations in the region and global. It implements and updates robust processes and applies strict controls in the whole order to delivery cycle. Due to the characteristics of its products and the variability of its business context, the dominant coalition is composed of its finance and legal brains. Finally, it invests heavily in planning functions—this is a planning organisation *par excellence*.

Although in theory being the subsidiary of a British company could cause resistance by the local population, this has not been significant. The fact that the company is deeply embedded in the Argentine market and sustaining significant employment of local people, helps overcome this potential problem. The company has developed a great awareness of changes in regulations and a high degree of sharpness and willingness for constant change which strengthens its position. Due to its Anglo origin it works towards heterogeneity and diversity turning the disadvantage of foreignness into an advantage. On the liabilities side are the difficulties to make foreign payments and to explain to the central management team in head office the local rules of the game, because key parts of them are not written.

As a result of all these factors, Nobleza Piccardo takes a truly clear *defender* type stance as its strategic choice. It is in a controversial and highly regulated industry, where it is second in the market. The Argentine subsidiary focuses exclusively on the local market. It combines a relentless adherence to planning with short-term flexibility to cope with an unpredictable institutional context. It also strongly adheres to global corporate standards and processes in search for efficiency.

4.3.5 The Governance Discussion

Nobleza Piccardo is extremely aware of the need for effective stakeholder management in its market. The key stakeholders are the government, the consumers and its clients, its distributors, its suppliers, anti-smoking activists and the senior management team at BAT head office. Curiously, its main competitor is also a key stakeholder with whom it needs to work together on regulatory issues and even pricing policies. Nobleza Piccardo applies a framework it calls *dialogue* to strengthen the links with its stakeholders.

In relation to the previous point, it is quite astonishing that pricing co-ordination in a de facto duopoly was spoken about quite freely—in any other consumer market business this would have caused serious legal actions against the companies. What is different in the case of tobacco compared to other industries? Maybe it is that in the tobacco industry where the taxpayer is a 70 percent majority stakeholder on sales price through duties, and where it is assumed that high prices deter consumption, price-co-ordination is accepted.

In terms of the three governance relationships, the one between the CEO and the rank and file, passing through local management at the subsidiary, has proven to be critical. It has led to a corporate culture of flexibility to adapt to abrupt local changes, combined with a powerful adherence to corporate standards. The latter has been key for the company in Argentina to preserve and increase structural intellectual capital embedded in its corporate business processes and in the BAT corporate innovations it introduces in the market.

On the remaining two dimensions of intellectual capital it also has a remarkable performance. Through its matrix regional and global organisation it offers its local subsidiary people opportunities for developing an international career and increasing its human capital. On the relational capital dimension it has incorporated its Corporate Affairs officers into the dominant coalition, together with legal and finance, thus reaching remarkable levels of relationships with its stakeholders.

Apart from a corporate culture in the subsidiary that relates very closely to the global corporate culture with, of course, ingredients of its local societal culture, not only has enhanced the intangible assets such as intellectual capital that are key to thriving in the knowledge economy, but also all the evidence seems to point to the fact that it has also developed a strong ethical corporate culture. It is notable that despite difficulties for the corporate headquarters in understanding all the intricacies of host country regulations, the corporation has opted for a high context approach to the market, where the company is solidly embedded. Over a century in the market plus extremely large investments in recent times, shows the commitment of the corporation to this market.

4.4 LOCAL MANAGEMENT MISALIGNMENT: A GOVERNANCE CHALLENGE

4.4.1 Background

Banco Santander is the leading bank in Chile in terms of market share, and it is considered one of the crown jewels in Banco Santander's portfolio of foreign subsidiaries. Its headquarters operates in a Latin cluster culture that, counterintuitively, is identified as more distant from the Latin America cluster than the Anglo one (GLOBE project, House et al., 2004). On the high context vs low context spectrum, Santander is off-centre towards the low context end. It emerges from the case study that despite the centre adopting an operational excellence value proposition, in the mind of local management in Chile the value proposition is confused and leaning more towards customer intimacy. This is not the result of strategy adaptation, but really a case of corporate governance ineffectiveness leading to strategy misalignment.

This Banco Santander Chile case was developed in the context of a study performed in 2004–2005 to identify criteria that would enable banks to maximise benefits from their ICT investments. In that project it was detected that there was a clear strategic misalignment between the corporate strategy defined at the centre, and the strategy being implemented in the subsidiary. That strategic misalignment was identified but out of the scope of the original study—so it is picked up now. This case is worked with the bank in its context at the time of that original study, and no effort is made to update the figures. It is not necessary because the purpose for using this case study is to extract governance lessons and not assess the state of the bank at the time of writing.

The strategy framework applied to study the strategic positioning of the bank is Treacy & Wiersema's *Value Discipline of Market Leaders* according to which value from the point of view of a client has seven dimensions:

- Price
- Quality of product/service
- Attributes of product/service
- Convenience of service
- Reliability of service
- Post-sales support
- Expert advice.

A corporation has different ways of satisfying the client's value expectation which the framework synthesises into three value disciplines: *Operational Excellence, Product Leadership* and *Customer Intimacy*. Each of these has a value proposition associated to it: *best total cost, best product* and *best total solution*, respectively. Each of these value disciplines gives a different priority to the seven dimensions of customer value and requires different core business processes to deliver the value proposition to customers. It also impacts the whole organisational design: types of organisational units, form of deployment of human capital, stance with respect to risk and failure, rigidity of business processes, dimensions for profitability analysis, priorities in terms of information systems, reporting and others.

The key lesson of the Value Discipline framework is that market leaders opt for one of the three value disciplines and are consistent in all its organisational design implications. What makes an organisation excellent in one value discipline makes it not-so-well performing in the other disciplines, simply due to organisational constraints. With this conceptual background in place, the next sections analyse Banco Santander Chile's value disciplines and observe the misalignments referred to above.

4.4.2 Overview of Banco Santander in Chile

Grupo Santander from Spain opened its first office in Chile in 1978, as a second floor bank. Four years later it acquired all assets and liabilities of a Chilean retail bank called Banco Español, and operated under that brandname until 1989, when it changed name to Banco Santander Chile. In 1993, Banco Santander Chile acquired Fincar and thus entered the mid to lower income personal financial services market. An important milestone was achieved the following year, when Banco Santander Chile listed on the New York Stock Exchange. A year after that, Banco Santander Chile acquired another financial services provider, called Financiera Fusa, and merged it with Fincar to give birth to its Banefe Division. In 1996 Banco Santander Chile merged with Banco Osorno (Banco Santander Chile, 2004, p. 16).

In 1999, Grupo Santander in Spain merged with Banco Central Hispano to form Grupo Santander Central Hispano. In Chile, this meant that Banco Santander Chile became a shareholder of Banco Santiago which had, in turn, merged with Banco O'Higgins two years earlier. This situation triggered a process by which Banco Santander Chile increased its stakes in Banco Santiago until it took full control by April 2002. Four months later the merger of both banks was approved by the banking authorities and shareholders, and by April 2003 full operational integration was achieved and the bank was re-launched as Banco Santander Santiago (Banco Santander Chile, 2004, p. 17).

To complement this history of mergers and acquisitions, during the 1994–1995 period Banco O'Higgins merged with the local operations of Banco Central Hispano from Spain and HSBC, therefore incorporating foreign shareholders. It also listed its debt in the US Stock Exchange (ADR). All these external demands added considerable rigour to its investment decision making, in particular ICT investments. In 1997 Banco O'Higgins merged with Banco Santiago. This was particularly complicated because the two banks had very different ICT platforms. Banco O'Higgins systems were enterprise wide, mainframe-based, while Banco Santiago's were much less structured, client–server based (they had over 48 servers). The bank decided to adopt the Banco de Santiago systems, but merging those two operations from a technology point of view was a failure. This led the merged bank to go out to look for a third-party core-banking system package and decided on Altamira (and back to IBM mainframe computers). As mentioned above, Banco Santiago was eventually controlled by Banco Santander Chile and their operations were merged in 2002. This last merger was a lot less traumatic than the previously mentioned one.

4.4.3 Banco Santander Santiago and Its Competitive Context

The Chilean banking system comprised, in December 2002, twenty eight institutions as a result of having followed the global trend of rapid consolidation. Taking an exchange rate of Chilean pesos 695.28 to the US dollar, at end of 2002, the total assets in the system amounted to some US$67 billion (SBIF, 2003, p. 35, 'Activo Circulante' plus 'Activo Fijo'), of which Banco Santander Santiago represented just under 23.9 percent (SBIF, 2003, p. 46). Having over US$5 billion and less than US$100 billion in assets, it is classified as a mid-sized bank on international standards, according to criteria adopted by the Tower Group. In terms of loans, the total Chilean banking system amounted, at the time, to US$45.6 billion (SBIF, 2003), of which US$11.1 billion (SBIF, 2003, p. 65) are managed by Banco Santander Santiago, which represents 24.4 percent of the market. The total amount of deposits in the

Chilean banking system in December 2002 were, approximately, US$41.1 billion (SBIF, 2003) of which US$9.4 billion were with Banco Santander Santiago (SBIF, 2003, p. 47), which represents a 22.8 percent market share. From these figures it emerges that Banco Santander's loan-to-deposits ratio was 1.18 which is worse than the industry average of 1.11 but quite healthy considering that in Chile there are strong tax incentives for people to save their surplus in thier pension fund rather than in bank accounts.

On the revenue diversification front, the Chilean banking system followed the global trend of increasing fee-based income as a proportion of total income. In the twelve year period from 1990 to 2002 fee-based income, for the banking system as a whole, grew from 6 to 18.8 percent of total income (SBIF, 2001, 2003). In December 2002, Banco Santander Santiago was just over the average of the system as its fee-based income represents just over 20 percent of underlying income. In its Annual Report in December 2003 (Banco Santander Chile, 2004, p. 35), Banco Santander Santiago compares fee-based income with Operational Expenses, and presents a ratio of 44.7 percent. On this measure, Banco Santander Santiago ranks first in the Chilean banking system.

Doing a strategic group analysis of the Chilean banking system it becomes clear that Banco Santander Santiago operates in the same strategic group as its rival BBVA. The general conclusion of that analysis is that a banks performance is related to how well it competes with the banks in its own strategic group and it is clear that Banco Santander Santiago has been more successful in both profitability and market share than BBVA Chile.

Banco Santander Santiago is one of the most efficient banks in Chile. As mentioned, its cost-to-income ratio (CIR) in 2003 worked out to be 43.6 percent, which was 6 percentage points below the system average and outstanding even at international standards. This is remarkable for an operation in a small country like Chile (Banco Santander Chile, 2004, pp. 29 and 35). Significant progress on this front was made in 2003 with respect to 2002, partly owed to a sharp drop in Operational Expenses due to efficiencies achieved as a result of the Santander–Santiago merger (Banco Santander Chile, p. 35). It would be interesting to do some in-depth research to understand the sources of such efficiencies, which probably derive from Banco Santander's ability to develop synergies across borders and build economies of scale.

Banco Santander Santiago reports a BIS capital adequacy ratio of 14.27 percent in December 2002, and 14.61 percent in December 2003 (Banco Santander Chile, 2004), which are not only significantly higher than the minimum requirement of 8 percent, but also higher than the Chilean banking system average of 13.9 percent in 2002 (SBIF, 2003, p. 10) and 14.06 percent in December 2003 (SBIF, 2004, p. 10).

As opposed to most of the other Chilean banks Banco Santander Santiago's strategy cannot be analysed without taking into account that it is part of a Latin American operation of a 'Euro-Iberoamerican Group', as it defines itself. According to Mr. Francisco Luzon, then Managing Director for the Latin America Division, 'We are the leading financial services organisation in Ibero-America, with a strong presence in the markets with the greatest potential (i.e., Brazil and Mexico), and in the most mature ones (i.e., Chile and Puerto Rico)' (Banco Santander Chile, 2004, p. 13).

The study concluded that it was evident that the operational merger of Banco Santander and Banco Santiago had an impact on the banks performance during the prior year. On the positive side, the merger had enabled a strong reduction in operational costs (over 15 percent year on year), which measured in terms of the CIR that went from 47.2 percent in December 2002, to 43.6 percent a year later (Banco Santander Chile, 2004, p. 35). On the negative side, in line with international experience, the merger has had an impact on quality of service as emerged from customer satisfaction surveys and client attrition rates. At the time of the study the bank showed impressive figures in terms of profit and profit growth, with a ROE that reached 24.2 percent.

4.4.4 Value Discipline of the Organisation

As observed above Banco Santander Santiago could not be analysed without taking into account that it is part of the Latin American operation of Banco Santander of Spain, due to that the Corporation has a strong culture and management style. Both the Group and the Chilean operation had set themselves ambitious goals for excellence: Banco Santander had proposed itself to become one of the ten top players in the World in its field; and Banco Santander Santiago aspired to become the best banking group in Latin America by 2006. As the original case study showed, achieving those objectives required making converge seemingly divergent initiatives, and ensuring that their ICT spend converted into shareholder value.

There was a difference in perception between the client-facing managers on the one hand, and the planning, staff and back-office managers on the other, as to which were the key dimensions of customer value. Banco Santander Santiago appeared to be in a transition from a value proposition of *best total cost,* to one of *best total solution.* This meant migrating from an *operational excellence* to a *customer intimacy* value discipline which, as described above, would have a major impact on organisation design, core processes, culture, measurement and reward system and information technology. The alarming issues were that senior management did not seem aware of the implications and that there were no signs of this being co-ordinated with the corporate head office that was clearly in an *operational excellence* value discipline.

On top of that, there appeared to be an idea to implement different value propositions for each market segment. For this to work, it would require implementing different value disciplines for each market segment and there the bank's leadership had not thought out how it would make these different cultures operate under one roof.

From the interviews to senior managers there was a dispersion in opinions on which were the critical dimensions of value from the clients' perspective and on which were the core processes in order to deliver the value proposition—this is consistent with having a transition in value discipline. It was also obvious in process design across the bank, controls weighed more than Client requirements, which is typical of an operational excellence organisation. Similarly, the bank had a utility view of technology, and its IT people were not seen as proactive service providers, which is an adequate vision for *operational excellence* but not so for *customer intimacy*. In *customer intimacy* the customer-facing processes and systems need to be agile and responsive to customer needs.

Although the integration of Banco Santander Chile and Banco Santiago was formally concluded, deep cultural differences still persisted between the legacy people of one or other institution. If the bank intended to retain talents, it would have to find a way of overcoming this. Training could have been a good way of doing so.

Business planning sessions were held every year, which enabled to 'land' the corporate global business plan onto a Chilean three-year plan, but this had not been accompanied by the required resource planning of people and technology. Moreover, it can be said that most ICT investments decisions were *management driven (strategic planning),* even though this responded to an ICT plan of Head Office, not of Banco

Santander Santiago. Some initiatives came from the market-facing business units, but they were not very significant and often fitted into corporate frameworks which made them drawn out and slow. Considering that (a) most ICT applications were aimed at reducing payroll costs which amounted to 60 percent of operational costs; and (b) in Head-Office's vision, IT's role was to push for more proven and efficient technology that is sustainable in time using world class solutions deployed globally, a misalignment of strategy and technology was taking place. This misalignment resulted from ICT investments being predominantly aimed at improving *operational excellence* when Banco Santander Santiago's three-year strategic plan was aiming at *customer intimacy*.

Interestingly, the bank was changing its front line staff (Client managers) who were good analysts and financiers but not necessarily good with people, and substituting them by people who were strong on people skills, such as teachers and social workers. These new front line people would operate by business rules contained in applications and workflows that were designed and defined by a small group of centralised experts. This was an innovative approach. The challenge here was, however, that concentrating knowledge in the centre is typical of an *operational excellence* model, not a *customer intimacy* discipline which is where the bank wanted to go (Treacy & Wiersema, 1995). In this value discipline, Clients expect to talk to people who really know their business. So, implementing this initiative would have required a strong effort on technology and on training (but training beyond requirements to use the technology—it means training on the business of the bank and of its Clients) which had not been planned (Watkins, 1998).

Banco Santander Santiago was remarkably good at focusing its operations on where it could win in the market. Unfortunately, however, quite often head office pushed it to be good at everything, and that is not possible. Related to this is that, in the view of local management, ICT projects had to be short and nimble. A project that required more than a year and a half should be rethought in order to reduce its scope, or it should be dropped. One of the problems at Santander-Santiago was that very big projects, that depart from this short and nimble concept, were imposed on them by Head Office.

4.4.5 The Governance Discussion

Local management in Chile gave a compelling reason for shifting from the global value discipline of *operation excellence* to one of *customer intimacy,* which was that in a small market like Chile's it was hard to grow for a market leader with nearly a quarter of the market share. A *customer intimacy* value discipline would enable it to grow on its current client base, that is growing without increasing its risk profile. This needs to be looked at from different lenses of governance.

There are two stakeholder groups involved in this situation, that of senior management at the global headquarters, and the management team at the subsidiary. The global team attempts to impose on the subsidiary a strategy based on operational excellence that optimises the attainment of global objectives. It does so by prescribing a model to follow and setting tough goals of growth in profitability for local management to achieve.

Under pressure from the centre to achieve demanding goals and in the absence of a strong corporate culture due to that growth in the subsidiary has been through a succession of relatively recent acquisitions, the subsidiary's management team is not on the same wave-length as the global operating model and seeks to optimise the functioning of the subsidiary by adopting a different operating model than that of the corporation. It is clear that neither the management at the centre nor the management team in the subsidiary seem to understand the organisational implications of changing the value discipline of the organisation.

This leads to analysing the governance relationship that should close the gap between these two diverting visions, which is the relationship between the CEO and the rank and file of the organisation. Some effort has been made as there are annual planning meetings to align plans between the centre and the subsidiary, but clearly it is not being successful. One of the factors that may be getting in the way of good understanding is that the societal cultures of the headquarters and of the subsidiary are at the antipodes of the GLOBE cultural clusters. Thus, the stances on risk, on power distance and on future orientation are radically different. It is quite probable that there are deep communications barriers between the two stakeholder groups.

Analysing the phenomenon through the lens of the Rizzuto strategy adaptation model, Chile and especially its banking sector operate under mature formal institutions, which should help overcome the mentioned distance in societal cultures between the two parts. Observing the business strategy problems of the model, it appears that the centre is emphasising the administrative and engineering problems while the subsidiary is focusing more on the entrepreneurial one. In Chile foreignness is often an advantage, especially if the foreign player comes from an Anglo-Saxon background. However, Spanish companies were very active in the public services sector privatisation of the 1990s and the public in general believes that level of service has fallen in all those companies taken over by Spanish investors—so that scepticism has spilled over to non-public service Spanish companies and Santander's high client attrition rate appears to be a consequence of this. This is probably compounded by the fact that at attempting to impose the global value discipline Santander is applying a low context approach that naturally causes resistance. All this has influenced the subsidiary's strategic choice towards the 'Analyser' stance, searching for efficiency in some segments and a more innovative approach in others.

A final word worth mentioning is that local management at Santander Chile needs to learn from the Wells Fargo case in Sect. 3.3. The value discipline shift from operational excellence to customer intimacy reminisces the cross-selling strategy and everything that went wrong at Wells Fargo. For this shift to be successful it must be sustained on a corporate culture platform where client-facing staff are centred on the best interest of their clients and the stance of cross-buying rather than cross-selling. Local management must ask itself if that culture and the appropriate incentives are in place before embarking on this new approach.

4.5 Cross-Case Analysis

These three cases give exposure to quite polar situations in terms of MNE strategy adaptation to host country conditions. There are clear differences in headquarters vs host country in terms of societal culture, where IBM and BAT highlight the issues in Anglo—Latin America relationships, and the Santander case highlights issues in Latin Europe—Latin America relationships. On the formal institutional dimension, the BAT and Santander cases illustrate the challenges of operating in highly regulated industries as opposed to the completely unregulated one of B2B technology as depicted by IBM. In terms of values discipline, the three corporations adopt operational excellence that are well adopted in the IBM and BAT subsidiaries, but not so by Santander Chile—lessons on culture can be extracted from this. In the two Argentine cases stakeholder management is critical for success while for the Santander case this is not so relevant. Finally, management of intangible assets is a key to success in the knowledge economy and some interesting comparisons on governance of IC in these three cases will be performed.

Although it is counterintuitive, the GLOBE project determined that societal culture in Anglo clusters is closer to the Latin America societal culture than the Latin Europe one is. Despite existing significant differences in *uncertainty avoidance, power distance* and *future orientation* the two Anglo cluster companies have managed to convey to their subsidiaries, operating in a highly volatile market as is Argentina, to adopt a corporate culture that is significantly different to that of the host country. This corporate culture manifests itself in the case of the two Argentine subsidiaries in the form of relentless planning and fluid dialogue between the different echelons of the organisation, as well as clear attention to stakeholder management. In the case of Santander this obsession with planning did not come through as such a key issue but that might be explained by that Chile is a more stable business environment than Argentina. On the power distance side, an open-door policy and closeness between the rank and file and the management echelons, or between managers and the local Board members, was not perceived. Power distance seems to be significantly greater at Santander Chile than at the two Anglo subsidiaries in Argentina.

The cases revealed the institutional disparities between Argentina and Chile. In Argentina the curiosity of formal institutions overlaid by a misty cloud of unwritten and particularistic norms in itself generates a challenging environment. This leads both Argentine subsidiaries to expend considerable resources and effort to simply understand the changing rules of the games they are playing. This is even more challenging for BAT than for IBM as it operates in a regulated business and needs to integrate Corporate Relations into the dominant coalition. In Chile Santander experienced a highly stable environment at the time of the research, with banking regulations setting clear rules of the game.

The value discipline framework was central to the original research on Santander Chile, but not so when the IBM and BAT Argentina cases were originally researched. However, going back to the data the value discipline of these two organisations emerge clearly as being operational excellence in both cases. The deep process orientation, the prioritisation of cohesion and order over innovation, the continuous search for efficiency, the standardised integration into global operations, the global transactional systems, their obsession with planning, the non-elitist cultures, the globalised products, the focus on profitability per transaction, are all indications of a strong adherence to the operational excellence model in both the headquarters or global organisations and their subsidiaries in Argentina. In contrast with this, at Santander the head office or global organisation is clearly in the operational excellence camp but it has not succeeded in conveying this to the subsidiary. The subsidiary is evidently looking towards client intimacy and the impression that emerged is that it is pursuing this covertly with respect to the head office. It is a strategy being implemented at the subsidiary without explicit approval from the centre, and without considering the organisational impact that this will have. The outcome observed when doing the data collection for the research is one of a hybrid value discipline at Santander's subsidiary in Chile; a symptom of this is the high degree of client churn or turnover.

Stakeholder management varies significantly across the three case studies. On the one hand, at the two subsidiaries in Argentina the local leadership teams give great importance to their stakeholder management of the headquarters. Challenged by the difficulties of explaining to Anglo cluster head offices the nuances of unwritten rules in their market, superlative effort was put into this communication. On the other hand, it was also found that stakeholder management of the head office at Santander Chile was far less visible. In fact, in all the interviews of senior management, the headquarters seldom came up and when it did it was more as a hindrance and source of barriers than as a positive resource. However, there was a larger coincidence between the three in the need and approach to management of Government as a key stakeholder—in Argentina because of the informality mentioned above, and in Chile because of the banking regulator's attempt to balance stability of the banking system with financial inclusion which spills over in pressure on Santander and the other banks. The extreme effort in stakeholder management with clients and suppliers perceived in the IBM case was not observed so important at BAT or Santander.

Of the three classic governance relationships, the one between senior management through subsidiary management to rank and file of the organisation is the one that offers insights in these cases. As a result of these relationships both IBM and BAT have developed strongly ethical corporate cultures in the subsidiaries, in defiance of the sometimes-low standards in this respect of the Argentine societal culture. It is fair to say that at Santander Chile there is also an ethical corporate culture, but building one is not as challenging considering that societal culture in Chile has higher standards according to objective corruption ratings. In imposing corporate values such as adoption of a corporate value discipline, clearly BAT and IBM have been more successful than Santander. A difference in how the three subsidiaries have arrived at where they are, is that the two subsidiaries in Argentina have grown internally over close to a century, while Santander has done so through a long succession of mergers and acquisitions in Chile, which makes constructing a local corporate culture similar to that at the corporate centre more challenging.

Finally, the three cases exhibit effective intellectual capital management capabilities which enables three successful subsidiary operations, but they seem to do so in slightly different ways. The three of them are extraordinarily successful in structural IC preservation and enhancement. IBM achieves this through developing strong integration of the subsidiary with global business processes; BAT does so by focusing on global brands, by investing in new production lines and distribution centres, and by spilling research and development findings at the centre over to the subsidiary; while Santander does so by setting up regional shared services, particularly in the information technology domain. IBM also appears to be effective in relational IC development through working closely with clients and suppliers, and Santander invests heavily in developing human IC through resources expended on staff training.

This cross-case analysis is summarised in Table 4.3.

The following chapter continues in the domain of international business but moves from strategy adaptation to the even more sensitive issue of coping with the risk of corruption in host markets.

Table 4.3 Summary of cross-case analysis

Factor/case	IBM Argentina	BAT Argentina	Santander Chile
Subsidiary's corporate culture	• Different to societal culture of host country • Relentless planning • Fluid dialogue between hierarchical levels • Low power distance	• Different to societal culture of host country • Relentless planning • Fluid dialogue between hierarchical levels • Low power distance	• Closer to host country societal culture • Planning, but not an issue • Less fluid dialogue between levels • Higher power distance
Institutional forces	• Formal institutions overcast by cloud of unwritten and particularistic rules: Challenging business context	• Formal institutions overcast by cloud of unwritten and particularistic rules: Challenging business context • More challenging than at IBM due to regulated sector • Highly developed Corporate Relations as part of dominant coalition	• Formal institutions with clear rules of the game
Value Discipline	• Operational excellence at corporate centre • Operational excellence well developed at subsidiary	• Operational excellence at corporate centre • Operational excellence well developed at subsidiary	• Operational excellence at corporate centre • Shift at the subsidiary, to customer intimacy
Stakeholder management	• Headquarters is key stakeholder • Government is a key stakeholder because of informality • Clients and suppliers for coping with pendular behaviour of economy	• Headquarters is key stakeholder • Government is a key stakeholder because of informality	• HQ does not seem so relevant with not-so-good communications (e.g. value discipline shift) • Government (in the form of banking regulation) is a key stakeholder because pressure of systemic stability vs financial inclusion

(continued)

Table 4.3 (continued)

Factor/case	IBM Argentina	BAT Argentina	Santander Chile
Key governance relationships	• Senior management through local management to rank and file • Resultant strongly ethical culture • Resulted in strong adoption of value discipline • Growth internally	• Senior management through local management to rank and file • Resultant strongly ethical culture • Resulted in strong adoption of value discipline • Growth internally	• Senior management through local management to rank and file • Resultant strongly ethical culture • Failing to adopt corporate value discipline • Growth through mergers and acquisitions
IC Management at subsidiary	• Effective IC management • Highly successful on structural IC via strong integration of subsidiary with global operation • Highly effective in relational IC via customers and suppliers	• Effective IC management • Highly successful on structural IC via global brands, investing in new production lines and distribution centres and capitalising on global R&D	• Effective IC management • Highly successful on structural IC via regional shared services such as ICT • Highly successful in human IC through training (Santander university)

References

Banco Santander Chile. (2004). *Informe annual 2003 [Annual report year 2003]*. Spanish Version.
British American Tobacco website [Online]. Available from: http://www.bat.com. Accessed 20 January 2013.
Faulkner, D. (2003). International strategy. In D. Faulkner & A. Campbell (Eds.), *The Oxford handbook of strategy* (pp. 651–674). Oxford University Press.
House, R., Hanges, P. J., Javidan, M., Dorman, P. J., & Gupta, V. (2004). *Culture, leadership, and organisations: The GLOBE study of 62 societies*. Sage (Dora Rizzuto) On line viewing: https://books.google.co.uk/books?hl=en&lr=&id=4MByAwAAQBAJ&oi=fnd&pg=PP1&dq=robert+house+globe+study&ots=7heDFw747y&sig=eUWbenmX4E_d1Wey60q51PfSkI8&redir_esc=y#v=onepage&q=robert%20house%20globe%20study&f=false.
Nobleza Piccardo brochure, paperback edition provided by the company in 2009.
Rizzuto, D. I. (2016). *The MNE subsidiary challenge: Adapting global strategy to the local cultural context—Two case studies in Argentina*. Thesis submitted

in partial fulfilment of the requirement for the degree of Doctoral Business Administration, Henley Business School, University of Reading.
SBIF. (2001). *Informacion Financiera Dicembre de 2000.* Superintendencia de Bancos e Instituciones Financieras.
SBIF. (2003). *Informacion Financiera Dicembre de 2002.* Superintendencia de Bancos e Instituciones Financieras.
SBIF. (2004). *Informacion Financiera Dicembre de 2003.* Superintendencia de Bancos e Instituciones Financieras.
Treacy, M., & Wiersema, F. (1995). *The discipline of market leaders, reading.* MA, USA: Addison-Wesley
Watkins, J. (1998). *Information technology, organisation and people.* Routledge Publishers.
Wilkins, M. (2009). The history of the multinational enterprise. In A. Rugman (Ed.), *The Oxford handbook of international business* (2nd ed., pp. 3–38), first published 2009. Oxford University Press.

CHAPTER 5

Challenges to Local Governance in International Business: The Risks of Corruption

5.1 Overview

This section will introduce the reader to the challenges of corruption that any corporation is subject to but especially those that operate internationally, where distance from the Centre and differing societal cultures add to the problem. The issue is aggravated by the increasing pressure to perform by staff in operational and client-facing roles.

Philp (2006) expresses that there is significant consensus in the literature on corruption as requiring three actors: Actor A that accepts a payment or a material benefit from an actor C at the cost of an entity B. C would normally not access this benefit without the intervention of A. A is usually the holder of a public office and B is the intended beneficiary of that public office such as society in general.

Within this framework there are many variations of corrupt activity. This chapter focuses on two forms of corruption, namely bribe and money laundering. While bribe is straightforward and defined as dishonestly persuading someone (in a position of power) to act in one's favour by a gift of money or other inducement, money laundering is more complex. It is the process followed by criminals with which they disguise the original ownership and control of the proceeds from illegal operations by making them appear to have derived from legitimate operations. Some of the most common techniques are smurfing, currency exchange and wire transfers.

© The Author(s), under exclusive license to Springer Nature Switzerland AG 2021
P. D. R. Griffiths, *Corporate Governance in the Knowledge Economy*, Palgrave Studies in Accounting and Finance Practice, https://doi.org/10.1007/978-3-030-78873-5_5

The four situations presented in Sect. 5.2 illustrate different forms of the phenomenon of bribing, while Sects. 5.3 and 5.4 present two variations of the phenomenon of money laundering.

5.2 Extortion: To Bribe, or Not Bribe?

5.2.1 Introduction

Imagine that you lead the local operation of a large international consulting firm in an emerging country, and you are confronted with one of the following situations:

a. After an intense pre-qualification process, your firm and its main competitor in the market are the only two shortlisted for a large management transformation project in a Government division. It is Saturday afternoon and your team of 6 experienced professionals has been preparing the proposal for over five weeks. They are now in the office working flat out with only four days to go. Unexpectedly, the telephone rings and you take the call. On the other end of the line is a voice familiar to you from the evening TV news shows. The Government minister comes through loud and clear that you should not submit this proposal: if you do, you can count yourself out of any future government work while this Administration remains in office. A key ingredient is that in this market, over 95 percent of your revenue comes from state-owned companies and there are no large private sector companies to whom offer your services.

b. You have been pursuing a major technology-enabled business transformation project at the local subsidiary of a multinational industrial company. This project is vitally important to you because of its size and visibility. There may be one more contestant still in the game, but you know that the whole process has gone impeccably well for your team and you sense that you are the clear forerunner. The Client's detailed queries indicate that the engagement may not quite be in the bag yet, but it is there for you to win or lose. As you are thinking about this your client manager for the prospect comes to you and says that his counterpart at the Client has told him that the contract is yours but you need to pay a $50,000 fee. An established 'Market Development' company will extend your firm a legal invoice for that amount, which is small, compared to the size of the contract. Now, your firm has no explicit policy on how to deal with this kind of situation. In fact, this issue has never been discussed or even mentioned in the management team meetings you have attended in head office. Yours is a young firm in a dynamic business sector: management meetings are focused on how to manage growth, not on how to handle the kind of unethical situation you are confronted with. You are 10,000 milesaway from the Centre and do not know who you could consult over the phone on such a sensitive issue.

c. A major banking system opportunity has opened in one of the largest state-owned banks. You assessed the requirements of the system, the risk profile of the project and the positioning of your competitors, and eventually decided your firm would not lead: your best option is to link up with one of the other contenders, and you are happy to take the back seat in the joint venture (JV). You would still have a sizeable amount of work if the JV gets awarded the project, so you invest heavily in putting high caliber people onto the proposal team, leaving your project manager in charge of day-to-day running of the proposal and relationships with your JV partner. You have no contact with the final Client as that is done by your counterpart in the leading party of the JV. After struggling to meet the deadline—just—you hear that the JV has been well qualified on the technical proposal and, after the commercial bid is opened, that you are placed to win. Two or three days later you are invited to lunch by the manager of your JV partner, and during the meal it emerges that the Client is ready to assign the project to your consortium, but a 3 percent fee needs to be paid. Your JV partner enquires whether you are prepared to support this with your share of the fees. As usual in these large and risky projects, you have built some float into the price, so the solicited amount could be absorbed as cost. While you listen, you reflect that your Financial Services practice is well behind its sales target for the year, and that this project would fill much of the gap. Your position is relatively safe as it is your counterpart that is taking the high risk of exposure if this should go wrong. But as opposed to the two previous cases, you now work for a traditional, well established consulting firm, where the issue is regularly discussed and thus are no doubts: any Partner, without exception, caught in dishonest or fraudulent conduct of this nature would be immediately ejected from the firm and possibly prosecuted.

d. You now work for a six-year-old management consulting firm that has been remarkably successful in expanding internationally. It now has a presence in the UK where it was founded, in Continental Europe, in Latin America, in Australia from where it is expanding around Asia–Pacific, and in South Africa. You are one of 20 partners and lead the Latin American operation. You and your partners meet twice a year to keep track of the progress of the firm and plan its development in the future. In the back of your and all your partners' minds is that you will make this business grow and in a horizon of a few years sell it to materialise the benefits of many years of experience and hard work. Based on your past international experience and learning from the implosion of Arthur Andersen after the Enron accounting scandal, that unethical activities in a single remote office can lead to the downfall of a global professional services firm, you persuaded your partners of the need to set up a code of ethics and you led the process of designing and implementing it. You also obtained approval and led the launching of a corporate responsibility services practice, where environmental sustainability would play an important part. You recruited a team of local specialists for this practice, but was finding it hard to obtain clients—business and government leaders were open and sometimes even eager to discuss issues of sustainability, but slightly more reluctant when it implied paying fees for it. But finally, you persuaded a local government to engage and carry forward an impactful project in the waste management area, creating a grand plan for a recycling centre and programme that would have great visibility in the county and beyond. Your contacts were the mayor and the planning director (a political appointment) that belonged to competing political parties but had a good working relationship. You helped them create the business plan to obtain funding for the project from a central government development agency and this initiative was successful. By that time you and your team had spent many unpaid hours, but there was an unwritten understanding that if the bid for central funds was successful, the local council would have to put the project out for tender, but you would be in a strong position to get selected. Many more hours of invested time elapsed but finally the tender process took place. You submitted a highly elaborate technical proposal and priced it competitively to ensure there would be no mishaps. The bids were opened in a public event and all seemed to be going as expected. The day after the bids were opened, your local expert who was responsible for developing the initiative comes to your office and says that we have been asked to make financial contributions in equal amounts for the parties of your two counterparts, for the election coming up a few months later where the mayor was standing for re-election and the planning director would be a candidate to the national parliament. It was a considerable amount that needed to come out of the project fees that were already stretched—but it was doable. You are in desperate need for a first paid project as proof of concept that there is market demand for a sustainability consulting practice.

These four situations clearly illustrate one of the toughest challenges that leaders confront in today's business environment: the pressure to perform, but to do so with integrity. So, the first aspect of this problem is, how does a business leader press her people to meet ever more demanding targets without cutting corners?

Having worked in multiple international firms in emerging markets for over twenty years, the four situations described above are not imaginary; they are a sample of real situations with which I have been confronted. It is from this perspective that the question of bribes will be addressed. Although brutally empirical, this section will apply the present state of theory on corporate responsibility to frame the problem and address the questions, 'Can bribes be avoided? Extortion resisted? Do businesspeople try? Do companies care?'.

5.2.2 Context

Corruption in the form of dishonest or fraudulent conduct by those in power, typically involving bribery, has been a part of man for several millennia. Mentions in the Bible and prior writings are plentiful, as are anecdotes of medieval times. Montesquieu describes how commerce was hampered by the prohibition of interest-taking by the Catholic Church and was consequently taken up by the Jews; how the Jews suffered constant extortions at the hands of nobles and Kings; and how eventually they reacted by inventing the bill of exchange or *lettre de change,* which made wealth invisible and such that it could be sent anywhere without leaving a trace. As Hirschman put it 'In this manner we owe...to the avarice of rulers the establishment of a contrivance which somehow lifts commerce right out of their grip' (Hirschman, 1997).

When 'moralising philosophy and religious precept could no longer be trusted with restraining the destructive passions of men' (Hirschman, 1997), Capitalism emerged as a system that would enable violent passions to be subdued by the relatively innocuous interest in acquiring wealth. For most of the 300 years since the advent of Capitalism, regrettably, performance has been rewarded far more than integrity: profit has usually ruled and ends have often justified means.

However, over the last 25 or 30 years the economic and political landscape in which businesses operate has changed significantly. When the Berlin wall fell in 1989 it was foreseen even by the most incredulous that the implosion of Marxism was coming. But what was not clear at the time was that Capitalism was also changing beyond recognition. While in the age of Darwinian capitalism, as late as the 1970s, it was acceptable for a Nobel laureate to say 'the business of business is business' (Friedman, 1970), this would be unacceptable thirty years later. The bar of acceptable business behaviour has been rising inexorably. Through technology and economic participation, people increasingly expect—and are in a position to demand—more visibility into Government and business activities. By law, precedent or standards of interaction, it has become ever more difficult to act in an unethical way (Tapscott & Ticoll, 2003). Pressure will grow still further for transparency in business practices, and for firms to act responsibly towards people and the environment. Such post-Darwinian capitalism involves what became known as corporate responsibility (CR).

This leads on to the second aspect to this problem. How can the ability of people in power to extort those trying to do their business be reduced?

5.2.3 *Embedding Integrity in the Corporate Culture*

Creating a culture that sustains both high performance and high integrity is probably the greatest challenge that corporate leaders face. Employees up and down the ranks are confronted with the temptation of fudging the accounts, securing low cost suppliers at the expense of child labour or bribing their way to lucrative contracts. This situation is becoming more serious as people at all rungs of the organisation are measured and compelled to perform, particularly when a business operates in an environment of government corruption (as happens in many emerging markets), or of extremely demanding customers in what is clearly a buyers' market, or when competition is unscrupulous.

So what tools do business leaders have to cope with this challenge? Essentially, the question is one of corporate governance. As pointed out in Sect. 2.2.1 corporate governance has three dimensions. Recapitulating, the first—and much the best known—dimension is the relationship of the Board with the CEO. This refers to how the Board designates the CEO, fixes her compensation and oversees and evaluates her performance. Within this dimension is the supervision of financial transparency through the work of the Audit Committee with the CFO. For those companies listed on the New York Stock Exchange, compliance with the Sarbanne-Oxley bill has given this dimension of corporate governance a high degree of urgency and visibility.

The second dimension of Corporate Governance is the relationship between the shareholders and the Board of Directors. It is essentially about how the shareholders select the members of the Board, and how the Directors look after the shareholders' interests, prioritising them over those of management. An essential part of this relationship is transparency: how does the Board report to the shareholders and keep them abreast of the state of the business?

The third dimension of corporate governance concerns the relationship of the CEO with the rank and file and is about how senior management instills a culture of extremely demanding performance with an unyielding commitment to integrity. Paradoxically, this is the dimension that has the greatest scope for making a difference but, as anticipated in Sect. 2.2.1 is the least referred to in the corporate governance literature. Certain companies have led the field by adopting a series of principles and best business practices that revolve around being ahead of regulators, going beyond formal financial and legal rules, giving employees a voice and holding business leaders accountable with integrity metrics. A pioneer and trendsetter on this front was General Electric (Heineman, 2007).

There is little doubt that significant progress in this field would be achieved if researchers and practitioners gave more attention to this CEO-downward view of corporate governance, with CEOs and senior managers trained to become stalwart supporters of the 'performance with integrity' corporate culture.

5.2.4 Transaction Governance Capacity

As seen in the opening of this chapter, corruption is about providing privileged access to resources and recognising the time value of money, while bribe is a special case of corruption defined as dishonestly persuading someone (in a position of power) to act in one's favour by a gift of money or other inducement. Interestingly, corruption in public administration is not given by the absence of rules; on the contrary, it is excessively detailed rules, or micro regulation, that gives power to public office holders. It is through micro regulation that they control access, transparency and therefore time.

As seen in Sect. 2.2.3, Prahalad (2005)[1] coined the term Transaction Governance Capacity (TGC) as the capacity of a society to guarantee transparency in the processes of economic transactions and the ability to enforce commercial contracts. A high degree of TGC is achieved by fulfilling three primary criteria: (a) giving stakeholders access to information; (b) designing and implementing clear processes that eliminate selective interpretations and (c) speedily completing processes. Complying with these three criteria builds trust in the system.

5.2.5 Discussion

From the previous paragraphs it emerges that the keys for avoiding bribes and resisting extortion require working within organisations and beyond them in what can be called the business ecosystem. Within organisations the focus should be on working from the CEO downwards in creating a culture of 'performance with integrity'. But work needs to be done with the business ecosystem as well, specifically in increasing TGC. Both of these principles have in common the need for transparency. These concepts are now tested with the four situations described in the introduction.

Before going into these analyses, it is relevant that the four cases described take place in different countries, but they all belong to the Latin America cluster as defined by the GLOBE project (see Sect. 2.2.3, Fig. 2.3) so societal culture is not significantly different between them. Moreover, connecting this to the institutional forces reviewed in

---

[1] Prahalad, C. *The Fortune at the Bottom of the Pyramid*.

Sect. 2.2.3 is that their formal institutions as characterised by legislation inherited from the Spanish tradition and heavy in detail. However, its excess in written constraints is not accompanied by effective enforcement.[2] What could be worse for TGC than intricate legislation that is not enforced? While the first and fourth situations described happen in two countries with some of the highest scores in the region in terms of Corruption Perception Index CPI (i.e. meaning they are the least corrupt in the Latin America region) cases two and three happen in countries poorly rated and therefore corrupt.

The context that does vary across these four cases is where the headquarters of the consulting firm is located. The first two cases involve the same firm that is headquartered in the Latin Europe cluster (i.e. Spain) and the third and fourth cases refer to two different firms located in the Anglo cluster (i.e. third in UK/United States and the fourth in UK). Surprisingly, from the analysis of Fig. 2.3, it is found that the GLOBE project arrived at that the Latin America societal culture is closer to the Anglo than the Latin Europe.

In the case of the call from the Minister, the Minister revealed some weakness in implying that he could block future initiatives but not the present one. If he could not block this one, it is because TGC is not as low as he intended to convey. But what this example really reveals are problems in the consulting firm derived from not having a well internalised culture of integrity. Had that culture been well engrained in the organisation, the person making the decision would not have hesitated, nor need to consult his head office.

The second case, that of the multinational company manager who demands a fee to award a contract, reveals a clear failing in TGC, and shows that these problems do not occur only in public organisations (this country scores low on CPI which means that its societal culture lives with public sector corruption that appears to spill over to the private sector). If the individual can impose that kind of extortion on a supplier, this reveals that its processes are not clearly defined; that there is opaqueness in the system; and that a particular individual had the ability to de-rail, or at least

---

[2] This insight emerged from a conversation with the late Dr. Antonio Mercader, Secretary of State for Education & Culture in Uruguay. Interestingly, Uruguay has no specific Ministry for Justice, but its functions come under the Ministry for Education & Culture. To have these three functions under one umbrella makes sense: What could have more impact on societal culture than education and the law of the land?

hold back, project awarding. Looking at the situation from the perspective of the other actor in this story, the manager of the consulting firm, it is quite possible that under the pressure to meet performance objectives and lacking a corporate culture that promotes integrity, the individual would have fallen into the temptation of bribe. Only a solid culture of integrity would have curtailed this.

The third case, that of the banking system project in a state-owned bank, reveals a breakdown in TGC in the bank. It is hard to believe that the bank had an ethical culture when the head of the organisation was engaging in this kind of practice. This highlights the difficulties of developing such a culture in a bank that is led by political appointments who do not have long-term 'skin in the game' for the institution's future. Furthermore, by having a political appointment in the joint role of Chairperson of the Board and CEO, the three key corporate governance relationships mentioned in Sect. 2.2.1 are distorted. The shareholder is the state, and clearly its interests are not well protected by a Board that engages in these practices. The relationship between the Board and management is distorted by the fact that one person is wearing a hat on each end of the relationship. The fact that the bank is carrying out this project is positive from both an operational and governance perspectives as the result would be to increase the organisation's structural intellectual capital, but clearly the Board is not in condition to be able to ensure that senior management implements an ethical culture in the bank through its relationship with the rank and file of the organisation. With respect to the JV lead firm, it does not have a firm ethical culture in place, otherwise it would not have turned to its junior partner for a contribution to the 'campaign contribution effort'. Only a strong integrity-laden culture in the consulting firm can be ethically rescued from this incident. Or maybe not. Maybe this firm took a hypocritical stance of not taking an active role in a major undercover corruption operation but did not push to avoid it taking place.

Finally, the case of sustainability services in waste management for local government. This case in a country that scores high in terms of CPI shows that even in those countries there can be a breakdown in TGC. Or maybe it is a limitation on CPI that it bases its scoring system on central government standards and does not reach out to local governments. From that perspective, what makes this case even more serious is that the officials involved are from the government and from the opposition parties. So where is the opposition's role of keeping the government accountable? This goes beyond weaknesses in the legal system to reveal weaknesses in the democratic political system, or the formal institutions in general. As theory indicates, when this happens informal institutions take over and that takes the form of tacit agreement between players that appear to be on opposite sides of the political system but have come to an agreement on a de facto modus operandi. In terms of the consulting firm, this situation shows that it is not enough to have an ethics code, an ethics committee and a structure that professes ethical standards. The ethical corporate culture of performance with integrity is not built into the organisation. There needs to be more ethical behaviours from the top of the organisation for this to get ingrained into the corporate culture.

Mapping these four situations onto the definition of corruption given in Sect. 5.1 reveals some interesting variations. In the first one, clearly the minister takes role A, while the competitor of the case analysed takes role C, and the public through the government department concerned is actor B. However, in this case there is a fourth actor that is the consulting firm being coerced to not submit its proposal and the loss to B is that it will not benefit from a proposal that is possibly more beneficial to the public interest. The second situation clearly maps onto the three actors of the definition of corruption, but has the peculiarity that B is not a public entity but a private sector multinational. Should this be defined as a case of corruption? There is certainly an immoral activity happening, but strictly speaking this could be classified more as a case of agency theory. Actor A is benefiting himself at the expense of the shareholders, but what about actor C? Actor C, the consulting firm, in this case is not making a payment to receive a benefit that it did not deserve. It is making a payment to unblock a right it had deservedly won.

Situations three and four, the state-owned bank transformation project and the local government waste management initiative, are cases of corruption by the book. What is notable about the three last cases is that in all of them the initiative for the corrupt activity was taken by actor A; in none of the cases was the initiative taken by actor C (in the first case it is not known which actor took the initiative). Like in situation two, in three and four actor C is making a payment to unblock a benefit it has deservedly won. Is there a moral difference between making a payment to access an undeserved benefit or making a payment to unblock a deserved one?

5.2.6   Conclusion

Addressing the questions of the opening paragraph of this section, bribes can be avoided but it takes hard work from many players. How many political parties have come into power with the promise of stopping corruption? Not many of them have succeeded, and in fact many have engaged themselves in questionable practices. When formal institutions decay and informal ones take their place in the form of societal cultures that accept corruption as a fact of life, it is hard to make changes. A corruption-accepting culture is a deep hole easy to slide into, but extremely hard to climb out from. Unfortunately, that is all too common in Latin America. Observed from the outside, one of the reasons that initiatives to recover from corruption have failed is that new governments think they can tackle it simply by changing people, but that is a recipe for failure. They should focus on systemic changes by concentrating on improving TGC.

Extortion can and should be resisted, but this requires leadership that measures its people's performance beyond purely financial outcomes. Despite being subject to fierce pressure to perform, businesspeople will avoid bribes and other forms of extortion if they operate in an organisation that lives by known codes of 'performance with integrity'. And it is fair to say that companies do care about operating in a morally uncertain environment: if they have an option, they will focus on markets where they know there is a high degree of TGC. And for those with poor TGC they will create the structure to avoid it. For example, many years ago IBM Argentina was caught out in a massive corruption case in projects for Banco Nacion, a state-owned bank—as a result of which it adopted the policy to no longer sell directly to the state in Argentina—it would do so through local distributors. Is that good enough? Does this mean that corruption is eliminated, or simply that it has taken an arm's length relation with it (i.e. like case three above)? This is an area where Boards need to get involved—they need to protect their shareholders' interests not just by focusing on the agency problem, but also by closely monitoring the 'CEO – rank and file' relationship in its push for an ethical corporate culture.

If these principles were more broadly diffused and adhered to, on the 'to bribe or not to bribe' dilemma, companies would go for the latter. The next section deals with a different aspect of corruption in international business: A case of drug money laundering through the banking system.

5.3 Laundering Drug Money: Rot from the Tail

5.3.1 Overview

This section moves from illegal coercion and bribing to a different form of corruption as money laundering. It develops a case study of the drug money laundering scandal at HSBC Mexico that spans over many years starting in the first decade of this century and which had deep implications for the bank's US operation. It explains the specific form of money laundering normally associated with drug trafficking from Latin America; it analyses the causes of the break-down of compliance at HSBC Mexico and USA; it describes its consequences and extracts lessons from the case and propose governance measures that can be taken to diminish the risk of this kind of incident happening again.

The author acknowledges the contribution of his *MSc Banking, Finance & Fintech* students at EM Normandie Business School in the investigation of this case. The students did this as an assignment for their 'Ethics and Corporate Governance in Banking' course. They are, in alphabetical order: A. Amouret, M. Degrave, S. Hecq, M. Madec, M. Ozdamar, A. Strantaris, H. Thomas and L. Zang. They deserve all the credit for the merits of the case, while the author takes full responsibility for the potential misrepresentations of reality.

5.3.2 The Organisation: HSBC

HSBC Holdings plc is a London headquartered universal bank of global reach. By 2020 it was the seventh largest bank in the world and the largest in Europe, both by assets (i.e. US$2.7 trillion) and by market capitalisation (i.e. US$169.47 billion). Founded by Sir Thomas Sutherland in 1865 as the Hong Kong and Shanghai Banking Corporation, it opened its first offices in Hong Kong and Shanghai that year. It was conceived since foundation as an international bank as its purpose was to facilitate the by then burgeoning trade between China and Europe, and to explore opportunities in commerce between China and USA. It is probably the most globalised bank with some 7500 offices in over 80 countries and territories across Africa, Asia, Oceania, Europe, North America and South

America. It has a headcount in excess of 230,000 employees to serve some 89 million customers.[3]

A truly universal bank, HSBC is organised into four business units: Commercial Banking, Global and Investment Banking, Retail Banking and Wealth Management and Global Private Banking. It positions itself as the bank whose strategy enables to connect customers to opportunities and it successfully sailed the trail winds of globalisation and the emerging of the wealthy and middle classes of the last 30–40 years.

The key actors in this narrative are its US and Mexican subsidiaries. HSBC Bank USA N.A. (HBUS) is its main US subsidiary, which operates from over 500 bank branches in the United States, manages in excess of US$200 billion in assets and serves some 4 million customers. It holds a national bank charter and its principal regulator is the Office of the Comptroller of the Currency (OCC) whose purpose is to ensure a safe and sound federal banking system for all Americans and is part of the US Treasury Department. HBUS is headquartered in McLean, Virginia, but its main office is in New York City. HSBC acquired its US presence through the purchase of several US financial institutions, including Marine Midland Bank and the National Bank of the Republic of New York.

With assets of US$40.6 billion Banco HSBC Mexico is the fifth largest bank in Mexico, with approximately 15,800 staff operating from 948 branch offices spread across the country. It is a part of the Grupo Financiero HSBC that together with its insurance, brokering, asset management and services companies conforms the largest financial group in Mexico.[4]

5.3.3 The Incident

The Mexican drug money laundering incident at HSBC developed over a long period. Indeed, as far back as 2003 and then in 2010, the US authorities had issued requests to HSBC to review its anti-money laundering practices. The fact that HBUS had classified its Mexican counterpart bank

---

[3] See https://www.bing.com/search?q=HSBC+Bank&filters=sid%3a4aaf37ad-af22-1e66-de25-d0df5dc6785d&form=ENTLNK.

[4] See https://www.advratings.com/north-america/top-banks-in-mexico.

HSBC Mexico Bank (HBMX) as low risk would in the end have a critical effect in the origin of the whole incident. Since 2007, the Mexican bank subsidiary of HSBC (HBMX) was put under close surveillance with regard to financial activities and in particular the capital flows it channelled to the United States. All banks, but especially those operating internationally, have in place an *anti-money laundering* (AML) policy, which stipulates the banking institution's willingness and preparedness to combat these fraudulent practices by any criminal organisation.

It was known that, since 2007, HBMX was channelling more Mexican capital through the United States than any other Mexican bank, which made it far more exposed to the risk of money laundering, especially when considering that Mexico is the hub of drug trafficking in the Americas. This fact was reported to the American commission of inquiry dealing with cases of financial fraud, after which the bank was constantly in the investigators' radar screen. In 2008, according to an HBMX internal report, 70 percent of the Mexican money laundered was smurfed through the bank. In 2010, the OCC issued a cease and desist order requiring HSBC to change its anti-money laundering policy and thus act to prevent such excesses. At that time it was found that there had been over 17,000 *suspicious activity alerts* that had not been reported in a timely manner to the US authorities; there had been a lack of due diligence to assess the risks incurred by other HSBC subsidiaries before opening correspondent accounts for them; there had been cash transaction worth US$15 billion between mid-2006 and mid-2009; there had been lack of oversight of the $60 trillion in annual wire transfers made by customers in countries considered low-risk by HBUS; and there was insufficient and inadequate staffing, resources and leadership in the area of anti-money-laundering and there were a high number of wire transfers to US-sanctioned counties such as Iran, Cuba, Libya and Sudan.

It was not until late spring 2012 that the story really came to light in a press release issued by the US Senate Subcommittee on Investigations, which explained that the Mexican HSBC group had channelled billions of dollars from drug cartels through the US banking system and used it to launder large amounts of money belonging to the same cartels. As a result of the investigations, HSBC had to agree to pay a $1.9 billion fine as part of a deferred prosecution agreement (DPA) for violating US laws designed to protect the US financial system. HSBC had to follow the agreement's recommendations for five years to avoid losing its banking license. It was determined that HSBC had laundered at least US$881 million of drug proceeds through the US financial system for international drug cartels, and had processed an additional $660 million for banks in US-sanctioned countries. According to a US Senate report, 'the US banking subsidiary failed to control more than $670 billion in wire transfers and more than $9.4 billion in physical dollar purchases from its Mexican unit'.[5]

It is surprising that the OCC allowed HBUS' anti-money laundering deficiencies to fester for so many years. It is alleged that this is so, at least in part, because on the one hand it treated HBUS' anti-money laundering problems as consumer compliance issues rather than safety and soundness issues and as such did not use formal and informal enforcement measures in a timely manner to impose anti-money laundering reforms in the bank. On the other hand, because it focused on anti-money laundering problems in specific banking units of HBUS without also examining them at the institution-wide level.

As a result of this case, HSBC's stock lost 16 percent of its market value. HSBC acknowledged that it had not been aware of the warning signs that drug cartels in Mexico were using its branches to launder millions of dollars, and also said that HSBC international staff had stripped identification information from transactions made through the United States. In 2013, in his intervention before the UK Parliamentary Banking Standards Committee, CEO Stuart Gulliver acknowledged that the bank's structure was 'not fit for purpose'. He also said that issues that should have been shared and scaled up in the hierarchy had not been done so.

5.3.4 The Money-Laundering Technique Applied Through HSBC Mexico

There are several techniques that criminals use for moving money internationally, a common one being *cuckoo smurfing*. For *cuckoo smurfing*, the criminals need help from a bank insider. Suppose a New York criminal owes a London criminal US$8000, and a London importer owes a New York supplier $8000. The London importer goes to her London Bank and deposits US$8000, with instructions to transfer the money to her New York supplier's bank. The London banker, working with the New

---

[5] See https://www.lexology.com/library/detail.aspx?g=2e625ec2-b2d9-4083-b2b6-8ad feefa2fbf.

York criminal, instructs the New York criminal to deposit US$8000 in the New York supplier's bank account. The London banker then transfers US$8000 from the London importer's account to the London criminal's account. The London importer and her New York supplier do not know the funds were never directly transferred. All they know is that the London merchant paid US$8000 and the New York supplier received his payment.[6]

The form used by Mexican drug barons (and others, such as the Colombians) is a more complex variation of this and is known as the *black market peso exchange* (BMPE). The cartels 'export' drugs to the United States or Western Europe where they get paid in the currency of the country where the drugs are sold. The drug dealers then contact a foreign currency exchange broker who holds pesos funds in Mexico, and they exchange the foreign funds for Mexican pesos. With that step the cartel operators fall off the radar screen of the authorities in the destination market of the drugs. The next step is for the broker to launder the money by placing it into Mexico's financial system. In order to achieve that, the broker contacts Mexican importers and tells them that he holds foreign funds suitable for the purchase of foreign goods. The broker then uses the foreign funds to pay the supplier on behalf of the Mexican importer and in the sequence receives Mexican peso denominated payment from the importer. In the final step the purchased goods are shipped to a Caribbean or South American destination, from where they are smuggled into Mexico. The importer takes possession of his goods and has the incentive that in the process he has avoided payment of import duties. So, in the BMPE process the drug barons need help from a forex broker and from the Mexican importer but not from an insider in the bank that does the wire funds transfer.

5.3.5 *Discussion*

The scandal was one of the darkest hours in the 153 years of HSBC history. As seen, it cost the bank US$1.9 billion in fines and placed it under a so-called deferred prosecution agreement. Despite having emerged from the financial crisis in a relatively strong position, while many devastated rivals needed to be bailed out by their governments, it

---

[6] See https://www.investopedia.com/terms/s/smurf.asp.

was not able to capitalise on this strength in the United States and Mexico as it spent much of the past seven years trying to repair the damage caused by these failures. The largest bank in Europe was forced to be on its hind foot for most of that period, as it invested billions of dollars in new processes and systems to revise its checks and controls.

What failed in the corporate culture of HSBC in Mexico and USA? From the analysis of the money laundering technique applied by the drug cartels, it appears that there was no direct involvement of the bank's staff in the procedures. The real issue was one of not carrying out the standard AML procedures and all its derivations such as 'Know your customer' (KYC), 'Account and transaction tracking' (ATT), 'Foreign account tax compliance act' (FACTA) reporting, and many others. From a corporate culture perspective, this does not seem to be a case of failures in ethics, but one of failures in business processes. As mentioned in Sect. 2.2.1 compliance operates at two levels:

> Level 1: The bank complies with regulations
> Level 2: The staff of the bank comply with internal systems and controls defined by senior management that are designed to lead to compliance with Level 1.

Clearly, the problem at HSBC was that compliance officers in the organisation did not do enough to interpret US regulations and translate them into internal policies and operational processes and systems. As a result of this the bank's operational staff were not given clear directives on how to act, and its compliance units were not doing their job of monitoring the operational staffs' activities. In other words, the failure here is one of structural intellectual capital. It appears, too, from the information gathered on the incident, that compliance staff was insufficient in numbers and in skills, so the problem is also one of human intellectual capital limitations. Recovering from this crisis required the bank to invest in both these forms of intellectual capital.

Having said all of this, one issue remains to be discussed. Over and above the processes and systems, senior management of HBUS and HBMX should have suspected by the volumes of transactions and where they were being generated, and especially after the early warnings from the regulatory authorities, that there could be illegal transactions. They also knew that their compliance procedures were not up to scratch. Were they turning a blind eye to the problem? Was the culture of performance with integrity tilted towards performance? It is quite probable that senior management at HBUS and HBMX did not have the incentives to detect the money laundering problem in its early stages.

In terms of the three key corporate governance relationships, it arises from the money-laundering incident that the 'CEO/Senior management vs rank & file' relationship was not successful in creating a corporate culture that maximised an intangible asset as important as intellectual capital. It emerges from the evidence, too, that critical thinking at all levels of the organisation was not working. People are not looking at the figures and internalising the story these figures are telling; there seems to be at all levels of the organisation a disregard for discovering patterns of behaviour, making sense of them, and prompting to investigate further. Furthermore, this leads to questioning the 'Board vs CEO' relationship—why isn't the Board demanding of the CEO that a corporate culture of valuing intellectual capital and generating critical thinking is developed?

Observing the problem from a stakeholder perspective, it is quite clear that the losers here were the governments of Mexico and USA through the double whammy of tax evasion and not being able to locate and detain a social problem as is drug trafficking. Losers, too, at the end were the shareholders through the impact of the fines on profits (and, thus, dividends) and the loss of reputation and steep drop in market valuation of the bank.

Finally, how does this money laundering incident map onto the definition of corruption? Looking at the three actors in a corruption scenario, it is interesting that the role of actor A, the public office, is taken by the bank (HSBC). The role of character B is the society in general, or more specifically the tax revenue offices and security forces in Mexico and USA. And the role of actor C is taken by the drug barons. In this case the corruption initiative is taken by actor C that drives the whole process. The cost, as always, is absorbed by actor B; but what is really curious is that actor A, in this case, acts through inaction. By not becoming aware of the money laundering activities, actor A is playing into the hands of actor C, the only beneficiary of the activity.

5.3.6 Conclusions

It is frustrating to see how in their role to protect shareholders' interest, well intentioned Board members pour over financial data that represent the past performance of the organisation, rather than looking at those aspects of the business that define its future performance. In the effort to overcome the agency theory challenge arising from data asymmetry, which Boards see as their central tenet, they lose sight of the importance of developing a corporate culture that enables achieving future performance.

What the HSBC case brings to light is that gross ethical failures are not always caused by failure to develop an ethical corporate culture. In this case a massive ethical failure that drove HSBC to nearly lose its banking license in the USA, an incident that would have had unpredictable consequences on the bank as a whole, potentially including its global demise, was caused by a corporate culture that was not necessarily unethical, but actually incapable of managing an intangible asset such as intellectual capital. It failed to construct the structural intellectual capital of compliance processes and systems, and the human intellectual capital of compliance staff. Rebuilding these intangibles took seven years of highly significant investments and, what is even more important, lost opportunities to exploit HSBC's relative financial robustness coming out of the Great Recession to expand its business. It is remarkable that HSBC's share price did not recover from the money laundering scam until this process was concluded.

Once more, this case brings to light how important it is for Boards to focus their attention on the 'CEO vs rank & file' governance relationship with an aim at ensuring that the organisation develops a corporate culture of performance with integrity. What makes this case different, is that it shows that in the knowledge economy creating a corporate culture of performance with integrity depends to a great extent of achieving a culture that safe-guards and permanently enhances the organisation's intangible assets such as intellectual capital.

The next section introduces another case of a bank involved in money laundering, but one where corruption arises from a different angle. This is the case of Danske Bank.

5.4 Laundering Easy Money: Rot from the Head

This section develops the case of the laundering scandal at Danske Bank's Estonian branch. The sources for the case are public domain data, including the lawyers' report to the Board of Directors that has been published (Bruun & Hieile, 2018). It needs to be pointed out that the mentioned report was commissioned by the Board of Directors to the legal firm *Bruun & Hjejle* that is the Bank's habitual provider of legal services so, strictly speaking, it does not qualify as an independent report.

The author acknowledges the contribution of his *MSc Banking, Finance & Fintech* students at EM Normandie Business School in the investigation of this case. The students did this as an assignment for their 'Ethics and Corporate Governance in Banking' course. They are, in alphabetical order: B. Baud, P.M. Donnefort, S. Le Francois, J. Michel, V. Sik, H. Tepraseuth and C. Veith. They deserve all the credit for the merits of the case, while the author takes full responsibility for the potential misrepresentations of reality.

5.4.1 The Bank

Danske is Denmark's leading bank, representing nearly 50 percent of the banking system at the time of the money laundering scandal analysed in this case study was revealed, thus one of the six systemically important institutions. It is listed on the Nasdaq OMX Copenhagen stock exchange, it has a total of 2.8 million individual and business customers, close to 2000 corporate and institutional clients, 237 branch offices and in excess of 20,600 headcount.

The bank's roots can be traced back to the founding of Den Danske Landmandsbank in 1871, which in less than 20 years became the largest bank in Denmark and by the beginning of WWI was the largest bank in Scandinavia. With deregulation and globalisation of the financial markets in the 1990s came a series of mergers and acquisitions with another two leading banks, Handelsbanken and Provinsbanken, to form a Danish banking powerhouse. This was followed by the acquisition of Danica in 1995 and the acquisition of BG Bank in 2001.

With little space to grow in its home market, Danske Bank engaged in an intense international expansion, mainly through acquisitions. It acquired banks in the Republic of Ireland, in Northern Ireland, in Norway, in Sweden and even as far reaching as Australia, giving it a presence in sixteen national markets. In this string of international acquisitions, that of the Sampo Bank from Finland in 2006 would prove to be lethal in the long term to Danske Bank's reputation as it was pivotal in the money laundering case. By 2019 Danske's assets were worth 1.5 times Denmark's gross domestic product and it had become a major actor in the European banking sector, especially in Northern Europe, and was ranked the 53rd largest bank in the world by assets (Bjerregaard & Kirchmaier, 2019).

With the acquisition of Sampo Bank came a series of subsidiaries in banking and insurance across the Nordic countries and the Baltic states. Among them was Sampo Pank in Estonia whose history goes back to 1992, shortly after the collapse of the Soviet Union. According to the Bruun & Hjejle (2018) report in 1992 two Estonian banking entities were established, Eesti Forekspank and Eisti Investeerimspank at a time when there were strong economic ties between Estonia and the Russian Federation. From close to its inception, Eesti Forekspank developed a strong client base of Russian individuals and corporations, which operated mostly in cross-border payments and foreign exchange transactions, and it eventually opened an office in Moscow in 1997 to better serve these clients. The following year Estonia suffered a major financial collapse as the Russian Economy deteriorated, which led the Estonian Central Bank to acquire controlling interests in both banks, and merging them into a new entity called Optiva Pank that became the third largest bank in the market. A few years later, in 2000, the Estonian Central Bank sold controlling stakes in Optiva Pank to Sampo Bank that in 2002 acquired the rest of the shares from the minority shareholders. In 2008, that is a year after its acquisition, Sampo Pank was turned into a branch of Danske Bank, and in November 2012 it took the name of its controller.

Danske Bank was renown for its ability to quickly absorb and integrate new acquisitions and a key mechanism for this was to replace the acquired bank's ICT systems by those of the Group, which meant that Danske could effectively impose its AML and risk management processes on the new branch or subsidiary. A crucial decision by Danske's senior management in this case is that it was decided not to substitute Sampo Pank's (Estonia) systems due to the high cost this would have had in relation to the volume of the bank.

5.4.2 The Incident

It was in the Estonian branch of Danske Bank, far from the crossroads of global finance, that a scandal broke out in 2018. Indeed, what originally was thought to be €8 billion ended up amounting to €200 billion of suspicious transactions passed through Danske Bank's accounts in Tallinn (capital of Estonia) and these €200 billion are the basis of this vast money laundering affair. The Danish bank admitted that most of these movements of funds were intended to launder money for the benefit of Russian, Moldovan and nationals of other former Soviet Union countries.[7]

More specifically, Danske bank started to launder money on a large scale in 2007 as "suspicious clients" opened accounts as soon as it started operations in Estonia. The Bruun & Hjejle report reveals that between 2007 and 2015 there were some 10,000 clients in Danske Bank's Estonia Non-Resident Portfolio that comprised mainly companies but also private persons, and another 5000 non-resident accounts not considered within the Portfolio. The expansion of this portfolio was strong from 2009 to 2013 and was then curtailed and closed in the 2014–2016 period.

The Non-Resident Portfolio used Danske Estonia essentially for money transfers. There were practically no loans to the 15,000 non-residents so they did not expose the bank to credit risk and thus did not cause need for regulatory capital. The Non-Resident Portfolio did, however, expose the bank to operational risk as during the 2007–2015 period there were 7.5 million incoming and outgoing payments and this number of transactions does not include payments between accounts held at Danske Bank Estonia. If all the 15,000 non-residents are included, that figure goes up to 9.5 million incoming and outgoing payments. These transactions were done in 32 different currencies, but mostly US dollars and euro. In terms of flow (that is value of the transactions) the 10,000 clients of the Non-Resident Portfolio represent the vast majority. At the time of the Bruun & Hjejle report, their investigation of the non-resident clients had reached the individual analysis of approximately 6200 customers, nearly all from within the Non-Resident Portfolio. The findings to that date reveals extremely serious AML shortcomings at the due diligence of customers (KYC) level, at the transaction monitoring and screening level and at the reporting suspicious customers and activities level. For example, in terms of KYC breeches, of the 6200 customers:

- 3500 were found to share addresses or other properties that have been identified as suspicious
- 1700 were found to have significant differences between revenue figures and payment activity

---

[7] See https://www.france24.com/fr/20180924-danemark-estonie-danske-bank-scandale-oligarque.

- 500 were found to be associated with money laundering schemes in the public domain
- 450 were detected to have suspicious characteristics or behaviours
- 50 were found to have suspicious counterparties in other banks.

Each customer is placed in only one of these categories—if they fit in more than one, they are placed in the one most relevan—so all 6200 clients analysed up to the time or the report had some suspicious characteristic!

With respect to monitoring and screening of transactions, there was a lack of identification of the source and origin of the funds used in the transaction, there was no screening of the clients against lists of politically exposed persons, there was no screening of incoming payments against sanctions or terror lists, and in general no automatic screening of incoming payments.

During the 2007–2014 period the non-resident portfolio generated an increasing share of Danske Bank's Estonian profits, with a mean of 60.4 percent and a standard deviation of 13.8 percent of profits before tax; it peaked with 79 percent of profits before tax in 2008 and of 76 percent in 2013. To put things into perspective it must be said that the Estonian operation was not significant within the Danske Group as a whole; during all that period the bank's Estonia assets were stable at approximately 0.5 percent of total group assets; however, it was far more significant in terms of overall profits before tax, with a mean of 4.6 percent, a standard deviation of 3.4 percent and a peak of 10.7 percent in 2011.

This money laundering incident had strong repercussions on the whole Danish financial system. It led to an investigation by the American authorities, the British National Crime Agency and a call from Brussels to open a Europe-wide investigation. Each state sought to establish whether dirty money had entered its territory. This case contributed to the deterioration of the Danske's financial ratings in Copenhagen and loss of market capitalisation, as its share price dropped from a peak of DKK 250 at the time that news of the scandal reached the markets, to half of that by April 2019.

It also had international ramifications as Danske could not act alone. For example, for its great volume of US dollar denominated flows, it needed correspondent banks. Initially, from 2007, it used JP Morgan Chase and Deutsche Bank. In the olden days, correspondent relationships were a gentlemanly game where the correspondent bank would trust that its client bank would have done the due diligence of its own customers and the transaction they were doing. However, this is no longer the case as responsibility falls upon all the institutions through which a fraudulent funds transfer circulates. So, in line with this, by 2013 JP Morgan Chase seriously suspected the origins of the funds and terminated its correspondent bank agreement with Danske Bank Estonia, which substituted it by Bank of America. By May 2015 Bank of America also suspected the origins of the funds and terminated its agreement that month. Deutsche Bank, however, continued until September 2015 when the situation was already untenable.[8] Deutsche Bank handled the largest number of suspicious money transfers that are estimated at over a million. Quite extraordinarily, a Deutsche Bank whistle-blower denounced this early on, but the bank did not report it until five years later, in February 2019. Even more surprisingly and telling about the cosy relationship between German banks and their regulators/supervisors, is that according to Reuters BaFin, defying all current principles of AML, would not take action against Deutsche Bank for that omission 'because Deutsche's role as a so-called correspondent bank was secondary to Danske'.[9] Other European banks such as Swedbank and Raffeisen Bank have also been drawn into the wake of this scandal.

Senior management at Danske Bank had many instances of red flag alerts to suspicious activity. In 2007, shortly after completing the acquisition of Sampo Bank, the Estonian financial services authority (FSA) came out with a critical inspection report on the subsidiary's AML standards and processes, and roughly at the same time Danske Bank at Group level was informed by the Russian Central Bank (through the Danish FSA) that there were clear indications of 'tax and custom payments evasion' and 'criminal activity in its pure form, including money laundering' estimated at 'billions of roubles monthly'. The termination of correspondent bank agreements by JP Morgan Chase in 2013 based on AML suspicions was a flagrant external signal that was ignored by Group management. A whistle-blower allegation from within the Estonian operation in 2013 followed by an Internal Audit report confirming weak AML procedures in 2014 was a fourth alarm not acted upon. Then there was a fifth external

---

[8] See https://calert.info/details.php?id=1716.

[9] See https://uk.reuters.com/article/uk-deutsche-bank-moneylaundering-exclusi/exclusive-deutsche-bank-took-years-to-flag-suspect-danske-money-flows-source-idUKKBN1WT288.

red flag when Bank of America terminated its correspondent bank agreement in March 2015. And all along experts in international corruption and the Organised Crime & Corruption Reporting Project (OCCRP), a network of international journalists specialising in organised crime and corruption, had been suggesting that the Estonian branch of Danske Bank is one of the favourite tax evasion vehicles for Russian, Ukrainian or Azerbaijani oligarchs.[10]

A corroboration of this is that in September 2018, Danske Bank admitted that its procedures for oversight had failed completely, and that its AML standards in Estonia were deficient. Following that the Chairman of the Board and the CEO had to step down, and in May 2019 the former CEO and another nine group senior managers were preliminarily charged in the case by the Danish State Prosecutor for Serious Economic and International Crime.[11]

5.4.3 Form of Money Laundering at Danske Bank

It is hard to know, at this instance, how much of the €200 billion is actually fraudulent and money laundering, due to the intrinsic secrecy of this activity and little information of what proportion of illicit transactions are detected. Global estimates given by the United Nations Office of Drugs and Crime (UNODC) give money laundering an annual range of between US$800 billion and US$2 trillion, or between 2 and 5 percent of global GDP. However, considering that all the clients analysed of the Non-Resident Portfolio have some basis of strong suspicion, it can be assumed to be extremely high. What may be easier to analyse is the method used for money laundering.

Apart from indicating that there are voluminous flows of funds, the Bruun & Hjejle report does not enter in details of how the procedures worked. Other sources indicate that it appears that in the Danske Bank case the methods used were shell companies, trade-based schemes and the purchase of valuable assets, but no details are given (Bjerregaard & Kirchmaier, 2019).

---

[10] See https://www.occrp.org/en/investigations/7698-report-russia-laundered-billions-via-danske-bank-estonia.

[11] See https://www.france24.com/fr/20180924-danemark-estonie-danske-bank-scandale-oligarque.

By shell companies is meant using companies to blur the identity of the individuals doing the transactions. These companies have no significant assets or operations and are often incorporated in tax havens, which offer the advantage of relatively low reporting requirements and are often used for triangulation of operations to generate profits in low tax domiciles.

Trade-based schemes use mechanisms such as over/under invoicing, over/short shipping, ghost shipping, triangulation, multiple invoicing to conceal illegal funds within the operations of legal companies. Some examples of this were given in the HSBC money laundering case, and another highly relevant example used often in Russia is 'mirror trading'. Mirror trading consists of buying shares in Russian blue-chip companies, in Moscow paying in roubles, and then offloading those shares on Wall Street and getting paid in US dollars. Trade-based schemes are often used in combination with shell companies.

The purchase of valuable assets such as property, racehorses, luxury cars, yachts, private jets, art artifacts, is a well-known way of investing illegal funds in an environment of reduced reporting requirements.

5.4.4 Discussion

It is no secret that individuals, mostly from Russia, are using the weakest links in the chain surrounding the EU to access the Western financial systems. The Danske Bank money laundering case in Estonia is a case in point. It is surprising though that at this stage of the digital universe physical proximity has any relevance. In the case of Estonia, and possibly all the other Baltic states, it appears that the driver is not so much the physical proximity to the EU, that is just a happenstance, but the cultural proximity to Russia that is the driver.

There are many stakeholders affected by the Danske Bank money laundering scam, but one of the ones worse hit is the Russian people through the tax evasion of funds to the tune of €200 billion. The 'Russian people' may not be very aware of this, but the Russian tax and financial services authorities certainly are, as was noted above by their claim to the Danish FSA early on in the development of the phenomenon.

If the Russian people are not very aware of their losses, the shareholders of Danske Bank certainly are. It is true that they must have been happy when the Estonian subsidiary contributed with an average of 4.6 percent to their bank's bottom line and thus their dividends, but that was clearly offset by the drop of 50 percent on their equity between the time the scam emerged and April 2019, not to mention the long-term effect of the bank's tarnished reputation as a result of the scam.

The employees of the Danske's Estonian branch was another severely hit stakeholder group as the bank, in effect, lost its banking license as it was requested by the Estonina SFA to close down its operation, and therefore they lost their jobs. But even before then, they operated in an organisation whose leadership did not promote a corporate culture of ethical behaviour and safeguarding of intellectual capital and they had to deal with 10,000 Non-Resident Portfolio unscrupulous and probably highly entitled customers with little respect for the bank's staff.

Danske Bank Estonia's clean clients were also a highly affected stakeholder group as quite unexpectedly and for no fault of their own were left without a bank account. Of course, they will have found other banks to take their business to, but nobody likes to have to prove their creditworthiness and go through the paperwork required for opening bank accounts and rebuilding credit history.

The Danish financial system as a whole suffered collateral damage as its biggest player got involved in corrupt operations and thus tarnished the reputation of Copenhagen as an aspiring international financial centre. The scam will not have done any good to the Estonian people either, as the reputation of their country hit the international headlines with negative consequences.

From the perspective of corporate governance and compliance, by deciding not to deploy the Danske Bank corporate ICT systems (and thus business processes) senior management failed to implement the minimum Level 1 compliance standards as described in Sect. 2.2.1 and this left the door wide open for Non-Resident Portfolio clients to launder their funds. As a result of not complying with Level 1 standards, the bank also failed to construct the ethical culture to enable Level 2 compliance and thus gave the opportunity for employees to bend the rules and circumvent the AML controls. This is particularly significant if it is considered that according to the findings of the GLOBE project (i.e., Fig. 2.3) Denmark is at the antipodes of Estonia on societal culture clusters. Knowledge of this should have alerted senior management that this would, in itself, cause significant risks. This risk was magnified by the approach of taking a high context stance and letting the local subsidiary carry out its own and independent strategy in terms of products and services. So, of the three characteristic sources of compliance breaches (i.e. customers, business, and bank-related) by not implementing its corporate systems and processes, Danske Bank's senior management enabled flagrant customer and bank-related compliance breaches.

The prior points confirm that Danske Bank failed to construct an ethical culture in its Estonian operation, but neither did it build a culture of preserving and growing the organisation's intellectual capital. With no corporate systems the Estonian branch was precluded from the *structural capital* that would have enabled the mobilising of the other two dimensions of intellectual capital, that is *human capital* and *relational capital*, to the organisation's benefit. In the knowledge economy this is lethal and therefore not surprising that its share price dropped by 50 percent.

Once again, it is clear that not having implemented the corporate systems was a gross error of judgment on the part of the CEO and senior management to the point that it makes an external observer wonder whether it was simple short-sightedness or outright intentional. The analysis of the three key governance relationships depicts that in the CEO vs Rank & File relationship it was not even attempted to create an ethical culture and one that preserves and increases intellectual capital. In terms of the Board vs CEO relationship despite there being clear and multiple signals that led to suspecting that things were not right in Estonia, the Board made no effort to question and ensure that senior management protect the interest of shareholders by implementing corporate AML systems and processes and developing an appropriate corporate culture.

Finally, mapping this case study onto Philp's corruption model depicted in Sect. 5.1, actor A is Danske Bank. On first analysis it would seem to be just the Estonian operation, but due to the evident ramifications leading to senior management at the centre, it would involve the whole of Danske Bank. Actor B and the loser in this corruption operation is the Russian people through its tax authorities, and actor C is the bank's Non-Resident Portfolio customers. From the analysis of the evidence it is clear that actors A and C are both actively involved in the operation but it is not easy to see, if that mattered, which of the two actors was the driver of the operation. Was it actor A that actively promoted this service and actor C took advantage of it? Or was it actor C that took the initiative and actor A turned a blind eye to it but capitalised on its advantages? It could, most probably, be some of both.

5.4.5 Conclusions

The decision to not implement the corporate ICT systems has proven to be a serious misjudgement on the part of senior management. The justification for this decision was that the implementation project to roll out those systems to the new subsidiary required a high investment in comparison to the size of the business. There is no information on how the business case was made and what criteria was applied but clearly it did not take into account operational risk. It is quite probable, too, that it was based only on tangible benefits. It is well established that in the knowledge economy basing technology business cases purely on tangible benefits is deficient and that qualitative benefits and risk analyses need to be included as well. ICT investments need to be treated as a portfolio, with different criteria for each segment of the portfolio. This is particularly so in a bank where informational and operational risk systems require being far removed from merely tangible benefits.

What should be expected of the Board in a case like this? The Board should have moved the decision away from the 'go-no go' decision on the corporate ICT systems, to that of 'keep or dispose of' the Estonian subsidiary. If the response to the latter had been 'keep', the decision on the ICT systems would not have been necessary and their implementation an integral part of retaining the Estonian operation. The Board vs CEO corporate governance relationship failed dramatically and responsibility for this should be placed squarely on the Board. The CEO and management team are pressed to perform and thus subjective on a decision such as making a large investment in a small business—it can be seen by them simply as a distraction from achieving the expected goals. Performance with integrity starts from the top and then trickles down the organisation in the form of an ethical corporate culture, and it is one of the key responsibilities of the Board to ensure that this happens. Furthermore, in the final analysis, it is possible that the CEO and senior management team considered the ICT implementation an operational decision, while in retrospect it is obvious that it was a governance decision. It was the Board's job to give it that category.

Governance problems in this case go much further than the decision on implementation of the ICT systems. As articulated in the description of the event and discussed in the prior section, there were many loud and clear external signals that there were money laundering irregularities in the Estonian subsidiary. Moreover, as if that were not enough, the simple careful analysis of the financial indicators of the Estonian operation should have raised questions on why an average of 4.6 percent of profits (and in some years nearly 11 percent) were being produced by a subsidiary that represented 0.5 percent of assets. The analysis in detail of financial ratios and acting as a result of them is a key responsibility of the Board.

Finally, this case shows how complex corruption cases that involve multiple jurisdictions can be. Actor B in the phenomenon, the one that bears with the cost, is in Russia (and some of the other former Soviet Union republics) but the laundering operations are carried out by actors A and C in Estonia; governance decisions to put the situation under control should be taken in Denmark by senior management of actor A; the case is investigated by financial authorities in the Euro area, in the United States and in the UK; and actor C operates through shell companies that will be based in domiciles other than all these countries. Looked at from this perspective, it is no wonder that national authorities have in effect declared themselves incapable of controlling this conundrum and delegated all responsibilities for policing these activities to banks. It is remarkable that banks are not compensated for performing those policing services, but are fined handsomely when they fail.

The final section of this chapter extracts lessons from doing a cross-case analysis of the bribe and laundering events.

5.5 Cross-Case Analysis

This chapter extracts lessons on corporate governance from cases in corruption. It looks at two quite distinct forms of corruption as are extortion and money laundering. It obtains from theory that corruption requires the existence of three actors, being the first a public office whose purpose is the attainment of benefit to the public interest and is regulated by a set of rules. The second actor is normally represented by a public entity that receives the benefits of the activities of the prior actor, the public office. And finally, the third actor is a private sector entity that relates to the public office to deliver products and services that will enhance the benefits of the public interest or entity. A case of corruption takes place when there is a distortion in the exercise of public office that leads to a gain in private interest at the expense of the public interest.

The analysis of the bribe cases confirms that corruption is about breaches in public interest. One of the four situations analysed included a bribe that deviated benefits from a private entity to an executive of the private sector who was in a position of power to extortion another private sector company through a procurement relationship—clearly there is an unethical situation and several failures in governance standards, but it cannot be classified as a case of corruption.

From the prior sections in this chapter, corruption in the form of money laundering tends to involve a greater number of people and leave a far more detectable footprint than bribes. It also takes more of a systemic approach and involves flows of large volumes of money over a period, while bribes tend to be more one-off transactions. Organisations have processes in place to detect cases of money laundering, while such protections are not at all common against bribes. Bribes are more secretive so, while there is order of magnitude estimates on volumes of money laundering, these are non-extant or even less precise, for bribes. Its secretism also leads to further crimes to silence witnesses. At the time of writing the Financial Times has released a story titled 'Silent witnesses' on a high-stakes case of bribes that targets Eurasian Natural Resource Corporation (ENRC) in which there are at least four suspicious deaths (Burgis & Watkins, 2020). For all these reasons bribes are harder to detect than money laundering. When detected, it is mostly through tip-offs and are investigated through auditing the accounts of those suspected to be involved. If the amounts are large, bribes may be followed by money laundering. When corruption is detected, as was the case with the two money laundering incidents studied, the bank's reputation is shattered and this has a severe impact on the market valuation of the organisation.

The bribe situations studied arrive at that this form of corruption needs to be combatted on at least two fronts, the private sector and the public office. On the private sector front, it is found that organisations need to develop an ethical corporate culture that creates the context for *performance with integrity*. This ethical culture of performance with integrity is created top-down through example and through the creation and diffusion within the organisation of a clear and well understood code of ethics, and well established channels within the organisation through which situations of extortion can be aired and dealt with in a corporate fashion rather than through the judgement of individuals in the front line of the organisation.

On the public front corruption through bribes needs to be combatted through strengthening *transaction governance capacity*, that is the simplification of the rules that regulate the public office. It is a common mistake, particularly in the Latin American countries, that highly detailed rules and regulations give objectivity to the processes. The cases of bribe analysed show the contrary: detailed rules curtail transparency and give power to the holder of public office as an 'expert' on those intricate rules and regulations.

It is not enough that broad and transparent rules and regulations are in place; even more important is that they are enforced. The situations of bribe reveal that in Latin America public office rules and regulations are extremely intricate but often poorly enforced—when this happens the voids left in formal institutions are filled by informal institutions such as societal culture. Societal culture determines, through customs and informally accepted ways of doing business, how the relationships between public office and the private sector work. The trouble is that in many countries in Latin America, as revealed by the CPI scores, societal culture accepts increasing levels of corruption as part of the way the world works. Experience shows that once that happens it is extremely difficult to recover, especially because societies frustrated by corruption tend to tackle the problem by replacing people rather than making systemic changes such as revising transaction governance capacity and making rules enforceable.

In the case of money laundering, combatting it is more focalised and needs to be done within the financial institution. Like combatting bribes, it requires developing an ethical corporate culture of performance with integrity in the bank, but in addition involves implementing clearly defined compliance processes and systems, and a compliance organisational unit with sufficient clout to ensure that the operational units abide by those processes and systems.

The study of the two money laundering cases shows how complicated it is to investigate these cases once they have been detected. By their very nature they involve multiple legal jurisdictions and apply a sophisticated three-stage process of cleaning black money by concealing audit trails to the origins of the funds. Although money laundering is a criminal offence that should be detected, chased and controlled by the state, governments have tacitly admitted that they are incapable of doing so and have pushed this responsibility onto banks. Banks get no benefit chasing money laundering and need to implement costly structures to carry out this duty. It is ironic that they are not compensated for this public duty when they get it right, and yet are severely fined when they fail!

From the two money laundering cases it can be seen that these phenomena can creep into the organisation bottom up as in the HSBC case where it all started in remote branch offices in Mexico without apparent knowledge by senior management in the initial stages, or it can do so top down with the knowledge of senior management as was the case at Danske Bank. It affects multiple stakeholder groups that vary from case to case, but two groups that seem to be common to all are the tax revenue offices of the countries whose citizens engage in the activity, and the shareholders of the bank whose dividends are reduced by fines that negatively impact their bottom line and whose assets are impacted by sharp drops in market valuation of the bank.

In both money laundering cases there are clear failures on the part of the Board of Directors. The Boards of both banks did not pay attention to clear early warnings from external sources that laundering could be happening at their bank. Neither did they question abnormally high flows of funds and contributions to profits, despite these signs sounding loud and clear in the financial statements. In both cases they turned a blind eye despite knowing that their banks did not have trustworthy compliance structures and methods in the locations where the money laundering was taking place.

Several clear lessons emerge from these cases on how Boards of Directors need to operate on governance in the knowledge economy. They need to monitor very carefully that the 'CEO vs Rank & File' relationship promotes an ethical corporate culture and one that preserves and increases the intellectual capital of the organisation. In particular, it needs to monitor that the bank's *structural capital* in the form of compliance processes and systems are implemented and abided by, as well as the *human capital* in the form of training their staff on compliance principles and processes. Interestingly, it emerges from the two money laundering cases that a corporate culture that promotes this *structural capital* contribute to building an ethical corporate culture.

Both money laundering cases refer to banks that have grown through acquisition, which leads to questioning if this was a factor that increased the opportunities for money laundering. Moreover, a powerful insight from these cases is that in the knowledge economy the business case for implementing corporate systems in newly acquired companies cannot be based purely on tangible benefits. The technology of the bank needs to be treated as a portfolio of ICT investments, with each category in the portfolio applying different qualitative criteria and risk assessments. Least of all can it depend exclusively on tangible benefits when the processes and system concerned refer to compliance. Boards need to bear in mind that compliance standards cannot be compromised depending on the size of the acquired subsidiary. If there are doubts in that respect, the decision needs to be escalated to one level. The decision cannot be whether or not to implement corporate standards; if there are doubts as to that, the question to be asked is whether the subsidiary should be kept or disposed of. It is also possible to define a two-tier standard of corporate systems consisting of using the corporate systems for the larger subsidiaries and a more agile approach, based on Regtech solutions,[12] for the smaller operations. But what cannot be compromised is the requirement to meet the highest standards in compliance.

Another important lesson from both the bribe situations and the money laundering cases, is that the Board of Directors in international banks needs to understand the societal culture of the regions where their subsidiaries operate. This understanding of the local societal culture should mediate to define to what degree the bank should operate in a *low context* or *high context* approach in that market. It should also help define the degree of power-sharing between the subsidiary and the corporate headquarters, and to what degree they can or need to adapt the corporate strategy to the local market. These are clearly governance decision that need to be discussed at Board level.

Finally, from the analysis of the four bribe situations emerge two interesting moral dilemmas that are not present in the case of money laundering. The first is whether there is an ethical difference between a private sector operator paying a public officer a bribe to obtain a benefit it would not have won legitimately, and paying a public office a bribe to unblock a benefit it has legitimately won. The other, less sophisticated, dilemma is whether it is valid for a multinational company to avoid bribe situations by selling to the state through independent local distributors, that is closing eyes and ears to what might be going on. Independently of the moral dilemmas, the responsibility of the Board is to protect the interests of the shareholders so, from that stance, it needs to assess the risk that any of these situations will have on the reputation of the company. This cross-case analysis is summarised in Table 5.1.

---

[12] By Regtech is meant the application of disruptive new technologies such as machine learning, distributed ledgers, business analytics to assisting banks meet their regulation compliance. Rather than the banks developing or buying these technology solutions, they normally outsource these services to smaller entrepreneurial companies that develop them.

Table 5.1 Synthesis of cross-case analysis

Factor/Case	Bribe situations	HSBC	Danske Bank
Corruption format	• Secretive • Hard to detect, normally through tip-off • Local actions and flows of cash • Very few people involved; all senior decision-makers • Public officer plays key role • Individual one-off approach	• Leaves footprint • Detectable through compliance processes • Cross-border actions and flows of cash • Multitude of 'footmen' involved in first stage; senior operators in stages two and three • Bank takes role of public office • Systemic approach	• Leaves footprint • Detectable through compliance processes • Cross-border actions and flows of cash • Direct participation limited to high net worth individuals and bank officers • Bank takes role of public office • Systemic approach
Stakeholder analysis	• Public interest affected; benefits diverted from public entities to corrupt officers (and private entities?)	• Mexican poor communities affected by growth of gang activity • US society affected by drug addiction • HSBC shareholders affected by fines that impact dividends and reputation impact that reduces market valuation	• Russian tax offices affected by revenue depletion • Danske shareholders affected by fines that impact dividends and reputation impact that reduces market valuation • Danske Estonia staff affected by harassment and then closure of subsidiary

Factor/Case	Bribe situations	HSBC	Danske Bank
Role of Board of Directors	• Boards of the participant private companies in some cases did not ensure a culture of 'performance with integrity'	• Board of HSBC did not ensure a culture of 'performance with integrity' • Board failed to pay attention to early warnings from external sources • Knew that the compliance structure in Mexico was weak and turned a blind eye	• Board of Danske Bank did not ensure a culture of 'performance with integrity' • Board failed to pay attention to early warnings from external sources • Failed to question abnormally high volumes of flow and profits • Knew that the compliance structure in Danske Estonia was weak and turned a blind eye
Combatting corruption	• Private sector: implement culture of 'performance with integrity' • Public sector: Implement transaction governance capacity by simplifying rules and enforcing them	• Implement culture of 'performance with integrity' • US regulation: Monitor suspect incoming flows	• Implement culture of 'performance with integrity' • Russian and Estonian regulators: Monitor suspect outgoing international flows

(continued)

Table 5.1 (continued)

Factor/Case	Bribe situations	HSBC	Danske Bank
Lessons for the Board of Directors on Governance in the Knowledge Economy	• Monitor carefully the 'CEO vs Rank & File' governance relationship to ensure that it achieves an ethical corporate culture that preserves and increases the intellectual capital of the organisation • Monitor that the bank's structural IC in the form of compliance processes and systems are implemented and complied with • A corporate culture that promotes the prior structural IC contributes to building an ethical corporate culture • Ensure that the bank's human IC in the form of staff training in compliance principles and processes is enhanced • IMPORTANT NOTE: Both HSBC and Danske bank grew by acquisition in the markets where money laundering occurred. Does this factor facilitate opportunities for money laundering? • In the knowledge economy the business case for implementing compliance systems at newly acquired units cannot be based purely on tangible benefits • If it is not worth implementing corporate systems in newly acquired units, consider disposing of them • Consider a two-tier corporate systems scheme for compliance, with a Regtech alternative for smaller units • When operating internationally, Boards need to understand the societal culture of the host countries and ensure that management is taking that into account for defining degree of power-sharing between subsidiary and corporate centre		
Ethical dilemmas that emerged	• Is there an ethical difference between paying a bribe to obtain an illegitimate benefit, or paying to unblock a benefit legitimately obtained? • Is it acceptable for a multinational to operate through an independent local distributor to sell to a state entity, and not monitor how that contract is obtained?		

Not only have governments tacitly declared themselves incapable of controlling money laundering as seen above; they have also declared themselves incapable of driving society towards a green economy. That is the subject of the next chapter.

REFERENCES

Bjerregaard, E., & Kirchmaier, T. (2019). *The Danske Bank money laundering scandal: A case study.* CBS Copenhagen Business School.

Bruun & Hjejle. (2018, September 19). *Report on the Non-Resident Portfolio at Danske Bank's Estonian branch.* Report commissioned by the Board of Danske Bank to Bruun & Hjejle legal firm.

Burgis, T., & Watkins, M. (2020, October 3). Silent witnesses. *FT Weekend Magazine*, pp. 14–19.

Friedman, M. (1970, September 13). The social responsibility of business is to increase its profits. *The New York Times*.

Heineman, B. W (2007, April). Avoiding integrity land mines. *Harvard Business Review*.

Hirschman, A. O. (1997[1977]). *The passions and the interests: Political arguments for capitalism before its triumph.* Princeton University Press.

Philp, M. (2006). Corruption definition and measurement. In C. Sampford, A. Shacklock, C. Connors & F. Galtung (Eds.), *Measuring corruption*. Ashgate Publishing Limited.

Prahalad, C. K. (2005). *The fortune at the bottom of the pyramid: Eradicating poverty through profits.* Wharton School Publishing.

Tapscott, D., & Ticoll, D. (2003). *The naked corporation: How the age of transparency will revolutionise business.* Free Press (Simon & Schuster, Inc).

CHAPTER 6

To be or Not to be: Principles for Responsible Banking

6.1 INTRODUCTION TO THE PRINCIPLES OF RESPONSIBLE BANKING

6.1.1 Overview

In this last chapter of the body of the book, there is a change in tack. While in the prior three chapters lessons in governance for the knowledge economy were extracted from some well-defined past experiences synthesised in a series of case studies, this chapter will focus on current developments that are also likely to condition banking governance in years to come. In Sect. 2.3 it was argued that one of the characteristics of the advent of the knowledge economy is that wealth has migrated from tangible to intangible assets; from material things to data as the buildings

---

The author is grateful to a group of his MSc Banking, Finance & Fintech students who in teams assisted in the research of the banks: L. Ayssi, J. Barre, A. Bosse-Platiere, C. Brosolo, R. Cizeau (Citi and Wells Fargo); S. Giacolletti, L. Laspeyres, K. Lawson Akpigo, T. Cudelou (MUFG and HSBC); T. Michaud, I. Sanogo, T. Thibault, C. Vermande, M. Wuensche (ICBC and JP Morgan Chase).

© The Author(s), under exclusive license to Springer Nature Switzerland AG 2021
P. D. R. Griffiths, *Corporate Governance in the Knowledge Economy*, Palgrave Studies in Accounting and Finance Practice,
https://doi.org/10.1007/978-3-030-78873-5_6

blocks of intellectual capital. With this comes the opportunity for organisations to relief pressure on physical resources and pursue sustainability. In Sect. 2.1 a four-dimensional framework of corporate responsibility was seen as the conceptual underpinning for sustainability, and three of these dimensions were amply discussed in the past three chapters. The one dimension that has been absent and will be the focus of this chapter is the environmental one: How do organisations integrate into their physical context? What is the role that banks can play to support society in its quest for environmental sustainability?

The UN-promoted Principles for Responsible Banking (PRBs) were launched by 132 banks from 49 countries, representing more than US$ 47 trillion in assets (or a third of the global industry) in New York City, during the annual United Nations General Assembly, on September 22 and 23, 2019. These PRBs, oriented at combating the climate crisis mainly by banks shifting their loan books away from fossil fuels as sources of energy,[1] were drawn out by UN officials and the representatives of 30 banks. It took over 18 months for the task force headed by Simone Dettling of the Geneva-based *United Nations Environment Protection—Finance Initiatives* (UNEP FI) to arrive at a final proposal. Illustrative of the difficulties met are that the principles have been defined as voluntary and non-binding, and that the signatories are given four years to flesh out their implementation plans.

The signatory banks commit through six principles to:

- Align their credit origination criteria with the 2015 Paris Agreement (COP-21) targets to contain and eventually reduce anthropogenic global warming.
- Set targets to increase 'positive impacts' and reduce 'negative impacts' on people and the environment.
- Work with their customers to encourage sustainable practices.
- Consult, engage and partner with relevant stakeholders to achieve society's goals.
- Implement their commitment to the Principles through developing effective governance and a corporate culture of responsible banking.
- Be transparent on how they report their progress and be accountable for outcomes.

---

[1] See https://www.unepfi.org/banking/bankingprinciples/.

Indeed, the agreement requires banks to consider the impact of their loans not only on their financial portfolio and loan book but also on society. These six principles have internal and external objectives; the first four focus on the external front and work towards using banks to entice their customers to adopt sustainable practices aligned with the COP-21 emissions reduction goals. On the internal front, the final two principles are about target setting and seeking to promote in banks effective corporate governance and a culture of responsible banking (i.e., mindfulness for stakeholders and greater transparency and accountability).

It will be contended that as they stand now, the *Principles of Responsible Banking* (PRB) are a toothless tiger. They are voluntary and non-binding. What is more important, by demanding the immediate and complete banning of finance to projects that are not green, it can be inferred that they disincentivise those banks that have a large client base in extractive, fossil fuels and other high-emissions industries to becoming signatories. If this is confirmed, the PRBs will be adopted by those banks with the least impact on curbing of greenhouse gas (GHG) emissions.

This chapter does three things. On the one hand, and in line with the previous chapters, it will analyse the characteristics and motivations of those banks that have become signatories, and those that have not, through the study of six cases presented in a brief synthesis. On the one hand, it will make the point that it would be far more effective for combatting the climate crisis to apply a loan book portfolio criterion with a roadmap to making the loan book greener. With that more flexible approach, it might be possible to bring more banks on board and make the principles, if not compulsory, at least binding. Finally, it will argue that once adopted, implementing the PRB poses significant challenges to overcome for which some guidelines are proposed.

6.1.2 History of Banks and the Climate Crisis

It is ironic that a set of principles on banking issued and agreed upon by a significant proportion of society, and the banks themselves, in a meeting held in New York in September 2019 should be called 'Principles of Responsible Banking'. What happened in the prior five hundred years of modern banking or even millennia since early banking activities started? Was banking not responsible then? Did society put up with irresponsible banking for all that time?

Reality is that the role of banks in society has expanded significantly over the years as society has put upon the players in a banking system many functions that originally were developed or should have been exercised by the State. In the early industrial economy the business of banking was business and their responsibility was financial towards their shareholders (Howard, 2014; Kusi et al., 2018); shortly afterwards, they also acquired fiduciary responsibility for the long-term financial health of another stakeholder group, their customers (Criddle, 2017; Demetriades, 2018; Kaufman, 2002; Martin, 2009; Shaikh et al., 2019).

In the transition from the industrial economy to the knowledge economy banks were given policing duties on fraud prevention; they served new stakeholder groups, the security forces and tax authorities, through activities such as 'Know your customer' (KYC), anti-money laundering (AML), suspicious activity reporting (SAR), bank secrecy act (BSA) and combating the funding of terrorism (CFT). Furthermore, in the early knowledge economy with the 'too big to fail' doctrine they were given responsibility to look after taxpayers money (Baker & McArthur, 2009; Kane, 2018; Massoc, 2020). This stakeholder-centred evolution of banking responsibility is summarized in Table 6.1.

Subsequently, as the knowledge economy progresses, bankers are given responsibility towards environmental authorities and NGOs for making it green by steering their investment portfolios away from environmentally unfriendly shares and doing environmental impact assessments of the application of their loans, and monitoring emissions mitigation activities of their clients (UN Environment, 2017).

The history of the engagement of banks with the climate crisis and climate risk initiatives is long and incremental, culminating in the recent Principles for Responsible Banking. The key milestones in this history are the following:

1991: The United Nations Environmental Protection Financial Initiative (UNEP FI) is launched with the participation of thirteen large banks such as DB, HSBC, Natwest, Royal Bank of Canada, Westpac.

1992: In the runup to the Rio Summit the UNEP Statement by Banks on the Environment and Sustainable Development is launched in New York.

1999: Both the Financial Institutions Initiative (FII) and the Insurance Institution Initiative came together to work more closely under the banner of UNEP FI and three working groups are created: Climate

Table 6.1 A stakeholder view of the evolution of responsibility in banking

ERA	Stakeholders	Responsibility	Activity	Key References
Early Industrial Economy: 'The business of banking is business'	Shareholders Clients	Financial Fiduciary	Maximise profits Pursue long-term financial health of Clients	Kusi et al. (2018); Howard (2014); Criddle (2017); Demetriades (2018); Kaufman (2002); Martin (2009); Shaikh et al. (2019)
Later Industrial Economy: 'TBTF'	Shareholders Customers Taxpayer	Financial Fiduciary Fiduciary	Maximise profits Pursue long-term financial health of Clients Protect taxpayers from need for bail-out	Baker & McArthur (2009); Kane (2018); Massoc (2020)
Transition from Industrial to Knowledge Economy: 'Policing'	Shareholders Customers Taxpayer Security Forces Fiscal Authorities	Financial Fiduciary Fiduciary Fraud prevention	Maximise profits Pursue long-term financial health of Clients Protect taxpayers from need for bail-out KYC, AML, SAR, BSA, CFT	Bergstrom et al. (2011); Chong & Lopez-De-Silanes (2015); Hartsink (2018); Joseph & Roth (2008); Marsh (2019); Metzger & Paulowitz (2018)

Change Group, Asset Management Group and Environmental Management and Reporting Group. That same year the UNEP FI North America support team is formed to assist US financial institutions operationalise sustainability goals.

2003: At COP-9 UNEP FI highlighted achievements on raising awareness among financial institutions on the issue of climate change and launched the creation of the Sustainable Energy Financial Initiative (SEFI) and the group's publication 'CEO Briefing on Emissions Trading.'

2008: The financial crisis prompted toughening of regulations demanding that banks capitalise and meet higher liquidity standards. In the US it was the Dodd-Frank Act and for international banking the new regulations were materialised in BIS III. These new standards emphasise the management of risk and introduce the concept of climate risk. Large institutional investors stated the need for Environmental, Social and Governance (ESG) standards in the companies they invested in and that they should become better long-term stewards.

2010: The Equator Principles (EPs) were proposed. It is a risk management framework adopted by the Equator Principles Financial Institutions, an unincorporated association of banks, for determining, assessing and managing environmental and social risk in projects. The EPs apply globally to all financial sectors and to four financial products: Project Finance Advisory Services, Project Finance, Project-related Corporate Loans, and Bridge Loans.[2]

2015: In the runup to COP-21 (Paris Agreement) UNEP FI conducted a study exploring the role that banking regulation can play in the transition to a green economy, and with the Financial Stability Board began to develop environmental impact guidelines for banks and the programme that emerged is known as the Task Force for Climate-Related Financial Disclosures (TCFD).

2016: Following COP-21 nearly twenty lending banks and investors (representing a total of $ 6.6 trillion in assets) launched the high-level UNEP FI Principles of Positive Impact Finance on how banks can contribute to achieving the UN Sustainable Development Goals (SDG).

2018: The TCFD began to pilot a programme for implementation with 16 partner banks, and participating banks started doing gap analyses on their existing climate-related programmes based on the TCFD guidelines.

2019: Following the UN General Assembly and within the frame of the Climate Week, the Principles of Responsible Banking were launched, developed by thirty banks under the auspices of UNEP FI and 132 signatory banks expressed they would abide by them, but rather symbolically because the Principles are voluntary and non-binding. This is summarised graphically in Fig. 6.1.

So, it took nearly 28 years to get to these Principles. The question is whether they will be adopted by banks as a core component of the

---

[2] See https://equator-principles.com/.

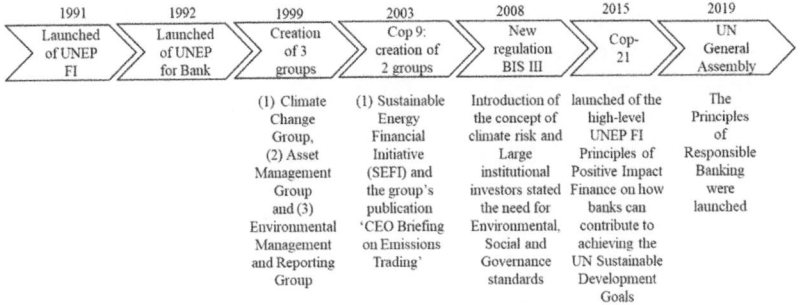

Fig. 6.1 History of banks' engagement with the environment (Griffiths & Baudier, 2021)

corporate governance, and if they do, whether they will really make a change in society and lead to the curbing of GHG emissions in line with the targets set by COP-21. The next section deals on the positive drivers for their adoption.

6.2 Drivers for Adoption

According to UNEP FI's website,[3] in the first year since the launch of the PRB, an additional 39 banks joined, making the total number of signatories 171; and since then to February 2021, another 29 came on board, taking the total to 200 (UNEP Financial Activity, 2020b). As will be seen in Sect. 6.4.2, becoming a signatory has a negative short-term impact on profits as it generates additional costs such as setting up the processes for environmental impact assessment of project loans, and leads to revenue loss from what would traditionally be considered low risk credit (e.g., financing an oil- or coal-burning power station). So, what do signatories see as mid- to long-term drivers for adopting the principles?

An interesting fact is that as exposed by Bloomberg[4] of the top ten banks in the world by market capitalisation, only three are signatories: Citigroup Inc., Mitsubishi UFJ Financial Group (MUFG), and Industrial

---

[3] As of September 3, 2020.

[4] See 'Biggest Banks Sit Out New Industry Commitment on Climate Goals' Kishan, Saijel, Chasan, Emily, Bloomberg.com, 9/22/2019. https://www.bloomberg.com/news/articles/2019-09-22/biggest-banks-sit-out-new-industry-commitment-on-climate-goals.

and Commercial Bank of China (ICBC). Each of these will be reviewed in turn to see what is driving them and compare them to find possible commonalities.

6.2.1 Citibank

Citibank is a global bank, founded in 1812. Its name has evolved over the last 210 years; it was formerly known as the City Bank of New York and later as the First National City Bank of New York. Citibank is controlled by Citigroup, one of the largest financial groups in the world. The bank has 2649 branches in 19 countries, including 723 branches in the United States and 1494 branches in Mexico where it is operated by its subsidiary Banamex, a market leader in that country. The U.S. branches are concentrated in six metropolitan areas: New York City, Chicago, Los Angeles, San Francisco, Washington, DC, and Miami. Aside from the U.S. and Mexico, most of the company's branches are in Poland, Russia, India and the United Arab Emirates. Citibank has approximately 200 million customer accounts and does business in more than 160 countries and jurisdictions. Citi provides consumers, corporations, governments and institutions with a broad range of financial products and services, including consumer banking and credit, corporate and investment banking, securities brokerage, transaction services, and wealth management Citigroup Governance (2021).

Citibank has been part of the United Nations Environment Programme Finance Initiative since 1997 and endorsed the Principles for Responsible Banking that have been facilitated by the UNEP FI and it became the first major U.S bank to do so.

In its *Environmental and Social Policy Framework* (July 2020)[5] Citigroup claims to be highly committed to combatting the climate crisis, despite being 'one of the largest financiers of carbon-intensive sectors such as oil & gas, power and industrials' and admits that it will not be easy to bring their business and the global economy into alignment with COP-21 objectives. It describes its three pillars as, first, *Low-Carbon Transition* through which it pledges to accelerate the transition to a low-carbon economy through its $250 billion environmental finance goal by 2025. Its second pillar is *Climate Risk* with the objective to measure, manage

---

[5] See https://www.citigroup.com/citi/sustainability/data/Environmental-and-Social-Policy-Framework.pdf?ieNocache=359.

Table 6.2 Signatories ranking table of fossil fuel financing since the Paris agreement—in billion US dollars (extracted from Banking on Climate Change, 2020)

Bank	Ranking	2016	2017	2018	2019	Total
Citi	3	43.066	46.090	46.101	52.409	187.666
MUFG	6	25.640	27.056	33.879	32.235	118.811
ICBC	18	19.307	13.731	15.196	20.706	68.940

and reduce the climate risk and impact of its client portfolio. Finally, *Sustainable Operation* aims at reducing the environmental footprint of its facilities and strengthen its sustainability culture.

Citigroups' second and third pillars are challenging but do not generate conflicts of interest between its commitment to the environment and its need for financial performance. However, in terms of *Low-Carbon Transition* it expresses as exclusionary criteria for financing new projects that they are large scale hydropower plants that have a generation capacity of over 25 MW, or that they are fossil fuel projects, including refined or alternative coal technologies, gas-to-liquid projects and natural gas projects. Citi is heavily involved in financing the shale oil and gas fracking industry, which is seen as highly detrimental to the environment in many ways other than GHG emissions.[6] It is also unfavourable for its balance sheet at this time (Reuters, 2020). Moreover, in the period since the signing of the Paris agreement on climate change and 2019, Citi has remained third in the league table on financiers to the fossil fuel sector (see Table 6.2).

In the final analysis, Citibank has defined public objectives linked to the attainment of sustainable development and expresses with deeds its intention to show that it is possible to make the banking industry an industry that is respectful towards the environment. In the first year of the PRBs there have not been too many tough decisions to make, but it will be interesting to observe going forwards how it manages to disengage from some of the overly sensitive sectors with which it is involved.

---

[6] See Fracking Fiasco: New report names Wells Fargo and JPMorgan Chase as main players funding U.S. shale bust—Oil Change International (priceofoil.org).

6.2.2 Mitsubishi UFJ Financial Group (MUFG)

MUFG is the leading global financial service group in Japan and among the ten largest banking institutions in the world on market capitalisation. The group states that its goal is to be the world's most trusted financial services group, which is an ambitious statement to live up to. MUFG has indeed been actively involved with sustainability over the last few decades, and its endorsement of the responsible banking principles is engrained into its strategy formulation, which states its strategic objectives in terms of sustainable development goals and ESG oriented investment. By the latter it means to choose investments following certain criteria such as how sensitive business models are to the environment and social concern, as well as the robustness of governance standards.

MUFG explains its commitment to the environment in its *For Environment* statement.[7] This is a brief document that expands on the TCFD recommendations and the Equator Principles but makes no mention to PRB. It presents seven streams of activity that could probably be consolidated into the three pillars stated by Citigroup plus an interesting fourth one developed by its securities arm on consulting services to measure and help reduce GHG emissions under the Clean Development Mechanism (CDM), applying U.N. procedures to create certified emission reduction credits and develop the necessary methodology to quantify GHG emission reduction. Having this expertise in place is a significant advantage for incorporating environmental impact assessment in its project finance origination and monitoring of GHG emissions mitigation activities by its clients throughout the life cycle of its loans.

On the support for clean energy front, MUFG states that it is acting as project finance arranger and lender for solar, wind and geothermal power generation projects and that through such initiatives it serves as a driving force behind the dissemination of renewable energy around the world. It also claims that, thanks to this, in 2017 and 2018 they were able to secure first place in the global ranking of financial institutions serving as lead arrangers in financing for renewable energy projects.

MUFG reinforces its commitment to responsible banking by setting up what appears to be an appropriate governance structure. Indeed, it has created a corporate social responsibility committee that reports straight

---

[7] See https://www.mufg.jp/english/csr/environment/business/index.html.

into the executive committee and is linked to all the divisions of the institution. Moreover, the group states to be stimulated and in synch with the Japanese government's effort to develop sustainability.

In terms of stakeholder management, there is no specific mention on how MUFG manages the conflict of interest between its commitment to the environment and the expectations of its shareholders in terms of returns on their investment. And, in fact, there are third party reports (Banking on Climate Change, 2020) that find that in the four years between the signing of the Paris agreements on climate change and 2019, MUFG is ranked the 6th biggest fossil fuel financier in the world, exceeding that of non-PRB signatories in its league, such as HSBC (see Table 6.2). So, on the one hand the group is publicly stating their intention to restrict financing GHG-emitting activities, but on the other hand they continue doing so in fossil fuels. While their strategy is driven towards sustainability, their financial activities are still heavily tied to those sensitive sectors. As shown by their fossil fuel involvement, a big challenge for PRB signatories such as MUFG is how will they manage to live up to their expressed engagement.

6.2.3 Industrial and Commercial Bank of China Ltd (ICBC)

With a market capitalisation of close to US$ 300 billion ICBC is the largest bank in China by this measure.[8] Over one-third of its shares are held by the Chinese state, which gives the government a strong lever to act upon green finance. The bank defines itself as one of the greenest banks in the world, aspiring to lead the green transition in finance. According to ICBC's Corporate Social Responsibility report its responsible orientation was adopted in 2007 by incorporating the performance of social responsibilities into its corporate vision (Industrial and Commerce Bank of China, 2007).

ICBC has been involved with the developing the PRB from the outset of the process in 2018. Among UNEP FI's 129 member banks, ICBC and Standard Bank formed the core group to steer the process of development of the principles with another 28 banks. According to ICBC the reason is that.

---

[8] World's Top Banks by Market Capitalization 2020 (advratings.com). Accessed 24 February 2021.

at present, as the climate and environmental issues are getting more and more acute, it has become the common goal and responsibility of global financial institutions to promote the financing for the development of green economy. (Industrial and Commerce Bank of China, 2019)

It also coincides and is aligned with some clear Chinese government policies, which may be the key drivers for the adoption of PRB. On the one hand, in 2018 Mr. Xi Jinping, the Chinese president, committed to cap greenhouse gas emissions by 2030 and to reach a net zero level by 2060, stressing the need for a green revolution, which appears impossible to reach without a responsible banking system. Quoting Mr. Inger Andersen, Executive Director UN Environment Programme, 'If finance will not move, the world will not move' (UNEP Finance Activity, 2020a). On the other hand, China is one of Africa's largest trading partners and is accused of dragging Africa down the road of debt overhang. Indeed, China does not grant official development assistance because it considers itself a developing country and is accused of opaque deals and the strategic use of debt to keep African states captive to its demands. It is, thus, reasonable to believe that ICBC's involvement with the PRB is aimed at improving the country's image and reputation. In line with its stated quest to become a green finance leader, ICBC claims to have developed a responsibility and incentive mechanism, which helps to identify any risks and ensure the enforcement of policies to promote its progress in green finance. More specifically, it claims to be implementing whole process management and a one-vote veto system through which it will embed the requirements of green finance in front, middle and back-office business processes; explore to include environmental and social risk factors in the customer/project risk assessment system; strengthen monitoring, identification, mitigation and control of environmental and social risk indicators; and, finally, exercise a green finance one-vote veto system throughout the whole process (ICBC, 2019). The one-vote veto system gives the bank the possibility to downgrade the financial activities of a client that has not adhered to the agreed requirements. Bank Directors in the regions have the right to use their veto, after monitoring and identifying the social and environmental risks of their clients.

ICBC states that in 2018 it issued the 'Risk Prompt on Financing Involved in Environmental Protection Supervision and Policy Adjustment', requiring all branches to raise environmental protection standards for customers from key industries and regions, strictly implement the 'one-vote veto system for environmental protection', observe the bottom line of environmental and social risk compliance, and strengthen risk management and control over high-risk customers.

The Special Report on Green Finance (ICBC, 2019) gives a detailed description on governance of environmental affairs at ICBC, and under the title of 'Strictly observing the bottom line of environmental and social risk compliance' it holds that the companies/projects financed by ICBC 'shall comply with the laws, regulations and regulatory requirements of host countries (regions) on environmental protection, land, health and safety'. It adds that ICBC will strictly abide by constraints on local ecological protection, environmental quality and the utilisation of resources. It is gratifying to see that ICBC proposes to abide by the law and regulations, but it does not develop how it will implement its commitment to the PRB—by all logic these go far beyond the minimum requirements of the dated laws that rule the land.

As in the cases of Citi and MUFG, ICBC's stated commitment to the PRB has not been accompanied by a reduction in financing fossil fuel initiatives, as it ranks 18th in the fossil fuel financing global league table (see Table 6.2). More seriously, it heads, with three other Chinese banks, the global rankings for financing coal mining and for financing coal power generation plants (Banking on Climate Change, 2020).

6.2.4 Synthesising the drivers for PRB adoption from the analysis of the three cases, it appears that the driver for adoption of PRB by these large banks is the pursuit of reputation through working towards addressing the climate crisis for which there is increasing conscientiousness around the world. This requires managing a conflict between the interest of society for creating a greener economy and that of its shareholders to maximise returns on their investment. However, this conflict is diminished by two factors. The first is that shareholders are coming round to accept that it is in the long-term interest of the bank and therefore of their investment to keep the climate risk under control. The other factor is that because the PRB are non-binding the bank has some flexibility to reduce its revenue loss by serving clients on environmentally marginal projects in the safety that UNEP FI will not apply its rules of expulsion too harshly on these flagship signatories. Proof of this is that the three banks studied have not diminished, and in fact increased their financing of fossil fuels in the four years that followed that Paris climate change agreement. The pressure has been low on this front as UNEP FI has spent the first year of adoption of the PRBs to develop its internal PRB governance processes rather than monitoring the signatories' real progress, and as the signatory banks have four years from the date of enrolment to flesh out their PRB plans.

The next section analyses three of the top ten banks by market capitalisation that did not enrol on the PRBs to see if there are any commonalities.

6.3 Reasons to Refrain from Adopting

The three top-10 banks by market capitalisation selected for not having signed up onto the PRB initiative are JP Morgan Chase, HSBC and Wells Fargo. This section will summarise case studies on each of them to understand why they have not signed up.

6.3.1 *JP Morgan Chase*

JP Morgan Chase, with over US$ 434 billion in market capitalisation[9] is the largest bank in the world on that measure. It is a universal bank that has grown to its current size through the absorption of over 1200 predecessors, among which are many venerable names in the banking industry such as J.P. Morgan & Co., The Chase Manhattan Bank, Bank One, Manufacturers Hanover Trust Co., Chemical Bank, The First National Bank of Chicago, National Bank of Detroit, The Bear Stearns Companies Inc., Robert Fleming Holdings, Cazenove Group and pat of what was Washington Mutual. It can trace its roots to 1799 in New York City as the Manhattan Water Company that opened a bank shortly after its foundation. It has a history with interesting connections such as the creation of the 'greenback' through the Legal Tender act of 1853 and of the Federal Reserve system in 1913; it played a leading role in financing the US railroads in the nineteenth century and the Panama Canal in 1904.[10]

Bloomberg states that JP Morgan Chase declined to comment on why they were not signatories to the PRB. Despite not signing up the bank revealed an interest for sustainability in October 2020 with the launch of a Paris Agreement aligned financing programme (J.P. Morgan Chase & Co, 2021a, b). This programme includes:

---

[9] See ADV World's Top Banks by Market Capitalization 2020 (advratings.com).
[10] See History of Our Firm (jpmorganchase.com).

- The launching of a Center for Carbon Transition (CCT) which is intended to provide corporate clients access to sustainable financing.
- Reaching carbon neutrality in its own operations by expanding its goals of renewable energy at 100%.

In its Environmental and Social Policy Framework (as of February 2020)[11] it also explicitly expresses climate-related activities it will not finance or invest in. It prohibits financing the development of greenfield coal mines and financing companies who derive most of their revenue from the extraction of coal; in fact, it goes further by pledging to phase out its credit exposure to this type of company by 2024. It also prohibits financing new coal-fired power plants unless they include carbon capture and sequestration technology in which case, they will be analysed case by case. It also prohibits financing oil and gas production activity in the Arctic and companies that engage in even more extreme activities such as illegal logging, wild animal trafficking and using uncontrolled fires for clearing land for farming.

JP Morgan Chase has defined enhanced review criteria for other sensitive sectors and activities such as hydraulic fracturing for extraction of shale oil and as oil sand development, where particular attention is paid to the technologies applied and the effects on water discharge, air pollution and ecosystems. Or transactions involving the construction of dams for hydroelectric power projects with more than 20 MW of installed capacity or dams for other purposes where the dam wall is greater than 10 m high. (J.P. Morgan Chase & Co, 2021c)

It will be interesting to see how JP Morgan Chase keeps to all these commitments taken up in 2020 considering that in the four years from the Paris agreement until 2019 it was the overall leader in fossil fuel financing (see Table 6.4) and is top of the league in four fossil fuel categories (see Table 6.3) and among the top in several others (BankTrack, 2020; OilChange International, 2020). It was also involved in financing the $400 million Gilgel Gibe Dam on the Omo River in Ethiopia, a controversial project that violates the UNEP FI principles due to its magnitude and that it does not contribute to sustainable development.

---

[11] See https://about.jpmorganchase.com/content/dam/jpmc/jpmorgan-chase-and-co/documents/environmental-and-social-policy-framework.pdf.

Table 6.3 Categories in which JP Morgan Chase heads the league table of fossil fuel financiers since the Paris Agreement—in billion US dollars (extracted from Banking on Climate Change, 2020)

Category	2016	2017	2018	2019	Total
Fossil Fuel Expansion	31.632	21.519	22.802	26.351	102.304
Fracking Shale Oil	10.480	10.124	12.190	10.436	43.231
Offshore Oil & Gas	6.195	3.453	2.389	6.799	19.556
Artic Oil & Gas	0.372	0.502	0.457	0.377	1.708

Table 6.4 Non-signatories ranking table of fossil fuel financing since the Paris Agreement—in billion US dollars (extracted from Banking on Climate Change, 2020)

Bank	Ranking	2016	2017	2018	2019	Total
JP Morgan Chase	1	63.986	70.654	69.028	64.925	268.593
Wells Fargo	2	35.504	54.931	63.237	45.242	197.914
HSBC	12	17.814	22.319	18.847	26.549	86.528

6.3.2 HSBC

The HSBC corporation has already been introduced in Sect. 5.3 as the seventh largest bank in the world by market capitalisation (i.e., US$ 169.47 billion) and the largest in Europe by both market capitalisation and assets (i.e., US$ 2.7 trillion). Despite not being a signatory of the PRB, there is evidence to support that awareness for the environment is incorporated into its strategy. Indeed, the concepts of sustainable finance and climate sustainability are major objectives in the group's strategy formulation and explicit governance policies and the bank has received external recognition for performance in this space as are The Banker 2020 Investment Banking award in three categories[12]:

- Investment Bank of the Year for Sustainability in its 2020
- Investment Bank of the Year for Sustainable SSA (Sovereigns, Supranationals and Agencies) Financing

---

[12] Awards | HSBC Holdings plc.

- Investment Bank of the Year for Green/Climate Action Bonds.

According to the group's Code of Conduct Ethics and the Environment the aim of the bank is to achieve net zero in its own operations and supply chain by 2030 or sooner and it commits to using the Paris Agreement Capital Transition Assessment (PACTA) tool to develop clear and measurable ways to achieve net zero GHG emissions. It also expresses its will to collaborate with others, such as its peers, central banks and industry bodies, to mobilise the financial system around a globally consistent standard for measuring GHG emissions, and developing an effective carbon-offset market. Furthermore, it commits to making regular and transparent disclosure in its progress in line with guidelines set out by the Taskforce on Climate-related Financial Disclosures guidelines, the already cited financial industry body that sets the standards for environmental disclosures, and to encourage its customers to do the same.

HSBC has a website titled 'Sustainable finance'[13] where it articulates its five pledges to be committed to the UN sponsored COP-21 target emission reductions. These pledges include providing US$ 100 billion in financing and investment to develop clean energy and low-carbon technologies by 2025; sourcing 100 percent of its energy from 'renewable' sources by 2030 with an interim target of 90 percent by 2025; reducing its exposure to thermal coal and actively managing the transition path for other high-carbon emitting sectors; adopting the recommendations of the TCFD; and lead and shape the debate around sustainable finance.

Digging deeper into HSBC's third pledge, that is reducing exposure to thermal coal, what it really means is 'discontinuing finance to new thermal coal mines and new customers dependent on thermal coal mining'. The emphasis here is on *new*, meaning it will not terminate support to current projects or current clients, but will work towards a less carbon-exposed loan portfolio going forward. However, there is no mention to the PRB.

With respect to its fifth pledge, to lead and shape the debate around sustainably finance, the bank is one of the founding members of the Climate Finance Leadership Initiative formed by Michael Bloomberg, UN Special Envoy for Climate Action. In this context, it states that

---

[13] See https://www.hsbc.com/our-approach/building-a-sustainable-future/sustainable-finance.

since 2015 it is working to bring together all the players in its portfolio to reduce GHG emissions in their activities and investments, and prioritising in its credit and financing decisions, companies with clear projects and intentions to reduce their GHG impact on the environment. During the same year, the bank issued its first green bond, raising €500 million to fund projects in the following sectors: cleaner transportation, climate change adaptation, energy efficiency, sustainable land use, waste and water management, renewable energy. Two years later, in 2017, the bank succeeded in mobilising US$ 1 billion dedicated to support the UN's SDGs through the issuance of a bond, that is claims to be the first of this type.

With respect to its internal management, HSBC claims success in reducing its total GHG emissions from 1 million tonnes of CO_2 equivalent in 2011 to just over half that in 2019; and its emissions per employee from 3.7 tonnes CO_2 equivalent per full-time equivalent employee (FTE) in 2012 to 2.3 tonnes of CO_2 equivalent/FTE in 2019 (ESG Update, 2019).

In terms of actual financing of the fossil fuels industry since the Paris agreement on the climate crisis and 2019, HSBC is twelfth on the global league table (see Table 6.4) and with a trendline that shows robust growth in the period.

6.3.3   Wells Fargo

Wells Fargo has been introduced in Sect. 3.3, but as a reminder and complement to that, it is a diversified, community-based financial services company, headquartered in San Francisco, California and has 7200 branch offices I its home country, Canada, the Northern Mariana Islands and the Caribbean. It serves 70 million customers of which over one-third are active mobile banking users.

Wells Fargo & Company was in New York on March 18, 1852 by Henry Wells and William Fargo. With its current close to US$ 2 trillion in assets and US$ 100 billion market capitalisation it is the third largest US bank. It is a universal bank with business in corporate banking, investment banking, wealth management, brokerage and pension fund management and, as seen in Chapter 3, it is heavily involved in retail and commercial banking with a broad offering of products and services. Wells Fargo declares to be committed to fulfilling its corporate responsibility by supporting diversity and social inclusion to ensure meeting the increasingly diverse needs of its customer base and to ensure that all of its employees are respected and have equal access to opportunities. Wells Fargo also expresses to support economic empowerment, by acting to strengthen economic opportunities in underserved communities to improve well-being and quality of life. On the environmental front, it says to be committed to acting effectively to accelerate the transition to a low-carbon economy and reduce the effects of climate change, 'by integrating its entire ecosystem'.

In this line, Wells Fargo's leadership states to believe that climate change continues to be one of the most urgent environmental and social issues of our time and says that it is working across the bank's value chain to help accelerate the transition to a low-carbon economy and reduce the impacts of climate change on its business, communities, employees, and customers.[14] In 2018 it announced that by 2030 it will have provided US$ 200 billion in financing sustainable businesses and projects, with more than half focussed on transactions that directly contribute to what it calls the *Clean Trillion* (e.g., renewable energy, green buildings, green bonds, alternative transportation), and the remainder on companies and projects focussed on sustainable agriculture, conservation, recycling, resource management, and other environmentally beneficial activities. It claims that by the close of 2019, Wells Fargo's tax equity projects represented 10.3 percent of all solar and wind generation capacity installed in the U.S. since January 2006.

In terms of climate change, Wells Fargo explicitly supports the principles of COP-21 including the goal of 2050 limiting the increase in global average temperature to below 2 degrees Celsius above pre-industrial levels. It says to be building a robust, centralised approach that seeks to integrate near- and long-term climate-related risk and opportunity considerations into decision-making (Wells Fargo, 2021).

Wells Fargo claims to have been the first bank to launch a blog to report on itd environmental management and ask for feedbacks from its stakeholders. It has committed to reducing its absolute greenhouse gas emissions from its American operations and has some external validation as it was awarded in 2013 the EPA Center for Corporate Climate Leadership the Climate Leadership Award, in the category of 'Excellence in Greenhouse Gas Management'. It also claims that same year Wells

---

[14] See https://www.wellsfargo.com/about/corporate-responsibility/environment/.

Fargo originated in excess of US$ 6 billion in funding for environmental business opportunities.

Despite this positive rhetoric and some achievements, Wells Fargo is the second largest financier for the fossil fuels sector in the four years from the Paris agreement on the climate crisis to 2019, as shown in Table 6.4 (BankTrack, 2020; OilChange International, 2020).

6.3.4 Synthesis of Reasons to Refrain from Signing

From looking at the declarations of these three banks, it emerges that in all cases their pledges are strongly aligned with the PRB, and hardly differ from the pledges made by the three banks analysed in the previous section that did sign onto PRB. So, why have these banks not adhered to PRB? If the justifications that a bank gives for becoming a signatory are to be taken with some scepticism, this is even more so for justifications for having not signed.

While the signatory bankers, UN officials and international government representatives were all congratulating themselves at the UN General Assembly gathering in New York in September 2019, for having reached the instance of signing PRB, the UN Assistant Secretary General Satya Tripathi is reported to have said at one of the panel discussions that the reluctance of some banks to commit is a signal that the principles have teeth and that some banks are not ready to be held accountable for their lending. This sounds more like exultation of the moment, than reality. The non-binding clause has made this tiger to be born toothless and it will be short-lived if something is not done about that.

There seems to be significant coincidence in the three banks analysed of scaling down coal mining and coal-burning power plants, but reticence in doing so with oil and gas: hydrocarbons are still very much the present and will remain so for the foreseeable future. Indeed, electric energy output from coal will peak in 2026, but gas-based power generation is projected to grow at a modest but consistent 0.6 percent year on year until 2050.[15] And although all the banks analysed pledge to promote renewable energy projects, there are not that many opportunities in this sector today. According to Bloomberg NEF only three firms in the S&P 500, making up 1 percent of the index's market capitalisation, are fully

---

[15] See https://about.bnef.com/new-energy-outlook/.

in this business, and even among private equity and venture capital firms, only US$ 11 billion was invested in non-fossil fuels in 2019. Looking ahead, projections are that between now and 2050 an expansion of 12 TW of generating capacity will be needed, requiring some US$ 13.3 trillion of which some 77 percent will go to non-fossil fuels, but take up will be gradual so banks need to properly time their transition. It is believed that it is this timing issue that is making these three banks unforthcoming to sign up for PRB at present. But it still remains to be answered why this affects JP Morgan Chase, HSBC and Wells Fargo, but not Citi, MUFG and ICBC?

Looking at the data, the signatories hold positions 3, 6 and 18th in absolute values of financing fossil fuels, during the 2016–2019 post Paris agreement period; while the non-signatories occupy positions 1, 2 and 12. There may be a pattern here, but why does Citi appear to be prepared to reduce fossil fuel financing and not HSBC? An explanation could be that fossil fuels weigh more in HSBC's loan book than in Citi's. So, the next step is to analyse the fossil fuel financing in the period 2016–2019 with respect to total assets, for the six banks. To make the assets comparable to the period of the flow of fossil fuel financing, the average assets between December 2015 and 2019 are taken. This is shown in Table 6.5 and some interesting information emerges.

As can be observed, the banks are now sorted by ratio of fossil fuel financing and the only change with respect to absolute values is that Wells

Table 6.5 Fossil fuel financing as a proportion of total assets

Bank	Assets 2015 (US$B)	Assets 2019 (US$B)	Asset average period (AvAsset) (US$B)	Fossil fuel finance (FFF) (US$B)	Ranking by FFF	FFF/AvAsset (%)
Wells Fargo	1787.63	1927.56	1857.60	197.91	2	10.7
JPMC	2351.70	2697.38	2524.54	268.59	1	10.6
Citi	1731.21	1951.16	1841.19	187.67	3	10.2
MUFG	2458.74	2892.97	2675.86	118.81	6	4.4
HSBC	2409.66	2715.15	2562.41	86.53	12	3.4
ICBC	3420.57	4324.27	3872.42	68.94	18	1.8

Note Data on assets is obtained from S&P (2020) and SAP (2016)

Fargo overtakes JP Morgan Chase by a marginal amount. Interestingly, fossil fuels weigh significantly more in the three American banks than in the remaining ones. But the question persists: this analysis does not explain why Citi is a signatory and HSBC is not.

6.4 Operational Challenges

6.4.1 The Long Tail of Environmental Sustainability

The PRBs are specifically about banks assessing the effect of their loans on GHG emissions. The signatory banks commit to not lending money to environmentally compromising through high GHG emissions projects for which the bank needs to perform an environmental impact assessment and estimation of its carbon footprint; this is not trivial. The *Greenhouse Gas Protocol* establishes three components of carbon footprint.

What the *Protocol* calls *Scope One* refers to direct emissions by the recipient of the loan (i.e., the company's own operation and processes).

Scope Two refers to the emissions of the utility company that supplies them with electric power (i.e., if they are based on coal generation that has a huge impact; if it is based on renewables then emissions are lower; and if it is on nuclear, lower still).

And *Scope Three* refers to the whole value chain, that is the suppliers down to extraction of raw materials, and the emissions of consumers when they use the product—so, for example, if the recipient of the loan is a car manufacturer, it must account for emissions from the iron ore and coal miners and steel smelters, through to the emissions of the consumers when they use their cars. As can be imagined, the company requesting the loan will commit to carrying out mitigation activities throughout the whole life cycle of the project (e.g., some of the relevant mitigation activities will be at the decommissioning stage of the project) and the bank is responsible that this is complied with. How does the bank keep track that those mitigation activities are executed and maintained throughout the life cycle of the project? This is not a minor issue either.

There are also difficulties in measurement and reporting. It is undeniable that corporate reporting on sustainability has increased dramatically over the last few years as shown in Fig. 6.1 however, many studies confirm that corporate reporting on sustainability is based on highly idiosyncratic *ESG* indicators calculated by external consultants in a relatively non-standard and often opaque way. This is corroborated by the

European Banking Authority (EBA) when it calls for 'promoting internationally consistent disclosures of key metrics Green Asset Ratios to support the identification, assessment and measurement of sustainability financial risks'. So, this means that sustainability reporting is unreliable for bankers and portfolio managers to compare initiatives across companies, and thus is not a trustworthy tool to manage their loan book or fund portfolio. Notwithstanding, there are some promising efforts to develop standard and transparent tools for this purpose, such as *TPI* that was awarded the *2020 ESG Assessment Tool of the Year* at the *Sustainable Investment Awards*, hosted by Environmental Finance.[16] The EBA is also looking in this direction and claims for a 'robust, evidence-based regulatory framework' (EBA, 2020). It argues for a single EU data platform of ESG-related information to support evidence-based decision-making (Fig. 6.2).

Companies have relative control over *Scope One* emissions by changing their internal processes or by outsourcing them. They have also some control over *Scope Two* by changing their energy suppliers to cleaner-based ones. But they have little control over *Scope Three*: they need to work with their suppliers to reduce supply chain emissions and change their products (which is arguably even more difficult) to reduce consumer emissions. Very few publicly traded companies report their *Scope Three* emission, but the good news is that these are highly concentrated. This is corroborated by *Climate Action 100+* that monitors 100 systemically important emitters that it claims account for two-thirds of annual industrial emissions plus another 60 that have leverage to drive the energy transition.[17]

So, the adoption of PRB has significant operational challenges that banks must overcome in order to take their role in greening the economy seriously. They must change their internal processes of credit origination to include the environmental impact assessment and GHG emissions measurement, and they must create the tools to be able to monitor emissions mitigations activities on the part of their clients, for the whole life cycle of the project.

---

[16] The *Transition Pathway Initiative* (TPI) is a global, asset-owner led intiative which asseses companies' preparedness for the transition to a low carbon economy (https://www.transitionpathwayinitiative.org/).

[17] Climate Action 100+ (http://www.climateaction100.org/) is an investor initiative to ensure the largest emitters of corporate GHGs take action in respect to the climate crisis.

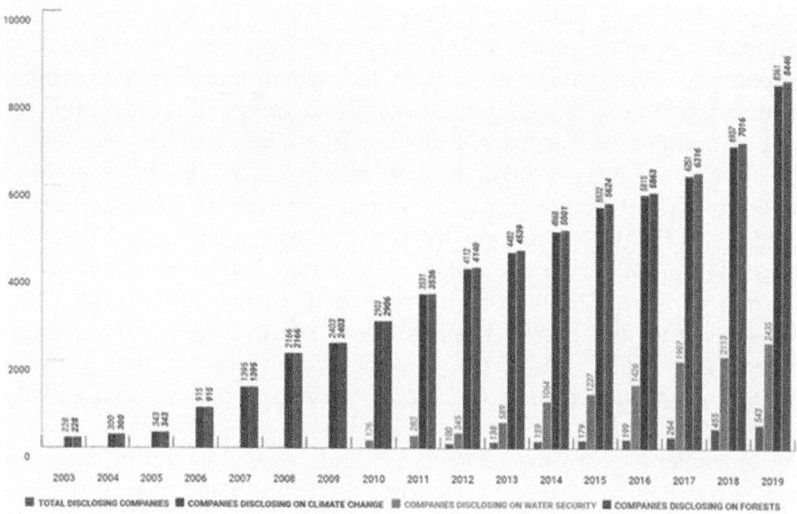

Fig. 6.2 Number of companies that engage in climate impact disclosure (*Source* Climate Disclosure Project [CDP] https://www.cdp.net/en/companies/companies-scores)

6.4.2 The Way Forward

From the analysis of the six large banks tackled in this chapter, it is interesting that there are no big differences between signatory and non-signatory banks on how they incorporate their environmental awareness into their corporate narrative. They all behave in a way that incorporates environmental sustainability into their strategy formulation much as predicted in Chapter 2 (Sect. 2.1.1, Fig. 2.1). So, the decision to enrol or not on the PRB programme appears to be based on their loan book and how they expect it to evolve. There is little visibility of this from the outside, and the fact that the signatory banks are given four years from September 2019 to flesh out their programmes means that external effects of strategy implementation are not yet available.

From the stakeholder management perspective, adopting the PRB creates an evident conflict of interest with the shareholders as this will have a double impact on returns on investment. On the one hand there will be a revenue loss on low risk financing of conventional coal mining and coal-burning powerplants, and an operational cost increase due to all the organisational changes that need to be put in place to cope with environmental impact assessments and monitoring the environmental performance of the projects they finance. Only Citigroup appears to acknowledge this, but even it does not give any indication of how it is managing this conflict of interest.

Supposing all the difficulties to reduce GHG emissions can be overcome, what will the real impact on taking control of the climate crisis be? Just to put things into perspective, anthropogenic GHG emissions amount, in total, to 55 billion CO_2 equivalent tonnes per year; of these, 37 billion tonnes can be traced to fossil fuel emissions and industrial processes (*The Economist*, 2020). Thus, the remaining 18 billion tonnes, or one-third of the emissions, are simply to keep 7.5 billion humans alive (i.e., breathing and eating) and therefore cannot be significantly acted upon without making ethically unpalatable decisions. So, when scientists and policy-makers talk about the need to reduce emissions by whatever target is set, it must be remembered that that must be achieved from the lower base of 37 billion. Thus, for the PRB to have some tangible effects, the broadest possible adhesion needs to be achieved.

Despite the impressive number of signatory banks and the volume of assets they represent, it is notable that only three of the top ten global banks by market capitalisation have signed on. Why are the others not in? From the analysis in Sect. 6.3 it is suspected that it is because they have a significant client base in the high-emissions sectors, and withdrawal from lending to them would have a large short-term impact on their financial results. However, from the figures given in the previous paragraph, the PRB initiative will only make a real contribution to the attainment of the COP-21 goals if a great majority of banks sign on, and especially those that serve the highest-emitting industrial sectors. This will not happen with drastic bans on lending. The focus must shift not on complete banning, but on emissions-portfolio management of loan books with incentives to move towards greener portfolios. Only that way will there be the broadest adhesion by banks and will the PRB have a chance of becoming compulsory and binding.

If the threat of abrupt losing of revenue is overcome through adopting this loan portfolio management approach, banks will have to work on the cost side of adopting PRB. Their operation will be significantly more complex both in the origination of loans and in the monitoring the environmental performance of their clients' projects throughout their life cycle as described in Sect. 6.4.1. They will have to count on bleeding edge technologies to achieve this without overburdening their operational cost. There is already research in artificial intelligence and distributed ledger technology (e.g., blockchain) to device effective solutions for these challenges.

A highly promising outcome of the analysis of the three American banks (i.e., Citigroup. JP Morgan Chase and Wells Fargo) is that they are all aligned with the COP-21 goals, even though the US government had walked away from the Paris agreement. Citigroup and Wells Fargo are explicit about this, and JP Morgan Chase is aligned de facto due to the policies it has adopted. If this happens in the US, it can logically be expected that this commitment is observed in banks headquartered in countries that have adhered to the COP-21 goals. Notwithstanding, governments cannot rely only on using PRB as a trigger for the green economy through their banks. For this gun to have any gravitas, it must be propped up by other factors. One is to have a robust carbon-tax scheme that would make GHG overly expensive for the polluter, and thus create the incentives for companies to internalise the cost of this externality. Having this in place would contribute to improving measurement and valuation and thus overcoming many of the limitations stated in Sect. 6.5. In this way, widespread carbon taxes would unlock the power of finance and motivate financiers to veer their loan books and fund portfolios away from fossil fuels towards more environmentally friendly ones. From dirty industries towards clean ones. These arguments are summarised in Table 6.6.

Picking up on the cited UN official, the PRB tiger was born toothless and if left that way it will be short-lived. It should be given its *green portfolio management* teeth and be supported by contextual measures such as effective carbon taxing. Otherwise, it will simply become another greenwashing activity for banks that have no flesh in the game.

Table 6.6 Governance factors in relation to the principles of responsible banking

Governance Factor	Impact
Signature of PRB	Six cases were developed, of which three are signatories (i.e., Citigroup, MUFG and ICBC) and three are not (i.e., JP Morgan Chase, HSBC and Wells Fargo). Notwithstanding, there is little difference between signatories and non-signatories on how they incorporate environmental awareness in their corporate narrative
Commitment to COP-21	Of the six cases analysed, all (i.e., signatories and non-signatories of PRB) are committed to COP-21. It is notable that the three US-based banks studied are committed to COP-21 despite their government having withdrawn from the Paris agreement
Operational impact	Double whammy on ROI: revenue loss from refraining to finance low risk projects such as traditional energy projects and increased operational cost due to environmental assessment and monitoring of mitigation actions
Stakeholder management	Adopting PRB creates a conflict of interest with shareholders: Reduced ROI. However, most shareholders understand that in the mid- to long-term they will have to move in that direction
Decision basis to enrol	Appears to be based on their loan book and how they expect it to evolve. It is suspected that those banks that do not enrol have a large client base in high-emissions sectors and an abrupt withdrawal from them would have large impact on short-term P&L
Incentives of policy	For PRB to have an impact, all banks need to sign on. However, a drastic immediate ban on loans to high-emission initiatives will not motivate those banks that have a large client base in those sectors
Proposed Approach	• Propose to focus on emissions-portfolio management of loan books, with incentives to move towards greener portfolios • Banks will need to work on the cost-side of environmental impact assessment and mitigation monitoring. There is an opportunity here for Fintechs and Regtechs to provide services based on advanced technologies such as machine learning and blockchain • The PRB alone will not have impact. They need to be accompanied by a powerful carbon-tax scheme that would make GHG emissions overly expensive

REFERENCES

Bergstrom, M., Svedberg Helgesson, K., & Morth, U. (2011). A new role for for-profit actors? The case of anti-money laundering and risk management. *Journal of Common Market Studies, 49*(5), 1043–1064.

Baker, D., McArthur, T. (2009). *The value of the too big to fail big bank subsidy, center for economic and policy research.* Issue Brief.

Banking on Climate Change. (2020). *Fossil Fuel Finance Report 2020*, authored by Rainforest Action Network, BankTrack, Indigenous Environmental Network, Reclaim Finance and Sierra Club (Banking_on_Climate_Change__2020_vF.pdf [ran.org]) downloaded on 24 February 2021.

BankTrack. (2020, September 24). *Banks and fracked oil and gas*, downloaded 15 February 2021.

Chong, A., & Lopez-De-Silanes, F. (2015). Money laundering and its regulation. *Economics & Politics, 27*(1), 78–123.

Citigroup Governance. (2021). Citi | Investor Relations | Corporate Governance Documents (citigroup.com). Accessed 1 February 2021.

Criddle, E. J. (2017). Liberty in loyalty: A republican theory of fiduciary law. *Texas Law Review, 95*(5), 993–1060.

Demetriades, G. (2018). The creation of express, resulting and constructive trust in banking transactions. *Journal of Financial Crime, 25*(2), 277–286.

EBA. (2020, July 16). *EBA supports EU Commission's actions towards a more sustainable European economy.* https://eba.europa.eu/eba-supports-eu-com mission%E2%80%99s-actions-towards-more-sustainable-european-economy.

Griffiths, P. D. R., & Baudier, P. (2021). Enabling responsible banking through the application of Blockchain. *Journal of Innovation Economics & Management.* Special issue Innovations for responsible and sustainable finance, forthcoming December 2021.

Hartsink, G. (2018). The digital identity of legal entities: Current status and the way forward. *Journal of Payments Strategy & Systems, 12*(1), 33–39.

Howard, C. (2014). Basel III's corporate governance impact: How increased banking regulations pose challenges to corporate compliance while simultaneously furthering stakeholder objectives. *Journal of Business Systems, Governance & Ethics, 9*(1), 9–49.

Industrial and Commercial Bank of China Limited. (2007). Corporate Social Responsibility Report [Online]. http://www.icbc.com.cn/icbc/html/dow nload/nianbao/2008/shehuizerenbaogao_2007e.pdf. Accessed 6 February 2021.

Industrial and Commercial Bank of China Limited. (2019). Special Report on Green Finance [Online]. http://v.icbc.com.cn/userfiles/Resources/ICB CLTD/download/2020/lvseEN20201116.pdf. Accessed 6 February 2021.

Joseph, L., & Roth, J. (2008). The criminal prosecution of banks under the US Bank Secrecy Act of 1970. *Journal of Securities Compliance, 1*(3), 208–312.

J.P. Morgan Asset Management. (2021). Sustainable investing [Online]. https://am.jpmorgan.com/gb/en/asset-management/institutional/investmentstrategies/sustainable-investing/. Accessed 6 February 2021.

J.P. Morgan Chase & Co. (2021a). Sustainability [Online]. https://privatebank.jpmorgan.com/gl/en/services/investing/sustainable-investing. Accessed 6 February 2021.

J.P. Morgan Chase & Co. (2021b). JPMorgan Chase Adopts Paris-Aligned Financing Commitment [Online]. https://www.jpmorganchase.com/ir/news/2020/adopts-paris-aligned-financingcommitment. Accessed 6 February 2021.

J.P. Morgan Chase & Co. (2021c). Impact [Online]. https://www.jpmorganchase.com/impact. Accessed 6 February 2021.

Kane, E. J. (2018). Ethics versus ethos in US and UK megabanking. *Journal of Financial Services Research, 53*, 211–226.

Kaufman, A. (2002). Managers' double fiduciary duty: To stakeholders and to freedom. *Business Ethics Quarterly, 12*(2), 189–214.

Kusi, B. A., Gyeke-Dako, A., Agbloyor, E. K., & Darku, A. B. (2018). Does corporate governance structures promote shareholders or stakeholders value maximization? Evidence from African banks, *Corporate Governance: The International Journal of Effective Board Performance, 18*(2), 270–288.

Marsh, B. (2019). How effective data management and automation can improve operational efficiency in onboarding and know your customer. *Journal of Securities Operations & Custody, 11*(4), 337–344.

Martin, W. (2009). Socially responsible investing: Is your fiduciary duty at risk? *Journal of Business Ethics, 90*(4), 549–560.

Massoc, E. (2020). Banks, power, and political institutions: The divergent priorities of European states towards "too-big-to-fail" banks: The cases of competition in retail banking and the banking structural reform. *Business & Politics, 22*(1), 135–160.

Metzger, J., & Paulowitz, T. (2018). Seeking common legal entity standards to facilitate cross-border payments. *Journal of Payments Strategy & Systems, 12*(4), 365–370.

OilChange International. (2020). *Fracking Fiasco: New report names Wells Fargo and JP Morgan Chase as main players funding U.S. shale bust* (September 24) Fracking Fiasco: New report names Wells Fargo and JPMorgan Chase as main players funding U.S. shale bust—Oil Change International (priceofoil.org) downloaded 1 February 2021.

Reuters. (2020). Exclusive: U.S. banks prepare to seize energy assets as shale boom goes bust | Reuters, downlowded 1 February 2021.

SAP. (2016). *Largest 100 banks in the world* S&P Global Market Intelligence, MI: Data Dispatch: Largest 100 banks in the world (snl.com) Downloaded 26 February 2021.

S&P. (2020). *The world's 100 largest banks, 2020* S&P Market Intelligence, MI: Data Dispatch: Largest 100 banks in the world (snl.com) The world's 100 largest banks, 2020 | S&P Global Market Intelligence Downloaded 26 February 2021.

Shaikh, A. I., Drira, M., & Hassine, S. A. (2019). What motivates directors to pursue long-term strategic risks? *Economic Incentives vs. Fiduciary Duty, Journal of Business Research, 101,* 218–228.

The Economist. (2020). *Briefing: Green investing,* June 20, p. 65.

UNEP Finance Activity. (2020a). Year One Update [Online]. https://www.unepfi.org/banking/bankingprinciples/progress/year-one-update/. Accessed 6 February 2021.

UNEP Finance Activity. (2020b). Principles for responsible banking [Online]. https://www.unepfi.org/banking/bankingprinciples/. Accessed 6 February 2021.

UN Environment. (2017). On the role of central banks in enhancing green finance [Online]. https://unepinquiry.org/wpcontent/uploads/2017/02/On_the_Role_of_Central_Banks_in_Enhancing_Green_Finance.pdf. Accessed 6 February 2021.

Wells Fargo. (2021). Corporate Social Responsibility Social Responsibility (wellsfargojobs.com). Accessed 24 February 2021.

CHAPTER 7

The Future of Corporate Governance

7.1 Overview

While in the prior chapters the narrative was case-driven, the first part of this chapter extracts seven concepts that emerge from the case studies and presents a narrative driven by those concepts with an intention of advancing theory and helping business leaders extract lessons that can be applied to their business challenges.

The second part of the chapter selects six dimensions relevant to corporate governance in the knowledge economy and uses them to develop twelve scenarios on how corporate governance in the banking sector will evolve over the next fifteen or twenty years.

7.2 Lessons on the Status of Corporate Governance

From the review of Chapters 3–6 and especially the synthesis table at the end of each of them, seven core concepts in governance emerge. These are:

- Stakeholder management
- Board of directors
- Governance relationships

© The Author(s), under exclusive license to Springer Nature Switzerland AG 2021
P. D. R. Griffiths, *Corporate Governance in the Knowledge Economy*, Palgrave Studies in Accounting and Finance Practice, https://doi.org/10.1007/978-3-030-78873-5_7

- Corporate culture
- Governance/Compliance Controls
- Intellectual capital management
- Business context.

The narrative of this section is organised along these seven core concepts with the objective of abstracting from the case studies some general conclusions pertaining to corporate governance in the knowledge economy.

In Sect. 2.2.1 it was said from analysis of the literature on corporate governance that although the relationship between shareholders and the board of directors and the relationship between the board and the CEO/senior management are well researched and developed in practice, much less is known or has been said on the relationship between the CEO/senior management and the rank and file staff, from a governance perspective. The case studies of the previous chapters show that getting this relationship right is key for success in governance in the knowledge economy.

The lessons from these case studies is that, from a corporate governance perspective, the whole point of the 'CEO vs Rank & File' relationship is to develop in the organisation a defined corporate culture, meaning by this one that is based on ethical values (i.e., Wells Fargo case) and that is respectful of the organisations intellectual capital as a key intangible asset (i.e., Orica and MW-CPG cases). In the case of multinationals, the corporate culture needs to have some adaptation to the societal culture of the host country (e.g., *power distance*, *uncertainty avoidance* and *future orientation* as was seen in the cases of IBM Argentina and BAT Argentina) but without losing the identity of the global organisation. Gauging this country by country is a sophisticated and critical task to get right. Santander Chile appeared not to have got it quite right; they did develop an ethical culture but they failed somewhat on the intellectual capital front and that resulted in misalignment in value discipline between the subsidiary and the corporate centre. In getting this right is essential to consider the societal cultures of both the country of the corporate headquarters and of the host country, and the GLOBE project societal culture clusters are an effective guide to understand what degrees of embeddedness in the host country are appropriate, and how power should be shared between the subsidiary and the corporate centre.

Failing to develop an appropriate corporate culture across the business units or subsidiaries can have a devastating effect in any business but especially in financial services, as the Wells Fargo Community Bank, HSBC Mexico and Danske Bank Estonia cases make evident. In these three cases culture failed on the ethical front, but also on the intellectual capital one. There was no application of corporate structural intellectual capital in the form of compliance processes, and the compliance officers were weak in comparison to the power of the business unit heads. There was also no development of human intellectual capital in the form of training on compliance standards for client-facing staff. Reflecting on the issues that arose from the case studies, the ethical and intellectual capital aspects of corporate culture are not totally independent from each other. A culture that is strong on the knowledge of compliance standards and processes will strengthen the ethical dimension of the culture.

Continuing on the corporate culture front, it is remarkable that IBM Argentina and BAT Argentina could develop such successful operations that developed and thrived for close to a century in a business context of weak formal institutions and a societal culture that differs significantly from that at the countries where these multinationals are headquartered. This, in an economy that not only is overseen by weak political institutions but also has extreme pendular movements of short and hard to predict cycles. Contrast this to Wells Fargo Community Bank, HSBC Mexico and Danske Bank Estonia that operate in stable economies. One factor that at least partially explains this difference is that the two Argentine operations have grown in that market through organic internal growth, while the latter three have done so by mergers and acquisitions. This has helped IBM Argentina and BAT Argentina develop a strong corporate culture aligned with the values of the corporate centre, which manifests itself, for example, in that these two Argentine subsidiaries have their corporate headquarters as one of their key stakeholders; this was not perceived in the other three cases. So, organic growth over a long period of time seems to be an enabler for a subsidiary's corporate culture that is in close synch with the corporation.

Traditionally the role of the Board of Directors has been to protect the interest of shareholders by closing the information imbalance between them and the management team in what has been denominated the agency problem that arose with the separation of ownership and management of corporations. For this to be effective, the Board vs. CEO/senior management relationship needs to operate fluidly. The cases studied show that this is hard to achieve as often the Board is uninformed or misinformed on what is happening in the organisation. These transparency breaches were evident in the case of Glamorgan FS where the Board was not informed on the implications of relocating a RHQ; at Wells Fargo on the seriousness of the implications of the sales malpractices; at Orica on the degree of implementation of the Standard Operating Model; at MW CPG on the status of ICT strategy and governance; at Santander Chile on the adoption of a value discipline different from that at the corporate centre. If the independent members of the Board of Directors are not informed on what is happening in the organisation, how can they protect the rights of the shareholders?

Based on what is observed in these case studies, the answer to that question is that in times of the data tsunami and information clutter that is ever more difficult. It is possibly naïve to think that the Board of Directors will be able to combat the agency problem directly by keeping abreast of everything that is happening in the organisation. The cases reveal that that is a lost game, but they also reveal a golden opportunity. The focus of the Board vs. CEO relationship should be on monitoring the CEO vs. rank and file relationship to ensure that the latter is operating to create a corporate culture that is ethical and that enhances the intellectual capital of the organisation. Why is an ethical culture so important?

Organisations in the knowledge economy operate in an overly complex environment where technological changes and the continual emerging of entrepreneurial, agile and innovative players demand that traditional organisations perform in the short-, mid- and long-term. While in the past the responsibility for corporate performance was at the head, through balance scorecards and other equivalent mechanisms the pressure and responsibility to perform has been pushed right down to the base and client-facing echelons of the organisation. Without an ethical corporate culture that counterbalances this pressure, staff fall into a dynamic that ends justify means and are tempted to cut corners to achieve their goals. That is evident in the four bribe situations and in the Wells Fargo Community Bank, HSBC Mexico and Danske Estonia Bank cases. The culture, thus, needs to be one of 'performance with integrity'.

The conjunction of a corporate cultural failure of 'performance with integrity' with the failure of intellectual capital management in the form of ignoring compliance standards and processes leads to the reputation disasters described in the Wells Fargo Community Bank, HSBC Mexico and Danske Estonia Bank cases, but it goes further than that. It was substantiated in Sect. 2.3.1 that in the knowledge economy innovation is not so much about products and processes, but about innovating business models. A corporate culture that does not protect and enhance the organisation's intellectual capital constrains innovation in business models as the Orica and MW CPG cases demonstrate.

The conclusion of the prior paragraphs is that the traditional role of the Board of Directors of attempting to close the information gap between management and shareholders is a lost game, unworthy of being pursued. The shareholders are far better served if the Board of Directors focuses on monitoring very closely the CEO vs. rank and file relationship to ensure that it promotes a corporate culture of 'performance with integrity' and of enhancing intellectual capital in the organisation.

Continuing with the role of the Board of Directors, the case studies detect multiple cases of Boards that do not react to early warnings of problems. At HSBC Mexico there were clear messages from the US banking regulators; at Danske Banks there were messages from Russian and Estonian regulators to the Board via the Danish financial services authorities. In the case of Danske there was also a whistle-blower and the resignation of two American banks to operate as correspondents of Danske Estonia Bank due to suspect money laundering activities. Less explicit but nonetheless obvious are abnormal flows and profits: Danske Estonia represented during the laundering period only 0.5 percent of total Danske assets but contributed with 8 percent of total global profits and nobody at the Board asked questions! On top of that, both the Boards at HSBC and at Danske Bank knew that their compliance structure in Mexico and in Estonia, respectively, was weak and they turned a blind eye. Similarly, at Wells Fargo the density of products was approaching eight when in the rest of the US system there was an average of three products per client. Does that not generate curiosity? This kind of behaviour from a Board is inexcusable.

The issue of whistle-blowers deserves a reflection. Governance efforts in many countries and organisations are said to be aimed at protecting whistle-blowers and encouraging them to come forward; however, this is illusionary. Whistleblowing has extremely negative connotations in many cultures where it is equated to snitching and thus held in deep contempt by peers, particularly in the lower echelons of society. It is also individualistic and non-systemic, and it comes after the damage has been done. It is far more positive to concentrate that effort in building an ethical culture, which prevents incidents rather than just denouncing them.

Moving towards stakeholder management, it is remarkable that in all the cases of poor governance (i.e., Glamorgan FS, Wells Fargo, Orica, MW-CPG) or where the organisation engaged in corrupt activities (i.e., HSBC Mexico, Danske Estonia) the stakeholder group most negatively affected was that of the shareholders both in terms of dividends due to fines and in market value due to reputation loss. If, as most would agree, the main objective of the Board of Directors is to protect the interests of the shareholders, these are issues of the highest importance for the Board. The Board needs to proactively push for robust governance standards and processes and as mentioned in prior paragraphs, proactively scan for areas of corruption risk. The organisation's employees are also an affected stakeholder group (i.e., Glamorgan FS, Danske Estonia Bank) by losing their jobs, and so are communities and government agencies through the promotion of local violence and tax revenue loss. In extreme cases where corruption in a too-big-to-fail bank puts the whole financial system at risk, the community through the financial services authority becomes a key stakeholder, too.

To reinforce the previous point, the IBM Argentina and BAT Argentina cases are examples of how good corporate governance has a positive effect on stakeholders through constructive relationships with government despite the challenging business environment due to weak formal institutions. This will be positive for shareholders and thus reiterates that it should be a focus of attention for the Board of Directors. It should be noted that in these two cases the corporate centre is a key stakeholder for the subsidiary. This is an integral part of the CEO through local management to the rank and file corporate governance relationship that, as mentioned above, the Board of Directors needs to nurture and monitor.

As an ending remark on stakeholder management, it is interesting that the customers emerge as an important stakeholder group in two cases with quite different connotations. The first is Wells Fargo where the customers are on the receiving end of the banks infamous cross-selling policy, by being sold and charged for products they do not need and do not know they have. The other case is IBM Argentina, in which the company develops a positive, collaborative, relationship with its customers to jointly overcome the frequent volatilities in the local economy.

Governance/compliance controls are a core need that emerges from the case studies and should be a focus of attention for the Board of Directors. Due to the very nature of corporate governance, these controls need to span across a broad front of activities. From the Glamorgan FS case it emerges that the Board needs to know when management commissions a technical study on geographic location of significant operating units, but then ignores the outcome of those studies and decides on criteria that transfers resources from shareholders to managers. From the cases of Wells Fargo Community Bank, HSBC Mexico and Danske Estonia arise the precautions that must be taken when a bank engages on aggressive sales strategies—the Board must ensure that it has complete visibility of these activities through appropriate controls and indicators. The ORICA case demonstrates that the Board needs to have visibility of the outcomes of a significant investment such as the implementation of a global or regional ERP system—it is interesting that the Board must have signed off a project of this magnitude, but did not follow up on the outcomes. At MW CPG, which has grown through acquisitions, the case shows how the Board of Directors needs to monitor how newly acquired units are integrated into the corporate fabric—in this case that job was not well performed and compromised the organisations capabilities for innovating business models. Similar lessons on integrating acquisitions emerge from the Santander Chile, HSBC Mexico and Danske Estonia. In short, any project or activity that requires approval by the Board of Directors, needs to be accompanied by a set of controls that enables the Board to monitor realisation of the benefits promised.

A special case of governance/compliance control is that pertaining to corruption, as arises from the bribe situations and the HSBC Mexico and Danske Estonia cases. Apart from precautionary actions such as monitoring the CEO vs. rank and file governance relationship to build a corporate culture of 'performance with integrity, the Board of Directors must monitor that the bank's structural intellectual capital in the form of compliance processes and systems are implemented and enforced. A corollary of this is that the business case for implementing the corporate systems in newly acquired units cannot be done based merely on tangible benefits, but must cover also intangible benefits and operational risk criteria. If an acquired organisation possesses units that are too small to justify the bank's corporate systems, it should seriously consider disposing of those small units. Alternatively, the bank might consider having a two-tier corporate systems scheme for compliance, with an option based on Regtech solutions for the smaller units. On top of all this, the Board of Directors must monitor that that the bank's human intellectual capital in the form of staff training on compliance principles and processes is enhanced. Finally, the Board of Directors needs to become aware of the hotspots for money laundering in its branch network and monitor international flows of funds from those areas.

The next core concept in governance is intellectual capital management which, as mentioned in Sect. 2.3.1, is essential to thrive in the knowledge economy and should be a concern for the Board of Directors. Several of the cases give indications on how to protect and enhance the organisation's intellectual capital. IBM Argentina achieves high standards of structural intellectual capital attainment by integrating the subsidiary into the global operation of its parent company, enabling it to share resources with other business units across the world; it also does so by working closely with clients on what it calls product roaming. BAT Argentina is also successful on this front and meets its objectives by investing in new production lines and distribution centres, plus capitalising from global research and development. Santander, Glamorgan FS and Orica take a different approach as they increase the structural intellectual capital of their subsidiaries through mounting global and regional shared services for functions such as IT and reporting. Santander also works on its human intellectual capital through training its staff at the Santander University.

Finally, a few words on the business context for organisations operating internationally and that are important from a governance perspective. The key challenges are how to cope with formal and not so formal institutions in the host country, and how to overcome the distance in societal cultures between the country of headquarters and that of the subsidiary. The IBM Argentina and BAT Argentina cases give clear indications of what it takes to be successful in a volatile context where formal institutions are overcast by clouds of particularistic and unwritten rules and regulations. They cope with this by investing heavily in corporate relations to the point that at BAT Argentina, which operates in a more regulated business sector than IBM, incorporates Corporate Relations into the dominant coalition of the subsidiary. A second characteristic is that they maintain at the subsidiary the highest standards of products, processes and services that is abreast of their best operations in the world. Thirdly, they grow in the market by organic growth rather than acquisition, which enables them to develop an extraordinarily strong corporate culture, which makes communications between the subsidiary and the corporate centre, straightforward and fluid. In fourth place they adopt in the subsidiary disciplines such as relentless dedication to planning that helps them cope with the volatility of the economy and the subsidiary adopts the corporate headquarters as a key stakeholder for the local operation. Finally, and based on the prior points, they carefully design a sensible distribution of power and decision-making between the corporate centre and the subsidiary, with an adaptation of the corporate strategy to the needs of the host market.

Abstracting from this discussion it is clear the Board of Directors plays a pivotal role in corporate governance in the knowledge economy. It is conditioned by the business context (i.e., its formal institutions and informal ones such as societal culture when the formal ones are weak) that is also influential on the stakeholders. Due to the advent of sustainability, there is a strong interaction between the Board of Directors and the stakeholder groups that are multiple as opposed to in the industrial economy when it was only the shareholders. On the one hand, the Board of Directors has a strong interaction with the corporate governance relationships (i.e., communicating with the CEO through the 'Board of Directors vs CEO' relationship) that in turn leads to influencing the corporate culture through the 'CEO vs rank & file' governance relationship, to build a culture that is ethical and protects and enhances the intellectual capital of the organisation. On the other hand, the Board of Directors also interacts strongly with governance/compliance controls that inform the Board on the state of compliance and which are changed by the Board to adapt to evolving demands of regulations. The governance/compliance controls influence the corporate culture to reinforce its ethical stance and enhance its intellectual capital on compliance issues. The corporate culture, in turn, influences intellectual capital management that has a knock-on effect on governance/compliance controls. This is synthesised in Fig. 7.1.

7.3 Uncovering the Window: Where Is Corporate Governance Heading?

7.3.1 Introduction to Scenario Planning

The Covid-19 pandemic is a reminder of what a complex system we live in, and how 'the linear thinking of simple cause-effect reasoning, to which the human mind can default, is not a good policy tool' (Flack & Mitchell, 2020). The causation paradigm is therefore not a good approach for predicting future development departing from current events, either. Living in a complex world requires embracing uncertainty and model systems that are adaptable to a broad range of possible futures—in line

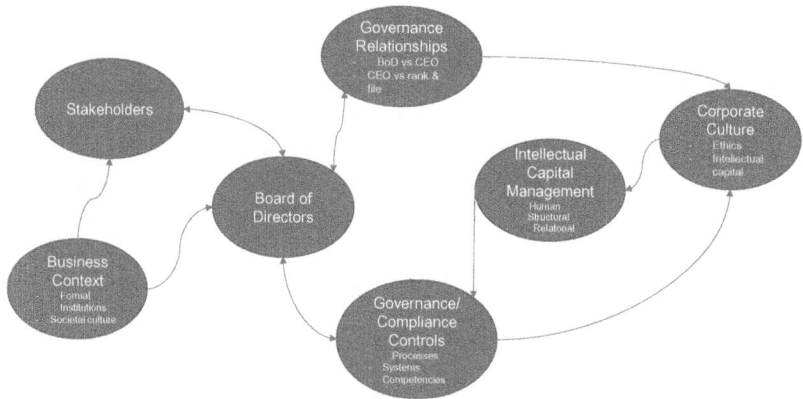

Fig. 7.1 Inter-construct influence and interaction model

with this the future of corporate governance in the knowledge economy will be done by applying scenario planning.

Essentially the method consists of adopting two variables that comply with certain characteristics:

a. They are External to the organisation—that is they are part of the business context and no ogranisation has significant influence over them. For example 'Growth of the Economy' that varies between two extremes: Recession and Strong Growth. This is one variable, of many possible ones, that measures the state of the economic context of the organisation. Another example of external variable, in the area of sustainability, would be 'Awareness for the Environment' that varies between two extremes: 'Complete disregard' to 'Extremely sensitive'. This would represent part of the social context for organisations in that market.
b. They are independent of each other. In other words, that the two variables are not correlated. The two variables given as examples in (a) above clearly comply with this condition.

Once two variables have been identified and decided upon, they are located on orthogonal axes to define four scenarios. If the two variables of the prior example are taken the scenario structure of Fig. 7.2 is obtained.

7 THE FUTURE OF CORPORATE GOVERNANCE   221

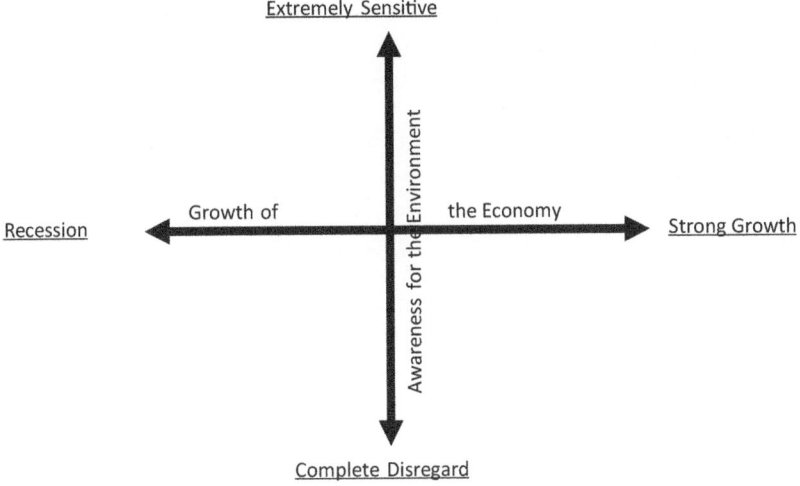

Fig. 7.2   Economy versus awareness for the environment

As can be seen the four scenarios are defined by: (a) High growth economy and a society extremely sensitive to environmental issues; (b) Recession and Extremely sensitive society to environmental issues; (c) Recession and Complete Disregard for the environment; and finally (d) Strong Growth economy and Complete Disregard for the environment by society. So those are the four scenarios that need to be developed in detail. This is done through research, brain storming, reflection or any other approach that helps drill down each scenario to an appropriate level of granularity. It is especially important that each of these four scenarios is given a name with a punch, that is, a name that generates emotional impact, and thus retention, on the reader.

For this projection six variables are selected to be combined into twelve possible scenarios of corporate governance in the knowledge economy. These are:

- Generation-Y driven cultural change as described in Sect. 2.3.3
- The adoption of Integrated Reporting <IR> as described in Sect. 2.3.4
- The development of artificial intelligence as describes in Sect. 2.3.2

- The governance of social networks and the Data Tsunami as described in Sect. Sect. 2.3.2
- Society's sensitivity to the issue of the climate crisis and GHG emissions as will be defined
- The adoption of the Principles of Responsible Banking as described in Chapter 6.

These will be combined in three scenario structures.

7.3.2   Scenario Structure No. 1

One variable is the adoption of forward-looking Integrated Reporting that can go from Low Adoption on one extreme, to Total Adoption on the other; another variable changes to society driven by the growing role (simply through sheer numbers) of Gen Y in the workforce and in the consumer market, from Low Impact to High Impact, giving place to four scenarios that could be called *Open Society, Unrealised Potential, Fragmented Society* and *Transparency for What?*, as shown graphically in Fig. 7.3.

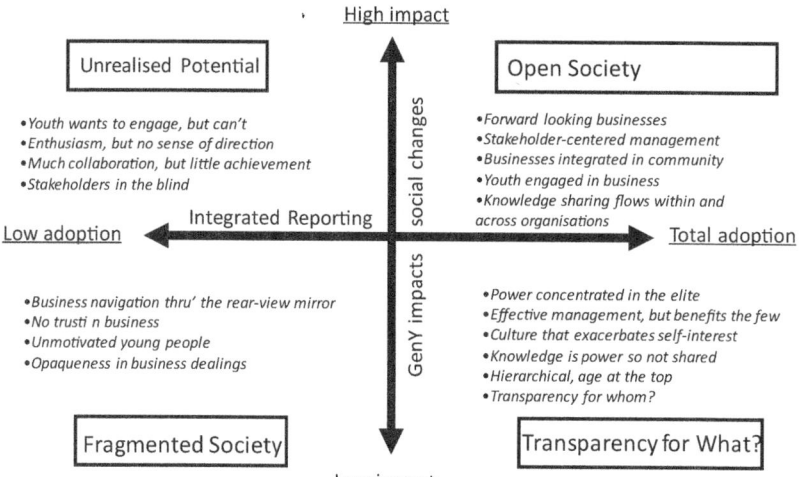

Fig. 7.3   Changes in approach to corporate reporting and in a Gen-Y society

Open Society: most observers will agree that this is the most favourable scenario in which corporate governance will have to be adapted to a society that has been shaped by the culture of sharing and collaboration of Gen-Y in which business has understood the benefits of transparency and looking forward rather than closedness and navigating through the mirror.

In this world businesses are extremely sensitive of the needs of the different stakeholder groups but understand that many of them have opposing interests and so come to terms with the fact that it must prioritise them, and communicate clearly those priorities. As a result of this business organisations are well integrated into their communities, contributing to the development of local knowledge workers and suppliers. The Board of Directors reviews intensely the CEO vs. rank and file governance relationship with an aim at ensuring that the business strategy for this market is adapted to the characteristics of the formal institutions and societal culture.

Within this context the Board of Directors know they have to focus on the future of the organisation, beyond what the financial statements say so they work on the 'Board of Directors vs CEO' governance relationship to keep abreast of developments, but most of all to ensure that the CEO is nurturing the corporate culture of ethics and upholding of this integration with the community. They live in a world where the <IR> has been adopted by most companies which gives them the tools to be able to make management accountable and also make the strategy and resource allocation transparent and comparable with other companies in the market and beyond.

It is interesting that Gen-Y people are engaged in business both as staff with growing responsibility and as consumers, keeping corporations to high standards of sustainability. The collaborative and sharing character attributes of these up and coming professionals are fitting to an economy where no organisation builds value on its own but cooperating with other organisations in their knowledge clusters.

In this world, banks and Fintechs collaborate and are making financial inclusion percolate into all echelons of societies both industrial and emerging. Technology is a strong enabler of these services.

Unrealised potential: In this scenario the maturing Gen-Y wants to engage with the business but finds it hard to do so in traditional structures where Board of Directors are moulded to old ways. The monitoring of performance of the organisation remains focussed very much on financial results observed through the traditional retro-facing financial statements. There are intergenerational conflicts in the corporate world; Gen-Y is now seeking positions of responsibility in significant numbers, and the mere volume of them injects much energy into the corporate world and society. However, that energy and enthusiasm have little sense of direction and are not being directed towards productive ends.

As expected, the influx of Gen-Ys in greater numbers is overflowing organisations with sharing and collaborations, but ineffective allocation of resources and narrow-minded business strategies are not leading to achievement. The knowledge economy offers many opportunities but corporations are not capturing them. Many of the Gen-Ys are changing jobs frequently, and an ever-growing number of them are leaving the corporate world and attempting entrepreneurial initiatives. Because Gen-Y also makes up a significant part of the consumer market, these new entrepreneurial initiatives believe they can interpret the needs of their potential clients so will make inroads into the different industry sectors.

The 'Board of Directors vs CEO' governance relationship is not operating transparently, so the Board is not able to promote through the CEO and senior management culture of integration into their communities.

Stakeholders other than, to a certain extent, shareholders feel that their interests are not being incorporated into the governance of organisations. This is reinforced by the fact that they are being kept in the blind and without visibility into the workings of the organisations they are engaged with.

This is a world where consumers have little attachment to old brands and institutions, so banks are suffering at the hands of Fintechs. New technologies are a barrier between the players of these two industrial sectors: Fintechs experimenting with bleeding edge technologies, and banks struggling to keep up with the services that Fintechs offer and are ever more in demand by the Gen-Y consumers.

Fragmented society: This scenario resembles the current status quo but with increasing intergeneration tensions due to Gen-Y being subdued by the older generations that do not open space for them to express themselves and find professional development in positions that enable them to display their character attributes of collaboration and sharing.

Together with their failure to access positions of responsibility and professional mobility, Gen-Y becomes an impoverished and disengaged component of society. They opt out of the property market and big-ticket consumer items such as electric cars. Financial inclusion is remarkably low compared to what would be expected.

Trust in business is at an all-time low, as corporations are managed through the rear-view mirror with no consideration for stakeholders. Businesses are not integrated in their communities and resort to purely financial decision criteria for relocating work. Western-style capitalism loses creativity and innovation, and thus loses ground in comparison with centrally planned economies such as China, which becomes the world's first economy and the undisputed leader in decisive technologies such as artificial intelligence and distributed ledger technologies.

Opaqueness is the name of the game, so the knowledge economy becomes a hindrance rather than an opportunity. Social networks and Big Data continue in the rise, but society is incapable of channelling them towards improving transparency.

The apathetic Gen-Y turn against the system but do not even enrol in activist initiatives to change the world. The third sector falls into a strong decline: The individualistic elder generations do not take leadership roles in this sector, nor contribute to their finances, and the young do not engage.

Globalisation becomes a memory of the late twentieth and early twenty-first century and gradually slides into the history books. Economies are closed and protectionist and the nation state gets a respite from its several decades of decline, together with representative democracy that remains in place in the Western world but with much distrust and low participation by young people.

With Gen-Y out of the financial system, financial inclusion decreases, and the Fintech sector loses dynamism. The banking sector becomes more concentrated in few traditional old institutions that become closed in themselves and serve mostly the low risk upper echelon of society. Their Boards of Directors become club-like and the 'Board of Directors vs CEO' governance relationship gives them little visibility of what is going on in the lower ranks of the organisation. The ambition of monitoring the 'CEO vs rank & file' relationship to ensure a corporate culture of performance with integrity and high regard for the organisation's intellectual capital fails to become a significant issue. All stakeholder interests are ignored, even those of the shareholders who are hijacked by the entrenched management teams.

Transparency for what? This is a polarised society, with power concentrated in a highly educated elite. The Western world order is characterised by a hierarchical society with effective management and value creation, but whose benefits are concentrated in the dominant coalition of ageing professionals, businesspeople, plutocrats and politicians.

The widespread adoption of the <IR> improves transparency but only among the dominant coalition. As a result of this there is differentiated stakeholder management, where some stakeholders such as shareholders, financiers, governments, selected customers and a small number of pro-establishment NGOs (e.g., environmental, poverty eradication and healthcare improvement in emergent countries) are well served, but the interests of others such as employees, trade unions, disruptive activists and mass consumers are shunted aside.

As Gen-Y has not managed to establish itself in positions of power, its core values of collaboration and sharing do not prosper in society. This is an individualistic society where knowledge is still power and thus shared as least as possible beyond small circles and mostly through leaks. Young people are disengaged and thus creativity and innovation are controlled from the top. Top-down design method innovation prospers but bottom-up crowd-innovation is in decline. Significant tranches of Gen-Y, particularly those that have opted out of the system and do not follow careers but tend to operate more in the gig or even informal economy are unbanked or underbanked—they do not have the creditworthiness to access banks.

The 'Board of Directors vs CEO' governance relationship is enhanced through transparency attained from the <IR> and is used to monitor the 'CEO vs rank & file' governance relationship to ensure that it develops an ethical corporate culture and one that enhances the corporation's intellectual capital.

In this scenario Fintechs are developing quite strongly but they are mostly backed by the banks and other institutional investors. For example, crowdfunding for lending is on the ascent due to the number of unbanked or underbanked young people, but the actual funding side of the relationship has been taken over by institutional investors. In a similar vein, the Fintech sector in general has morphed from a sector that competed with banking, to one that works with banks to help them digitalise and overcome the constraints of their legacy systems.

7.3.3 Scenario Structure No. 2

This is a scenario structure of technology development and its governance, where one variable is the development of artificial intelligence in the form of machine learning, which goes from a low degree of development to one of high development. The other variable is referring to the growth of social networks and its outgrowth Big Data and their governance, which goes from an extreme of highly controlled growth through strong governance, to one of wild growth, completely out of control. This is depicted in Fig. 7.4 and, as can be seen, defines four scenarios that are titled *Knowledge panacea, AI Dependency, Cyber chaos* and *Stagnation*.

Knowledge panacea: In this scenario machine learning has achieved notably high levels of development and humans have managed to keep under control through good governance the accelerating use of social networks and the massive growth in Big Data or rather the data tsunami that this produces. Machine learning has started to evolve in its unsupervised learning format, by which it has gone beyond the running of algorithms designed by humans but is actually creating knowledge from scratch. The thoughtful scientists and professionals are starting to elicit concerns on what the future of this technology might be. Will

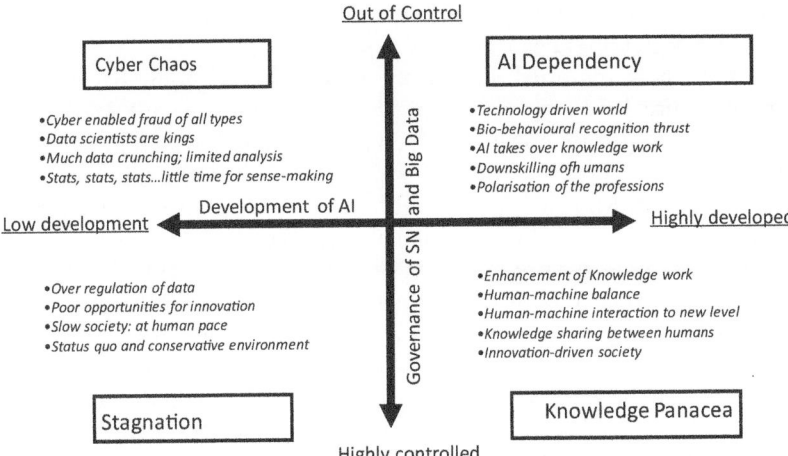

Fig. 7.4 Interaction of the development of AI and the governance of social networks and Big Data

it develop consciousness and therefore self-interest? They realise that progress cannot be detained, as the potential benefits to humanity are colossal in many ways, and not least that it will help better understand the human mind and intelligence, but the threats are enormous if it is not properly governed. That is the greatest challenge to humanity, how to govern the evolution of AI in its machine learning form.

Fortunately, Big Data growth that was of significant concern up to the recent past, has now come under control. Humanity has managed to define important issues in relation to ownership of data through a combination of imposing on social networks a subscription business model rather than an advertisement-based one, by organising people in collective action and thus increased bargaining power with respect to the social network companies, and some legislation, ownership has been turned back to the individual. Governance over the content of social networks has also progressed significantly, albeit at the cost of free speech, through the use of algorithms to give less visibility and viral control to dubious content, through creating non-governmental social media councils for moderating content, and through getting the social media companies to keep data audit trails. Social network companies have enrolled battalions of content-moderators that operate under this new framework alongside machines, and thus the social network companies internalise the externalities they have created in the form of the data tsunami. In this way post-truth society has been contained or reversed.

As a result of the prior actions, the knowledge economy has become a more secure landscape for professional development and knowledge work has been greatly enhanced. Human- machine interaction has been taken to a new level and one in which the human–machine relationship is balanced. Knowledge sharing between humans is thriving and this, together with the balanced human–machine coexistence, is a great boost for an innovation-driven society.

With the assistance of machine learning to trawl data, corporate governance is strengthened. Transparency leads to empowerment of all the stakeholder groups, be they prioritised by the corporation or not. The 'Board of Directors vs CEO' governance relationship is balanced and normally works well, and serves the Board of Directors to monitor the 'CEO vs rank & file' governance relationship to achieve an ethical culture of performance with legitimacy, and a culture that protects and enhances the organisation's intellectual capital. The latter is key to success for business in this scenario.

Open banking is by now fully developed and led to a banking sector that has fragmented vertically through the action of account aggregators that facilitate transfer of individuals' and firms' financial data between financial services companies. The banking industry's new structure resembles the traditional insurance industrial organisation, where incumbent banks retain their core function of managing credit risk, while an assortment of other companies do the client relationship functions, Fintechs do the client onboarding and identity verification through multiple forms of bio-recognition, Regtech companies take over functions such as KYC and AML, and yet others perform functions such as securitisation and other risk distribution operations.

AI Dependency: Machine learning has started to evolve in its unsupervised learning format, by which it has gone beyond the running of algorithms designed by humans but is actually creating knowledge from scratch. The thoughtful scientists and professionals are starting to elicit concerns on what the future of this technology might be. Will it develop consciousness and therefore self-interest? They realise that progress cannot be detained, as the potential benefits to humanity are colossal in many ways, and not least that it will help better understand the human mind and intelligence, but the threats are enormous if it is not properly governed. That is the greats challenge to humanity, how to govern the evolution of AI in its machine learning form.

In this scenario, social networks are flourishing out of control, contents are really difficult to differentiate between true or false, data is used to manipulate from elections to consumer preferences, and the data tsunami is seriously affecting people's lives in the form of privacy breaches and identity intrusions and simulations. Human intelligence is simply overwhelmed and incapable of sensemaking in this context, which means humanity needs to rely on artificial intelligence for pattern recognition and simply being able to cope.

This is a technology-driven universe where artificial intelligence takes over most of the knowledge work leading to a polarisation of the professions into a few superstars that learn to work with machine learning, and the great majority who are out of work and need to re-cycle into other roles. The roles available are mainly in the service sector (i.e., personal services, nursing, teaching) and appropriate only for those who have the required emotional intelligence and empathy. One of the very few positive developments is that these occupations, traditionally left behind in terms of material compensation, become highly valued.

In this universe, the work that was previously performed by droves of highly trained investment bankers and wealth managers has been substituted by algorithms designed by a handful of Ph.D. holders. What is left for the displaced bankers? They will have to find jobs in the personal services industry (if they have the empathy attributes!) or driving Ubers until Uber cars become fully self-driving. That is, people displaced from knowledge work will be downskilled. This is a defining characteristic of the technological revolution happening in this scenario. While in all previous technology revolutions machines took over mechanical, repetitive and manual office work from humans, which led humans to have to upskill and do more knowledge intensive jobs, in the artificial intelligence revolution this process is reversed.

In this universe, corporate governance needs to rely heavily on artificial intelligence to cut through the data tsunami as data is confusing. Members of the Board of Directors need to apply intense critical thinking to not let themselves by carried away by news headlines. The Boards of Directors engage in great efforts to ensure that management segregates seed from chaff to keep stakeholders well informed. They also use the 'Board of Directors vs CEO' governance relationship to monitor the 'CEO vs rank & file' relationship to develop an ethical performance with integrity culture that is also vigilant of the organisation's intellectual capital. Interestingly, this corporate culture is less critical in this scenario because most of the transactions will be done by AI rather than people, and AI does not have ethical conflicts; and the intellectual capital of the organisation is, to a great extent, embedded in the algorithms of AI.

The banking sector is heavily digitalised in this scenario, for which it works closely with Fintechs. With the development of AI and the serious opportunities and threats presented by the data tsunami, there is a vast space for Fintechs to develop—these Fintechs hardly employ any people as their services are fully digitalised. Open banking is underway, but there is great concern about cybersecurity. Due to the uncontrolled data tsunami, one of the areas of opportunity that Fintechs develop to great success is that of bio-behavioural identification—each individual is recognised by seven to ten different criteria, from the simple iris, facial and fingerprint recognition, to the sophisticated recognition of body movement and key board touch characteristics.

Cyber Chaos: The scenario takes its name from the fact that the data tsunami is completely out of control while AI has not lived up to its promise, so humanity is left to fight this dragon with the toothpick of human intelligence as its main weapon. Indeed, social networks are flourishing out of control, contents are really difficult to differentiate between true or false, data is used to manipulate from elections to consumer preferences, and the data tsunami is seriously affecting people's lives in the form of privacy breaches and identity intrusions and simulations. Confronted with this situation, the human mind is assisted in the task of segregating the seed from the chaff by a myriad of disjointed and limited technology tools that humanity has available for different aspects of pattern recognition and sensemaking of the data.

In this scenario the data scientist is king—this is without the slightest doubt one of the most sought after professions. Statistics are applied in multiple forms to almost every aspect of human life, as for example on security issues. Cyber-enabled fraud of all types is everywhere. The challenge for data scientists is that so much time has to be devoted to number crunching that analysis and sensemaking is always limited.

From a governance perspective, much effort in corporate governance is spent on ensuring that management feeds valid data to the different stakeholder groups. The fact that it is so difficult to segregate the seed from the chaff, defines that information facilitated to stakeholders is always minimum, to ensure that it is valid. The Board of Directors needs to monitor that the 'CEO vs rank & file' governance relationship promotes a corporate culture that is ethical and a guardian of the organisation's intellectual capital, but also one in which people are expected to be critical thinkers. In this universe no data can be accepted on face value—everything needs to be questioned.

The banking sector is conservative in its outlook and has failed to digitalise. The fact that AI has not developed as expected, has led banks to become highly sceptical and dubitative at the time of selecting technologies to adopt. Because of these difficulties and added that technology decisions are of high impact in an industry that is as information intensive as banks, the banks turn to Fintechs to develop and actually operate many of their digital activities. Open banking has not developed due to the cyber-data risks and the lack of sophisticated AI tools to assist account aggregators in their consolidation and exchange of data.

Stagnation: For all its promise to change the world, AI in its machine learning format has not delivered. The great promise, unsupervised learning, did not evolve further than the successful resolution of complicated games such as Go or chess. In the world of real problems it faced the barrier that the real world does not give enough cases for trial and error and learning even in an entire human life-time. AI is also limited in that it does not have a general intelligence, but just specialisation in a narrow knowledge domain, so it does not have the versatility in terms of diversity of problems it can tackle and this becomes another barrier to experience.

The lagging behind of AI is potentially a big problem in the world of the data tsunami but fortunately, Big Data has now come under control. Humanity has managed to define important issues in relation to ownership of data through a combination of imposing on social networks a subscription business model rather than an advertisement-based one, by organising people in collective action and thus increased bargaining power with respect to the social network companies, and some legislation, ownership has been turned back to the individual. Governance over the content of social networks has also progressed significantly, albeit at some cost of free speech, through the use of algorithms to give less visibility and viral control to dubious content, through creating non-governmental social media councils for moderating content, and through getting the social media companies to keep data audit trails. Social network companies have enrolled battalions of content-moderators that operate under this new framework alongside machines, and thus the social network companies internalise the externalities they have created in the form of the data tsunami.

The problem with the lag in AI development is that this slows down society to the speed of the human mind. The regulation of Big Data exacerbates this slow down with over regulation of data, which in turn leads to poor opportunities for innovation. All this tends to maintain the status quo and determines a highly conservative environment for doing business. Young people emigrate in search of more prosperous opportunities.

In synch with the other aspects of the corporation in this scenario, corporate governance is very conventional. Indeed, there is awareness about stakeholder management being important but the organisation's bandwidth is narrow so most attention is given to the traditional group of shareholders. Because there is little progress in AI the role of humans is essential for maintaining the reputation of the organisation and its intellectual capital, so creating through the management team an ethical corporate culture that nurtures the organisation's intellectual capital is of critical importance and one of the key objectives of the Board of Directors.

Due to the poor development of AI and the conservative stance of the business community digitalisation of banks has not picked up very strongly. Notwithstanding, Open Banking is one of the new rules of the game and is evolving at a significant rate leveraging that data protection in an environment of highly controlled social networks and Big Data make cybersecurity less of an issue. Fintech's have emerged to take the role of account aggregators, and to give back-office services to the banks. Although AI has not evolved, other technologies such as distributed ledger technologies have, and cryptocurrencies are at last gripping hold as payment alternatives.

7.3.4 Scenario Structure No. 3

This scenario structure is about the climate crisis and the role that banks take in controlling this phenomenon. As depicted in Fig. 7.5 the first variable *Sensitivity towards the climate crisis* is referring to how sensitive and involved in combatting GHG emissions society becomes, and it goes from *low* sensitivity to *high*. Low sensitivity means that society is not concerned with the environment because people do not believe in anthropogenic

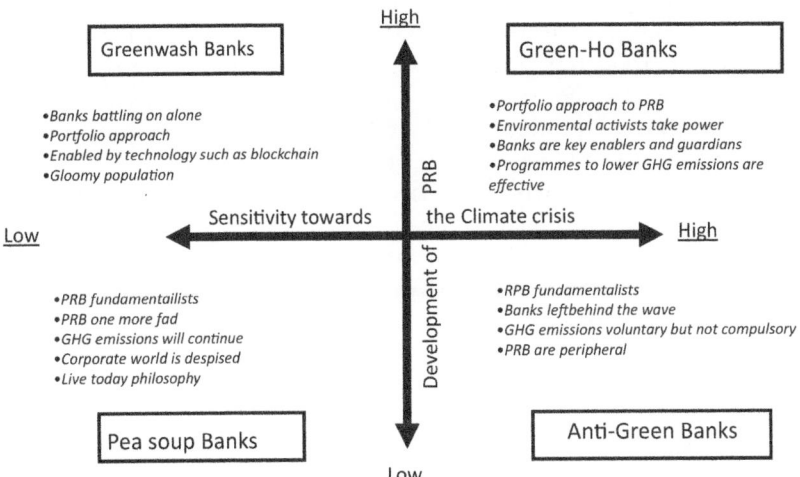

Fig. 7.5 Interaction of sensitivity towards the climate crisis and the PRB

climate change or are sceptical about humans being able to make a difference in containing GHG emissions. High sensitivity is referring to that people are extremely involved and will not consume products and services that are not carbon neutral.

The second variable is referring to the role that banks are given, and that they accept, in containing GHG emissions through including environmental impact assessment in their loan origination processes, as explained in detail in Chapter 6. By *low* development of the Principles of Responsible Banking is meant that the principles remain voluntary and non-binding, while *high* development means that the principles become compulsory and applied by all banks. As posited in Chapter 6, achieving the high development situation will require banks to manage their loan book as a carbon emissions portfolio with clear targets to migrate to a greener portfolio. The four scenarios produced by the interaction of these two variables are called *Green-Ho Banks*, *Greenwash Banks*, *Pea Soup Banks* and *Anti-Green Banks* and will be now described.

Green-Ho Banks: In this scenario society is highly committed to containing GHG emissions and has delegated in banks to drive the effort. Environmental activists take a high-power role in society and are vigilant of the whole supply chain of products and services. They will internalise the *Greenhouse Gas Protocol* criteria as described in Sect. 6.4.1 to monitor emissions from the extraction of raw materials through the logistics and production processes until arriving at finished products and services (scope 1); the emissions from the energy they consume (scope 2); to the emissions produced in the full life cycle of the product until its decommissioning and recycling (scope 3).

Banks and environmental activists are curious allies as the latter see the former as the instrumental force to make change happen. It has been accepted that banks approach their loan book as a carbon emissions portfolio that must become greener over time, and banks have accepted the Principles of Responsible Banking as compulsory. Banks will incorporate detailed environmental impact analyses based on the *Greenhouse Gas Protocol* criteria, tracking scope 1, scope 2 and scope 3 type emissions in their loan origination processes. Not only will they do the environmental impact analysis but they will also monitor throughout the life cycle of the initiatives they are financing, that the receivers of the loans carry out the emissions mitigation activities that they have committed to when requesting the loan.

From a governance perspective, the environmental departments of national and local governments, and the environmental NGOs are highly significant stakeholders for the banks and the Boards of Directors will act through the 'Board of Directors vs CEO' governance relationship to ensure that there is transparency with these stakeholder groups. The banking regulators have incorporated environmental departments in their organisations, to create rules based on the Principles, and supervise their compliance. Shareholders remain being important stakeholders, too, and need to be engaged to accept the dividend reduction that will result from their bank refraining to do low risk business with high-emissions companies and from the increased operational cost that will result from these complicated environmental-related processes. It is fair to say that by this time most shareholders have accepted that there is no alternative for banks to take. The Board of Directors needs to ensure that the 'CEO vs rank & file' governance is working to create a corporate culture that includes sensitivity to the environment as part of its ethos, and that enhances the structural IC of the organisation by including environmental impact in its processes and the human IC by training staff on the Principles of Responsible Banking and their implications.

Banks are protagonists in the drive towards a green economy, working side-by-side with environmental NGOs. However, they are not able to adapt all their internal processes to analyse environmental impact at the time of assessing a loan request, and least so to monitor mitigation actions throughout the life cycle of the initiatives they finance. The competences required are distant from the traditional credit risk capabilities of banks but there is much at stake here. Just like in AML and guerrilla finance, they have been delegated this role by governments without being specifically compensated for its accomplishment; however, they will be taken to court and severely fined when they get it wrong. As a result of this, a cluster of Fintechs and Regtechs specialising in these areas have emerged and banks partner with them. These Fintechs use AI and blockchain technologies to deliver their services.

The outcome of all this activity is that GHG emissions control programmes are effective and the tide is turning towards emissions reductions and the Paris Agreement targets start to look achievable.

Greenwash Banks: Banks and environmental activists are curious allies as the latter see the former as the instrumental force to make change happen. It has been accepted that banks approach their loan book as a carbon emissions portfolio that must become greener over time, and banks have accepted the Principles of Responsible Banking as compulsory. Banks will incorporate detailed environmental impact analyses based on the *Greenhouse Gas Protocol* criteria, tracking scope 1, scope 2 and scope 3 type emissions in their loan origination processes. Not only will they do the environmental impact analysis but they will also monitor throughout the life cycle of the initiatives they are financing, that the receivers of the loans carry out the emissions mitigation activities that they have committed to when requesting the loan.

However, banks and environmental NGOs are swimming against the current as society at large is still not sensitive towards GHG emissions reduction actions. Governments have delegated in banks to pursue a greener economy, but through scepticism or through individualism or through plain disregard for future generations, this is a gloomy population that is not prepared to change its consumption habits to reduce emissions.

From a governance perspective the environmental departments of national and local governments and environmental NGOs are significant stakeholders that banks have to keep well informed on their carbon portfolio evolution, but the situation is tricky with shareholders who question why they should be giving up dividends when the rest of society is not really committed or even interested. The Board of Directors wants the CEO and management team to have compliance with the Principles of Responsible Banking as part of their balance scorecard and compensations, but find some resistance and the 'Board of Directors vs CEO' governance relationship is tense and has some opaqueness in this area. The Board of Directors also needs to ensure that the 'CEO vs rank & file' governance relationship is working to create a corporate culture that includes sensitivity to the environment as part of its ethos, and that enhances the structural IC of the organisation by including environmental impact in its processes and the human IC by training staff on the Principles of Responsible Banking and their implications.

Banks are lone wolves together with government and environmental NGOs in the drive towards a green economy. However, they are not able to adapt all their internal processes to analyse environmental impact at the time of assessing a loan request, and least so to monitor mitigation actions throughout the life cycle of the initiatives they finance, so they engage Fintechs and Regtechs specialising in these areas to make this operational. These Fintechs and Regtechs will use AI and blockchain technologies to deliver their services.

The outcome of all this activity is that GHG emissions control programmes are only partially effective but banks use this to improve their corporate image and highlight it as part of their contribution to society, with an intention of improving their reputation.

Pea Soup Banks: The world is in a shamble with respect to GHG emissions and pollution in general. Air and water quality are a pea soup type disaster, GHG emissions are growing at beyond all prediction rates and this is felt in the form of natural disasters due to climate-related events. Environmental NGOs are swimming against the current as society at large is still not sensitive towards GHG emissions reduction actions. Through scepticism or through individualism or through plain disregard for future generations, this is a gloomy population that is not prepared to change its consumption habits to reduce emissions and Western governments have realised that and have ceased to pursue a greener economy.

The banking community and the environmental communities started the Principles for Responsible Banking with great enthusiasm, but this wore off quickly. The natural evolution of managing the principles as a carbon emissions portfolio striving to become GHG emissions-neutral and reaching a point when they would become compulsory never materialised. Banks realised that this caused them more problems than benefits so they just let them fall off the radar screen of the environmentalist and die-off gradually. They remained voluntary and non-binding so in this context, only a few die-hard environmental fundamentalist banks apply them. The Principles of Responsible Banking have become just one more management fad. A cynical population that cares only about here and now renewed its despising of banks and this sentiment spilled over to the business world in general.

From a corporate governance perspective, stakeholder management has simply become shareholder management and most shareholders declare themselves against their bank abiding by the Principles. The environmental issue and sustainability in general have fallen off Board meeting room tables. A corporate culture that respects performance with integrity and that withholds the intellectual capital of the organisation are still valid, but neither includes issues related to the environment.

Traditional banks show relief in that they do not have to perform the green economy driver role, and are pleased to be able to keep their shareholders happy by not putting carbon emissions restrictions on their loan portfolio nor on their investment portfolios. They are also happy that the risk of their portfolio degrading due to the markets punishing large GHG emitters has vanished.

Anti-Green Banks: In this scenario society is highly committed to containing GHG emissions and environmental activists take a high-power role in society and are vigilant of the whole supply chain of products and services. They will internalise the *Greenhouse Gas Protocol* criteria as described in Sect. 6.5 to monitor emissions from the extraction of raw materials through the logistics and production processes until arriving at finished products and services (scope 1); the emissions from the energy they consume (scope 2); to the emissions produced in the full life cycle of the product until its decommissioning and recycling (scope 3).

The banking community had thought that it would be positive to be in synch with society and started the Principles for Responsible Banking with great enthusiasm, but this wore off quickly. Due to the declining power of Western governments and the disagreements between banks, the natural evolution of managing the principles as a carbon emissions portfolio striving to become GHG emissions-neutral and reaching a point when they would become compulsory never materialised. Many banks realised that this caused them more problems than benefits so they just let them fall off the radar screen of the environmentalists and die-off gradually. The Principles remained voluntary and non-binding so in this context, only a few banks that are environmental fundamentalists, most of which have no stakes in GHG emissions-heavy industries such as mining and power generation, adopt them. The Principles of Responsible Banking have become just one more management fad. An environmentally engaged society that is overly sensitive to GHG emissions maximised its despising of banks and this societal sentiment spilled over to the business world in general.

From a corporate governance perspective, bank Boards of Directors have taken a defensive mode on environmental issues. Most banks have not adopted the Principles of Responsible Banking but their Boards of Directors are aware of the risks of lending to heavy GHG emitters so credit to these sectors is limited, but in a disorganised way, with each bank adopting its own criteria. The 'Board of Directors vs CEO' governance relationship is full-on to review how loans to emitters are being managed, and the Credit Committee and Risk Committee of the Board are permanently vigilant. Environmental NGOs are powerful stakeholders that banks are diligent in keeping at bay, but the highest priority for banks is their shareholders.

The banking sector falls behind the wave of environmental consciousness and sustainability that is ubiquitous in society in general. The sector is split between a few banks that are highly compliant and a majority that are not but take precautions to cover up their environmental impact. The argument of the latter is that it is government's responsibility, not theirs, to drive society towards a green economy and they use securitisation and other techniques to get these non-environmentally friendly loans off their balance sheets as protective measures. A significant number of Fintechs that offer banks environmental impact assessment services have emerged—banks engage them but more to decide which loans they should get off their balance sheets than to be environmentally compliant.

It is expected that these scenarios will assist business leaders to interpret the business context of their organisations in years to come. Finally, having covered the fundamental groundwork, the next and final chapter will address the research question and gives some concluding remarks on the positioning that corporate governance needs to take in the knowledge economy.

Reference

Flack, J., & Mitchell, M. (2020). *Uncertain times.* Aeon Essays. https://aeon.co/essays/complex-systems-science-allows-us-to-see-new-paths-forward.

CHAPTER 8

Final Reflections and Concluding Remarks

An appropriate ending to this book is to go back to the research questions presented in chapter 1 and respond to them. With respect to how corporate governance can deal with the predominance of intangible assets over tangible ones, the response is two-fold. On the one hand the organisation needs to develop a strong corporate culture that has commitment to protecting and enhancing intellectual capital in all its forms: human, structural and relational. For this to happen the Board of Directors must operate through the 'Board of Directors vs CEO' governance relationship to ensure that senior management is acting through the 'CEO vs rank & file' governance relationship to construct that corporate culture. On the other hand, the organisation must strive to be able to account for and thus manage intellectual capital. The <IR> is presented as a promising initiative to do exactly that. The scenario structure No. 1 in Sect. 7.3 presents four possible scenarios for this in which 'Open Society' shows its potential. Of course, <IR> is an initiative in early stages that may not succeed—but there is no doubt that it is showing a route to account for and manage intangible assets, among which is intellectual capital. If <IR> fails, there will be some other initiative with a similar philosophy and objectives that will follow it.

With respect to how to adapt corporate governance to deal with multiple stakeholder groups many of which may have opposing interests,

© The Author(s), under exclusive license to Springer Nature
Switzerland AG 2021
P. D. R. Griffiths, *Corporate Governance in the Knowledge Economy*, Palgrave Studies in Accounting and Finance Practice,
https://doi.org/10.1007/978-3-030-78873-5_8

this is a key aspect that needs to be looked at carefully by the Board of Directors. Of course, the world was easier in the industrial era when 'the business of business was business' and there was only one overarching stakeholder group as were the shareholders, but the need for sustainability has led to this new reality where multiple stakeholders are to be dealt with. As shown in Fig. 7.1, the business context in the form of formal institutions or informal ones will have an incidence on the stakeholders that need to be considered.

In this space the organisation needs to make tough decisions; it is about prioritising among competing sustainability initiatives and thus stakeholders. As long as the organisation is clear in its priorities and transparent with its stakeholders, it will be able to defend its position effectively. The Board of Directors needs to ensure that management is informing the stakeholders and that the Board itself interacts proactively with them. A key conclusion arrived at is that Boards need to move beyond the agency problem as filling the information gap between management and the stakeholder groups is a lost battle. It is far more productive to develop a corporate culture of 'performance with integrity' as the best protection for the interest of stakeholders. The scenario structure No. 3 in Sect. 7.3 describes the possible scenarios (i.e., *Green-Ho Banks*) where the bank prioritises the environmental dimension of sustainability and shows how even environmental activists can become close allies and significant stakeholders that need to be looked after by the bank.

In terms of the effects of the challenges of digitalisation in the era of the data tsunami and risks of cybersecurity, Fig. 7.1 presents the positive loop of having in place appropriate governance/compliance controls that will reinforce a corporate culture oriented to protecting and enhancing the organisation's intellectual capital, which in turn strengthens intellectual capital management that has the knock-on effect of improving governance/compliance controls processes, systems and competencies. Achieving this positive spiral requires making good decisions in terms of technology. In scenario structure No. 2 the *Knowledge Panacea* is achieved by an optimal human–machine interaction taken to new levels, promoting knowledge sharing between humans and applying technology to carry out multi-dimensional bio-recognition types. Of course, this depends on external factors such as that the social networks and the data tsunami are under control and that technology such as AI in its machine learning form is highly developed. If this is not the case, the organisation will have to accommodate itself as best as possible in one of the other three scenarios.

For multinationals to deal with the tension between headquarters and the subsidiary due to the need to combine the corporation's ethical culture with the institutional forces of the subsidiary's host market, the model in Fig. 7.1 shows that the Board of Directors needs to process the signals it is receiving from the business context to act through the 'Board of Directors vs CEO' governance relationship to ensure that the 'CEO vs rank & file' governance relationship is contributing to build a robust corporate culture at the subsidiary. Here, the model in Fig. 7.1 highlights another positive loop: the robust corporate culture at the subsidiary leads to more effective intellectual capital management that in turn leads to stronger governance/compliance controls that inform the Board of Directors. A cue for the Board of Directors that this is working is that the subsidiary takes the corporate headquarters as one of its key stakeholders and that there is a fluid and transparent communication between the subsidiary and senior management at the centre. Experience indicates that this is easier to achieve when the growth of the subsidiary is driven by organic growth rather than by mergers and acquisitions.

Finally, all the prior responses show what a pivotal role the governance relationships 'Board of Directors vs CEO' and 'CEO vs rank & file' play in achieving an effective corporate governance in the knowledge economy.

This prepared the ground to address the overall question *What changes need to be incorporated into corporate governance to cope with the challenges posed by the transition to a knowledge economy?* The short answer to this is that in the knowledge economy Boards of Directors need to go beyond the agency problem that was their traditional concern, to focus on monitoring that the organisation develops a robust corporate culture that promotes 'performance with integrity' and that enhances its key intangible asset, intellectual capital. And most important of all, corporate governance itself moves from being just one dimension of sustainability as shown in Fig. 2.1 to becoming the great protagonist that ties together corporate culture, stakeholder management, a sustainable business strategy that addresses the organisation's new challenges in an innovative business model, as represented in Fig. 8.1.

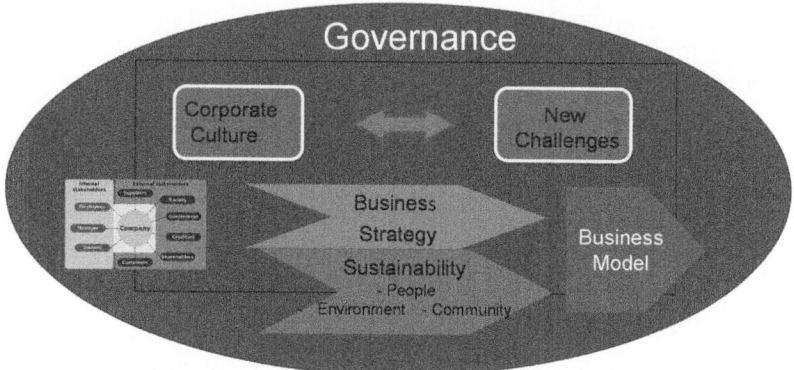

Fig. 8.1 Corporate governance as the great integrator

Index

A

Accountability, 9, 18, 44, 183
Acquisition, 54, 66, 79, 83, 86, 87, 89, 90, 99, 100, 108, 109, 120, 128, 133, 137, 139, 161, 162, 165, 174, 178, 213, 217, 218, 243
Administrative problem, 113, 124
Agency theory, 151, 160
AI Dependency, 227, 229
Anti-Green Banks, 234, 238
Anti-money laundering (AML), 154–156, 158, 162, 163, 165, 166, 168, 169, 184, 185, 229, 235
Argentina, 4, 54, 59, 75, 79, 86, 105–125, 135–139, 152, 212, 213, 216, 218
Artificial neural networks, 38, 39
Audit, 73, 86
Audit trail, 173, 228, 232

B

Baltic states, 162, 167
Banco Santander, 126–131
Bank Secrecy Act (BSA), 184, 185
Basel Committee of Banking Supervision (BCBS), 20
Benefit realisation, 76, 82, 86
Best practices, 77, 83, 94
Big Data, 1, 4, 10, 37, 47, 225, 227, 228, 232, 233
Black market peso exchange (BMPE), 157
Board of Directors, 3, 19, 68, 97, 147, 160, 174, 175, 177, 178, 211–219, 223–226, 228, 230–232, 235, 236, 238, 241–243
Born global, 117
Brazil, 25, 54, 58, 59, 64, 75, 79, 130
Bribe, 4, 141, 145, 148, 150, 152, 171–173, 175, 214, 217

British American Tobacco (BAT), 4, 105, 115–118, 121–123, 125, 134–137, 212, 213, 216, 218
Bruun & Hjejle, 160, 162, 163, 166
Business context, 16, 18, 55, 56, 96, 122, 124, 138, 212, 213, 218–220, 239, 242, 243
Business ethics, 18, 21, 23, 47
Business model, 8, 9, 34, 36, 37, 45, 99, 100, 109, 117, 190, 215, 217, 228, 232, 243
Business process, 16, 77–79, 83, 88, 92, 94, 115, 125, 127, 137, 158, 168, 192
Business unit, 73, 77, 78, 87, 107–109, 113, 116, 119, 132, 154, 213, 218

C
Capital adequacy, 130
Capital allocation, 46
Capital allocation decisions, 44
Carbon footprint, 9, 202
'CEO vs rank & file' relationship, 3, 4, 97, 98, 101, 160, 169, 174, 178, 212, 214, 215, 217, 219, 223, 225, 226, 228, 230, 231, 236, 241, 243
Chile, 4, 25, 54, 59, 69, 75, 116, 126–131, 133–139, 212, 214, 217
Citigroup Inc., 187
Climate crisis, 10, 37, 182–184, 188, 193, 198, 200, 203, 205, 222, 233
Cognitive computing, 38, 39, 47, 115
Collaboration, 2, 31, 36, 47, 223, 224, 226
Combating the Funding of Terrorism (CFT), 184, 185
Communications plan, 85
Competencies, 115, 242

Competitive landscape, 2, 119
Compliance, 18–21, 29–31, 123, 147, 153, 156, 158, 160, 168, 173–178, 213–217, 219, 235, 236, 242, 243
Compliance risk, 20, 53, 193
Consumer packaged goods, 89, 90, 94
COP-21, 182, 183, 186–188, 197, 199, 205–207
Corporate citizenship, 8, 106
Corporate control, 72
Corporate culture, 5, 21, 23, 25, 29, 30, 41, 47, 65, 72, 73, 88, 90, 96–98, 101, 114, 115, 125, 133–135, 137, 138, 146, 147, 150, 151, 158–160, 168, 169, 174, 178, 182, 212–215, 217–219, 223, 225, 230, 231, 235–237, 241–243
Corporate governance, 1, 3–5, 7, 9, 18, 19, 21, 31, 47, 48, 55, 75, 77, 88, 89, 96, 98, 113, 126, 147, 150, 159, 168, 170, 171, 183, 187, 211, 212, 216, 219–221, 223, 228, 230–232, 237–239, 241, 243, 244
Corporate leadership, 113
Corporate responsibility (CR), 7–13, 15–19, 31, 46, 47, 55, 65, 144–146, 182, 198
Corporate standards, 53, 77, 88–90, 95, 97, 98, 101, 124, 125, 175
Corporate values, 18, 99, 137, 139
Corruption, 4, 5, 9, 18, 23, 26–29, 31, 115, 137, 141, 145, 146, 148–153, 159, 160, 166, 169, 171–173, 216, 217
Corruption Perception Index (CPI), 27, 149, 150, 173
Cost of delivery, 56, 58, 60–63
Cross-selling, 7, 66–71, 134, 216

INDEX 247

Culture, 4, 8, 19, 20, 23, 25, 28–30, 41, 43, 47, 65–67, 69, 71–75, 88, 95–101, 111–113, 123, 126, 130, 131, 134–136, 139, 147–150, 158, 160, 168, 169, 177, 183, 189, 212–215, 223, 224, 228, 230, 243
Customer intimacy, 13, 59, 126, 127, 131–134, 138
Cyber Chaos, 227, 230
Cybersecurity, 3, 230, 233

D

Danske Bank, 4, 7, 160–169, 174, 176–178, 213, 215
Data tsunami, 3, 37, 38, 214, 222, 227–232, 242
Deep learning, 38, 39
Deutsche Bank, 164, 165

E

Engineering problem, 25, 112, 124, 134
Entrepreneurial problem, 25, 112, 123
Environmental, Social and Governance (ESG), 15, 186, 190, 198, 202, 203
Estonia, 162–169, 171, 176, 177, 213, 215
Estonian Central Bank, 162
Ethical bank culture, 29, 30
Ethical corporate culture, 3, 47, 74, 125, 137, 151, 152, 160, 170, 172–174, 178, 214, 226, 232
Ethical management, 106
Ethics, 9, 18, 21, 22, 29, 31, 110, 144, 151, 158, 172, 223
Europe, 15, 24, 107, 118, 135, 149, 153, 157, 158, 161, 196

European Banking Authority (EBA), 15, 203

F

Factors of production, 31, 32
Financial services (FS), 1, 3, 4, 13, 16, 31, 36, 41, 48, 53–55, 57, 58, 63, 73, 97–99, 127, 130, 143, 190, 198, 213, 214, 216–218, 229
Fintech, 2–4, 41–43, 48, 181, 207, 223–226, 229–231, 233, 235, 236, 239
Formal institutions, 3, 26, 110, 114, 122, 133, 135, 138, 149, 151, 152, 173, 213, 216, 218, 219, 223, 242
Fragmented Society, 222, 224
FTI Consulting, 69
Future orientation, 26, 44, 45, 111, 123, 133, 135, 212

G

Glamorgan, 4, 54, 57–59, 61, 63, 64, 97–100, 214, 216–218
Glass-Steagall, 66
Global governance, 101, 105
Globalisation, 3, 10, 23, 44, 77, 78, 118, 154, 161, 225
GLOBE project, 23, 126, 135, 148, 149, 168, 212
Green-Ho Banks, 234, 242
Greenhouse gas emissions, 88, 192, 199
Greenwash Banks, 234, 235

H

Headcount reductions, 85
High context, 23, 88, 96, 125, 126, 168, 175

Host market, 4, 25, 105, 137, 219, 243
Human capital, 30, 99, 100, 125, 127, 169, 174

I
IBM, 4, 36, 38, 105–115, 122, 128, 134–139, 152, 212, 213, 216, 218
Incentives, 15, 42, 56, 65, 74, 85, 129, 134, 157, 159, 192, 205–207
Industrial and Commercial Bank of China (ICBC), 181, 188, 189, 191–193, 201, 207
Informal institutions, 3, 25, 26, 151, 173
Innovation in business model, 36, 47, 87, 215
Intangible assets, 2, 4, 23, 31, 33, 35, 37, 44, 47, 48, 91, 96, 100, 125, 135, 159, 160, 181, 212, 241, 243
Intangibles, 2, 11, 22, 31, 34, 35, 44, 46, 83, 86, 88, 115, 160
Integrated reporting (IR), 43–46, 48, 221–223, 226, 241
Intellectual capital (IC), 2–4, 22, 30, 34, 37, 47, 48, 91, 96, 99, 115, 125, 135, 137, 139, 150, 158–160, 168, 169, 174, 178, 182, 212–215, 217–219, 225, 226, 228, 230–232, 235–237, 241–243
Intellectual capital management, 115, 137, 139, 212, 214, 218, 219, 242, 243
Internal controls, 20, 53, 73, 99
International growth, 99, 107
Investigations, 27, 65, 69, 70, 153, 155, 161, 163, 164
Investment decisions, 44, 83, 95, 128

J
JP Morgan Chase, 181, 194–196, 201, 202, 206, 207

K
Knowledge & Sustainability (K&S), 31, 32
Knowledge economy, 1–4, 8, 11, 23, 31–37, 40, 41, 43, 44, 46–48, 87, 88, 91, 96, 99, 115, 125, 135, 160, 169, 170, 174, 178, 181, 184, 211, 212, 214, 215, 218–221, 224, 225, 228, 239, 243
Knowledge network, 42
Knowledge Panacea, 227, 242
Knowledge sharing, 42, 228, 242
Know your customer (KYC), 20, 158, 163, 184, 185, 229

L
Latin America, 53–55, 57, 58, 63, 75–78, 85–87, 118, 126, 130, 134, 135, 144, 148, 149, 152, 153, 173
Leading practices, 79, 94
Learning reinforcement, 39
Low context, 23, 126, 134, 175

M
Machine learning, 38, 39, 47, 175, 207, 227–229, 231, 242
Macmillan SPIRIT, 10
Mexico, 4, 7, 54, 75, 79, 130, 153–159, 174, 177, 188, 213–217
Miles & Snow, 25, 123
Mitsubishi UFJ Financial Group (MUFG), 181, 187, 189–191, 193, 201, 207

INDEX 249

Money laundering, 5, 20, 141, 142, 152–155, 158–161, 163–167, 170–175, 178, 215, 218
Moral dilemma, 175
Multinational, 4, 53–57, 75, 113, 122, 142, 149, 151, 175, 212, 213, 243
MW CPG, 4, 89–95, 97–100, 212, 214–217

N
Nasdaq OMX Copenhagen, 161
Nobleza Piccardo, 115–125
Non-Resident Portfolio, 163, 164, 166, 168, 169
Norwest Bank, 66

O
Open innovation, 36
Open Society, 222, 223, 241
Operational excellence, 13, 78, 88, 126, 127, 131–136, 138
Organised Crime & Corruption Reporting Project (OCCRP), 166
Orica, 4, 55, 75–79, 81, 83, 85–88, 97–100, 212, 214–218
Overhead cost, 80, 85
Oversight Committee, 69, 70, 74, 99

P
Paraguay, 116
Paris agreement, 182, 186, 189, 191, 194–196, 198, 200, 201, 206, 207, 235
Pea Soup Banks, 234, 237
Performance with integrity, 5, 147, 148, 151, 152, 159, 160, 170, 172, 173, 177, 214, 215, 217, 225, 230, 237, 242, 243
Peru, 116

Polycentricity, 25
Power distance, 26, 28, 112, 123, 133, 135, 138, 212
Principles of Responsible Banking (PRB), 4, 5, 182, 183, 186, 187, 189–194, 196, 197, 200–207, 222, 233–238
Productivity, 31–33, 40, 91
Productivity paradox, 91
Product leadership, 13, 127
PwC, 69, 109

Q
Quality of service, 55, 56, 58, 60, 61, 63, 130

R
Regtech, 175, 178, 207, 217, 229, 235, 236
Regulated industry, 13, 31, 124, 134
Regulation, 3, 11, 20, 21, 28, 110, 113, 114, 122–125, 135, 138, 148, 158, 173, 175, 177, 186, 193, 218, 219, 232
Relational capital, 30, 125, 169
Reporting, 2, 14, 15, 18, 20, 35, 43–46, 48, 55, 72, 73, 77, 98, 113, 127, 158, 163, 167, 202, 203, 218, 222
Reputation, 1, 13, 20–22, 36, 48, 71, 73, 97, 120, 159, 161, 168, 172, 175, 176, 192, 193, 214, 216, 232, 237
Return on investment (ROI), 80, 207
Risk, 11, 20, 43, 44, 65, 71–73, 84, 85, 100, 127, 133, 137, 143, 153, 155, 163, 168, 170, 174, 175, 184, 186, 187, 189, 192, 193, 199, 204, 207, 216, 217, 225, 229, 235, 238
Risk management, 84, 162, 186, 193

Rizzuto model, 26, 88, 96, 112
Roam up, product/service, 112, 115
Robert Solow, 91
Rometty, Ginni, 38, 109
Russia, 167, 171, 188

S

Sales malpractices, 66, 68, 70, 100, 214
SAP, 55, 75, 76, 78, 79, 81–83, 85–88, 90, 94, 124
Shared services, 55, 64, 77, 88, 89, 137, 139, 218
Shearman & Sterling, 69
Signatory banks, 182, 186, 194, 200, 202, 204, 205
Social change, 31, 41
Societal culture, 3, 5, 23, 26, 31, 47, 88, 111, 113, 115, 122, 125, 133–135, 137, 138, 141, 148, 149, 152, 168, 173, 175, 178, 212, 213, 218, 219, 223
Stagnation, 227, 231
Stakeholder, 8, 10–12, 14, 18, 19, 21, 22, 28–30, 46, 54, 64, 65, 98, 100, 106, 114, 115, 123–125, 135, 136, 138, 148, 159, 167, 176, 182–185, 191, 199, 204, 207, 211, 213, 216, 219, 224–226, 230, 232, 235–238, 242, 243
Stakeholder group, 2, 4, 8, 11–14, 16, 29, 30, 46, 53, 54, 72, 73, 89, 96, 97, 112–114, 133, 168, 174, 184, 216, 219, 223, 228, 231, 235, 241, 242
Statistical pattern recognition, 38
Strategic group analysis, 129
Strategic misalignment, 126
Strategy, 3, 4, 8, 10, 15–18, 23, 25, 26, 30, 32, 34, 36, 44–46, 54, 57, 66, 72–74, 77–79, 84, 88, 95, 96, 99–101, 105, 109, 111, 112, 116, 118, 119, 121–123, 126, 130, 132–134, 136, 154, 168, 175, 190, 191, 196, 204, 214, 217, 219, 223, 224, 243
Strategy adaptation, 5, 25, 99, 100, 105, 126, 133, 134, 137
Structural capital, 30, 96, 100, 169, 174
Subsidiary, 4, 26, 96, 105–107, 109, 111, 113–117, 122–126, 133, 134, 136–139, 142, 154–156, 162, 165, 167, 168, 170, 171, 175, 176, 178, 188, 212, 213, 216, 218, 219, 243
Supervised learning, 39
Suspicious activity alerts, 155
Sustainability, 5, 7–10, 13–15, 18, 19, 23, 31, 33, 54, 144, 145, 150, 182, 185, 189–191, 194, 196, 202–204, 219, 220, 223, 237, 239, 242, 243
Sustainable business model, 8, 9, 12, 15, 18, 46, 47, 72–74, 101
Systems architecture, 95

T

Tangible benefits, 45, 80, 83, 88, 170, 174, 178, 217
Transaction governance capacity (TGC), 28, 148–150, 152, 172, 173, 177
Transparency, 9, 13, 18, 28, 44, 48, 65, 74, 98–100, 106, 110, 146–148, 173, 183, 214, 223, 225, 226, 228, 235
Transparency for What, 222, 226
Trust, 7, 10, 14, 20–22, 26, 29, 44, 66, 71, 74, 106, 148, 164, 225

U

UK, 13, 54, 64, 118, 144, 149, 156, 171
Uncertainty avoidance, 26, 111, 122, 135, 212
United Nations Environment Protection Financial Initiatives (UNEP FI), 182, 184–188, 191, 193, 195
United Nations General Assembly, 182, 186, 200
Unrealised Potential, 222, 223
Unsupervised learning, 39, 227, 229, 231

USA, 41, 66, 118, 153, 154, 158–160

V

Value discipline, 13, 59, 61, 127, 131–139, 212, 214
Venezuela, 75, 86
VW, 7, 73

W

Wells Fargo, 4, 7, 65–74, 97–100, 134, 181, 194, 196, 198–202, 206, 207, 212–217
Whistle-blower, 165, 215

CPI Antony Rowe
Eastbourne, UK
August 26, 2021